ELVIS SPEAKS!

The Performer
"My moment of glory is being
on the stage and singing and feeling
all the love the audience sends to me . . .
It's beyond any mortal high."

The Man
"I've never had a lasting love affair
like everyone else—
and I'm a person too . . .
Do you realize I'll never know
if a woman loves me—or Elvis Presley?
Me, not the image. I'm real."

The Legend
"I'm not concerned anymore about the fans.
They're wise enough
to see through any lies.
But what about Lisa?
What is she going to think about her daddy
when she grows up?"

The Superstar
"Don't forget, Larry, angels fly
because they take themselves so lightly."

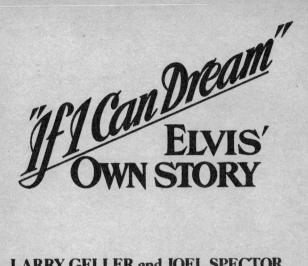

"If I Can Dream"
ELVIS' OWN STORY

LARRY GELLER and **JOEL SPECTOR**
with **PATRICIA ROMANOWSKI**

AVON BOOKS ◢◣ NEW YORK

The photographs numbered 1, 2, 3, 4, 11, 12, 13, 14, 15, 16, 17, 18, 19, 20, 21, 23, 24, 25, 27, and 28 are from the author's collection. Numbers 5 and 7 are from the Eddie Fadal collection and are used with his permission. Numbers 6 and 29 are used by courtesy of Sid Shaw, The Elvisly Yours, Ltd., Fan Club. Numbers 8 and 10 are from the Vernon Presley Collection, courtesy of Aurelia Yarborough. Numbers 9 and 22 are used by courtesy of Sean Shaver. Number 26 © 1978 Graceland Associates.

AVON BOOKS
A division of
The Hearst Corporation
105 Madison Avenue
New York, New York 10016

First Avon Books Printing: August 1990

Printed in the U.S.A.

RA   10 9 8 7 6 5 4 3 2 1

*This book is dedicated
to fans of Elvis Presley
everywhere.*

INTRODUCTION

It was an unusually hot and humid Wednesday. Already at eight o'clock in the morning, the sweet fragrance of magnolias hung heavy in the air. I pulled my car up to the mortuary gate, and after a security check, two policemen escorted me to an office. Then six others flanked me and Charlie Hodge, Elvis Presley's longtime associate, and all of us made our way to another building several hundred feet away. Though I didn't lift my eyes from the ground I could hear people wailing as they pressed against the gates. There was the whir of automatic-camera shutters and overhead the buzz of helicopters bearing newspeople, all training their cameras on us, hundreds of feet below.

When we reached the second building, another pair of police officers parted to allow us by. Inside, another dozen or so policemen and several somber men, each dressed in a dark, conservative business suit, awaited our arrival. As Charlie and I passed, each man nodded—a silent gesture of sympathy. The quiet was finally broken when another police officer approached and said softly, "Mr. Geller, will you please follow me?"

We continued down a long corridor, at the end of which was an open door. My heart pounded furiously, and although I'd spent the previous eighteen hours trying to brace myself, I knew that nothing could have prepared me for the sight that grew clearer with each step.

There, lying on a table with a worn black leather cushion, covered up to his neck with a plain white sheet, was my friend Elvis.

I stood paralyzed before him. An officer grabbed my upper arm to support me. "No, no," I said, tears streaming down my face. "I'll be all right."

As I stared into Elvis' face I was trying to convince myself of what I knew was the truth. *Elvis died yesterday,* I told myself. And yet another part of me couldn't believe it. Through the years, I'd seen Elvis asleep hundreds of times, and standing there I asked myself, why doesn't he just open his eyes, sit up, grin, and say, "What the hell is goin' on here, Lawrence? The joke's over. Let's go home."

But as the seconds ticked into minutes, the truth overpowered whatever desperate fantasy my mind was trying to sustain.

Feeling faint, I steadied myself against the table. I placed my hand gently on Elvis' cool, smooth forehead, closed my eyes, and said, "I love you, Elvis. I know you're aware of what's going on. You're free again. No more suffering, Elvis. You're back with God." When I opened my eyes, it struck me that while Elvis—the man I knew and had loved as a dear friend for nearly fourteen years— was somewhere and could hear my words, what lay before me wasn't my friend but a piece of clay; a worn, useless physical body. Making that distinction helped me to focus on the task at hand. I opened my bag and removed my tools and hair preparations. As I unpacked I heard myself saying, "Elvis, I'm here. I know how you would want to look."

I'd never worked on a cadaver before and pray I never have to again. This was the most unsettling ordeal of my life, made more difficult and gruesome by several incidents I hadn't anticipated. One reason Elvis looked so unfamiliar was that prior to our arrival the funeral home's cosmeticians had coated Elvis' face and hands with a bizarre, unnatural-colored makeup, which Charlie and I objected to and asked them to remove.

When we finally began our work on Elvis, a procedure I'd envisioned taking maybe thirty minutes, it consumed nearly two hours. Everything seemed wrong. I hadn't anticipated a full half-inch of white undergrowth and so was forced to ''dye'' his roots with a wand of mascara borrowed from a female attendant before I trimmed the hair.

In all the years I'd worked for him, I'd never thought to collect the pieces of his hair that fell to the floor. But that day the vision of people rummaging through the mortuary's garbage, searching for locks of Elvis' hair, flashed before me so I gathered up the clippings and placed them in my bag. Next I struggled to work his full head of limp, baby-fine hair into some semblance of Elvis' classic style.

The work done, I packed my things and got ready to leave for Graceland, where we would await Elvis' noon arrival. Charlie and I tearfully embraced and remarked on how well he looked, how he must know we were there. As we stood there staring, an attendant pulled the sheet off Elvis' body, exposing a grotesque X of stitches running diagonally from shoulder to hip, holding closed the autopsy incisions.

''Why did you have to do that?'' Charlie cried.

The attendant apologized, muttered something about time running short and procedure, then left the room. There was nothing more for us to do, and several policemen appeared, ready to accompany us back to our cars.

The morning had the feel of an interminable, suffocating nightmare, and I looked forward to being at Graceland. I knew that Elvis' father Vernon and his daughter Lisa Marie, and so many other friends and relatives would be grieving, too. I hoped that during the ten-mile drive back I could compose myself. What was there left to say to them?

What I witnessed on the way back, however, only heightened the sense of unreality. All along the route stood thousands of people; most were crying, all were gazing blankly in disbelief. Overhead, news helicopters hummed. What were they looking for? I wondered. In the past eleven months, when the thought of Elvis' dying crossed my mind, as it had so often, I envisioned a great outpouring of sadness from his fans and the world, but nothing like this. Everywhere I looked were strangers whose pained, anguished expressions seemed to mirror my own feelings.

As I drove back to Graceland I thought about all the things he still had to live for: his daughter, his father, his music. Yet he seemed to have given up, and no one truly knows why. Perhaps that explained some of my anger at him for dying the way he had.

A Memphis paper ran a most poignant banner headline: A LONELY LIFE ENDS ON ELVIS PRESLEY BOULEVARD. Reading it, I heard Elvis say something he'd said a thousand times: "People think I'm lonely, but I love that lonesome feelin'. I know what people will think. 'Yeah, Elvis is an old recluse like Howard Hughes. He's holed up in his house, and he's a prisoner.' Bullshit! I love my life. I wouldn't trade my position for anything or anyone. I've earned it. It's what I've wanted all my life." What Elvis failed, or chose not, to see, were the negative aspects of anything or anyone he loved. In that, he was an average human being.

I was also eager to get back to Graceland to write in my diary, a collection of notes I'd begun keeping in November of 1976. I didn't know then why I started writing down incidents and conversations with Elvis, but re-reading those entries and recalling the period before I started the diary reveals that there is no question that by late 1976 Elvis had reached a crisis in his life. And although it is clear today that the odds were firmly stacked against him, that whatever opportunities he might have had to change his life, to direct it along another course, were long gone, Elvis' tragedy is that once they were within his grasp.

Elvis never kept his own diary; he rarely even wrote letters. During his life, however, he conceived of ways that he might have communicated to the world what was really important to him. In the sixties he recorded albums of gospel music. In the seventies, although he didn't write songs, he chose to record songs that expressed and reflected his personal trials and disappointments. He hoped to make films to explain certain aspects of himself, such as his love of karate's spiritual elements or his feelings about the writers and philosophers whose words he loved and tried to live by. Elvis also wanted to establish a permanent foundation that would provide funds for a range of charitable causes. These were plans he didn't live to carry out.

That there was a chasm dividing the public Elvis from the private Elvis was something he knew too well and felt very sharply. As his life moved to a close, as his physical and emotional pain increased, as the once comfortable, safe world he'd created to protect himself turned dark and hostile, he often said to me, "The world knows Elvis. They don't know me."

The idea of writing his own book, telling his own story, was one of the several obsessions that drove him in his last months. He spoke of it often and asked me to help him express his ideas. Large portions of my diary were devoted to faithfully recorded notes of our conversations. These we planned to work into the book Elvis wanted to write.

As I drove through Memphis that August morning, watching through my own tears the world mourn my friend's death and trying to find a way to express my own terrible grief, it seemed to me that finishing the project we had begun together would be the best thing I could do for myself and for him.

CHAPTER

1

From the very beginning, the basis of my relationship with Elvis was our pursuit of life's spiritual aspects. Our mutual interest in esoteric philosophies, religions, teachings and arts struck many people as bizarre and unorthodox, a perception I honestly couldn't fully appreciate, since I'd grown up with these things. My own introduction to these subjects came from my parents, Bernard and Annabelle (Cookie) Geller, a middle-class Jewish couple.

Both my parents were first-generation Americans. My father, who had grown up in Harlem and as a young man frequented the Cotton Club, was something of a rebel. Rather than go to work in the family's garment business, he joined Borah Minnevitch's Harmonica Rascals, vaudeville's number-one harmonica group. Among the other Rascals was one Lee Jacobs, who would later find greater fame as the actor Lee J. Cobb. Today the idea of a harmonica group sounds quaint, but as my father described it to me the various harmonica acts were like the doo-wop singing groups of the fifties, in that each had its own sound, style and look, and the competition among them was keen. He later joined another outfit, Joey Hoffman's Ragamuffins, and stayed with them until 1933, when his impending marriage to my mother led him to assume a more respectable position in the family trade.

Their first child and only son, I was born on August 8, 1939, in Elmira, an upstate New York town. In 1947 my parents decided to move to California, partially because I suffered from severe chronic asthma, which the brutal New York winters exacerbated. Another reason was that my mother's parents, to whom she was very close, had relocated to southern California. We arrived in Los Angeles on October 16, 1947, ready to make a new start.

From the moment I set eyes on my new home, I loved everything about it, from the perpetually summerlike weather to its reputation as the home of the stars. Just being inside the Hollywood city limits was exhilarating. From as early as I could remember, I had loved movies. My father frequently took my younger twin sisters, Judy and Elaine, and me for drives along Sunset Boulevard, followed by a meal in a restaurant known for its star clientele.

We weren't Orthodox Jews, but we observed all the high holidays, and many of our neighbors were Jewish as well. In fact, locals referred to our neighborhood, the Fairfax district, as the "Borscht Belt." My family lived the postwar American dream of comfort, prosperity and security, something I realize only in retrospect. That sense of safety and certainty shattered in 1951.

One weekend that year, I traveled with my Cub Scout pack to the Malibu hills for a weekend campout. As we rode home along the Pacific Coast Highway, I felt compelled to stare at the ocean and think about my grandmother. It didn't make sense to me: What does my grandmother have to do with the Pacific Ocean? I kept asking myself.

The bus deposited me at the corner of my block, and as I made my way up the street to our house I couldn't shake what you'd call, in eleven-year-old parlance, a creepy feeling. Inside the house I saw a lot of people besides my parents: my uncles and some other relatives. Taking me aside, someone told me gently that my grandmother had died. From what the police could ascertain, she had been walking in Santa Monica that Saturday afternoon when someone accosted her—who we never found out—and forced her into a car. Then she was robbed and strangled, and her body was dumped into the ocean. Because she was wearing a fake-fur jacket, a gift from my grandfather, the police surmised that her killers believed she had money.

My grandmother's murder was a crime more typical of 1980s New York than California of the fifties, and everything about it—the randomness, the brutality, the injustice—weighed on us all, though my mother took it especially hard. She had never dealt with death before, and contemplating her mother's fate led her to question the very meaning of life. Finding no solace, she immersed herself in such works as *Basic Principles of the Science of the Mind* and *The Healing Power of Balanced Emotions,* by Dr. Frederick Bailes, *Specific Meditations for Health, Wealth, Love and Expression,* by Dr. Joseph Murphy, and other titles. She attended lectures and classes given by Dr. Bailes, Dr. Murphy and the world-renowned author and teacher Dr. Ernest Holmes. With Dr. Ester Sirkin, she studied at the School of Divine Science.

My twin sisters were considerably younger than I, and my father was at work all day. Though I was only twelve, I became my mother's junior partner in her quest. She would discuss with me what she had read and studied, often quoting from Dr. Holmes *The Science of the Mind.* The basic philosophy underlying these works was simply that we each have inherent powers to direct the course of our life by understanding and tapping into key universal principles. My mother and I would talk about these subjects for hours almost every day, and I remember these wonderful conversations. Mom was surprised at how quickly I grasped fairly sophisticated, complex ideas; they made perfect sense to me.

My father, who was very concerned about my mother's grief, supported her in these pursuits and frequently accompanied her to meetings and classes. Before long he became especially intrigued by the healing processes. He joined the Church of World Messianity and developed the skills of johrei (pronounced jor-ray), a Japanese method of healing specific parts of the body by focusing healing energy—sometimes though not always by direct touch— on the corresponding spiritual centers, or chakras.

My father was adept in the art of johrei, as was evident

from the stream of people who came to our home almost every evening. I never really understood what my father was doing, or how, until one night when I awoke feeling as though my heart were on fire. My father placed his open hand about three inches above my chest and calmly explained that he was healing me, as he had done during many of my nighttime asthma attacks. When I asked him why he practiced johrei on me only when I slept, he confided that he had been worried I'd resist the treatment and that people who heard about it would scoff. That struck me as odd, because *I* understood it and knew it was real. When I told my father that I wanted to learn about johrei, he was pleasantly surprised and agreed to teach me. Over time I gained knowledge of the inner techniques of healing. As a focal point, my father also wore around his neck a crystal. I guess you could say he was one of the first New Agers; at least, he was the first I knew. My parents' attitudes and encouragement planted the seeds for the lifelong spiritual quest I'd embark on several years later.

In the meantime I was the prototypical fifties L.A. teen. We lived near Fairfax High School, and among my buddies was Phil Spector, later to become a renowned rockand-roll record producer. Rick Nelson, the radio and TV actor and future teen idol, attended a different school, but we met at a mutual friend's party and went to other parties together after that. My favorite memory of Rick is being driven home from a party by his parents, Ozzie and Harriet Nelson, and briefly experiencing the odd sensation that I was living in a television program.

Phil Spector and I became good friends sometime around 1954 or 1955, when he, his mother and his sisters moved from New York into a house that was situated kittycorner from ours on Ogden Drive. Phil had been into rock and roll as far back as junior high school, so we had that in common. We were lucky to grow up just before rock and roll went mainstream, while it was still dominated by the wilder, more expressive black rhythm and blues. My favorite artists then were Johnny Ace, the Checkers, the Chords, Clyde McPhatter and the Drifters, Fats Domino,

and Bo Diddley, the stars of what I call the "pre–rock and
roll" age. Our first conversation was all about music.

"I really like music," Phil said. "I play the accor-
dion."

"Oh, really? I play the drums."

And with that, we started our own little rock group. It
was so informal we didn't even bother to name ourselves,
and we never performed in public. Of course, only a few
years later Phil would become world famous for his records and, unfortunately, in some ways better known for
his legendary eccentricity. Admittedly, even back then Phil
was hardly your average kid. Some kids in our clique didn't
like him because he was so quiet and withdrawn. A few
of the guys even pressured me to get rid of him, but I
refused. I really liked him, despite the fact he always
walked several paces behind the rest of us whenever we
went out. He was a good guy, and although we drifted
apart later, I was always happy that he found success doing
what he loved.

The fifties were the first era to recognize teenagers officially as different from young adults, and there was probably no better place to spend your teen years than Los
Angeles. My friends and I were deeply into style. The
skin-tight pegged pants that looked as though they'd come
on only over a coat of Vaseline, the T-shirt with the cuffed
sleeves holding packs of cigarettes, and, of course, the
incredible, gravity-defying pompadour with the duck's-ass
back comprised our uniform. And my comb was practically attached to my hand. We weren't bad kids, but we
thought that bad guys were cool, so we tried emulating
them as much as we could and still be safe. Our idols
during the midfifties were Marlon Brando, for his por-
trayal of the quintessential punk rebel in *The Wild One*,
and James Dean, of course.

The most compelling thing about guys like Brando and
Dean was that they represented something brand-new, a
violent and definite break from all that had come before.
Their very presence on the scene gave form to the thoughts
and longings of teens everywhere. Some thirty-five years
after the fact, these explanations sound a little dusty, and

it's all been analyzed before. But for those of us who grew up then and experienced those emotions firsthand, words can never do justice to how it felt. Another reason for my attraction to Brando and James Dean was that I wanted to act. I belonged to our school theater group, the Thespians, and was president of the school orchestra.

Around 1955 or so, I started playing my conga drums at friends' parties, and eventually on the afternoon television program, *The Art Laboe Show*. Art "Oldies but Goodies" Laboe, one of the most popular local disc jockeys, hosted a daily dance show patterned after *American Bandstand* that was broadcast from the KHJ Building on Vine and Fountain streets. Not only a nice guy, Laboe was clearly the hippest jock in town and something of a hero for promoting early rock concerts starring Ritchie Valens, Buddy Holly and other rock founders.

One day in early 1956 he announced a new song by a new sensation, a guy none of us had ever heard of, Elvis Presley. I recall quietly learning against my conga drums and being totally amazed by "Heartbreak Hotel." It was such a strange record, with its deep, dark echo, and Presley's voice, so anguished and powerful, was stunning. Now, as then, I still think of "Heartbreak Hotel" as a record that came out of nowhere. There was nothing like it before.

Of course, "Heartbreak Hotel" had been preceded by just under a year and a half's worth of regional and country hits on Memphis' Sun Records: "That's All Right," "Blue Moon of Kentucky," "Good Rockin' Tonight," "I Don't Care If the Sun Don't Shine," "Milkcow Blues Boogie," "You're a Heartbreaker," "Baby, Let's Play House," "I'm Left, You're Right, She's Gone," "Mystery Train" and "I Forgot to Remember to Forget Her." None of them, except for an RCA Records rerelease of "I Don't Care If the Sun Don't Shine" in 1956, reached the pop chart, so very few of us on the West Coast knew of Elvis. But within days of hearing "Heartbreak Hotel," Elvis was all we heard. If my friends and I weren't talking about him, his voice was coming through our radios. Then, as now, Elvis was everywhere.

Not long after, my friends and I got the shock of our young lives when we saw a photograph of Elvis. Because of his sound and his name—what kind of name was "Elvis"?—we had assumed the singer was black. He was white! Not only that, at just twenty-one, he wasn't much older than we. And he was beautiful, almost unsettling so, and exotic, almost too pretty for a guy. A lot of boys my age would have hated Elvis if it hadn't been for those tough-guy sideburns. With them, he had to be cool. Except for a handful of movie actors, like Brando in *The Wild One,* nobody we knew in real life wore them. In fact, Elvis started growing his after seeing Brando. "I was different, and I didn't care," he later told me.

The next great leap that Elvis made into our collective teenage consciousness was through television. We couldn't wait to see Elvis in action, and when we saw him on *Stage Show* or on Milton Berle's or Ed Sullivan's program it was a true revelation. He was wild, free, cocky and powerful—everything we wanted to be, and more. He might sing raucous rockabilly, sentimental ballads or hard blues; he might wear the wildest cat clothes or be forced into stuffy tails. Those details didn't matter, because Elvis' style and presence transcended everything around him. When he sang a gospel hymn, "Peace in the Valley," on *The Ed Sullivan Show,* I loved that too. Whatever it was, he had it; however it was that he did it, there was no question: Elvis was the King.

Nineteen fifty-six belonged to Elvis. From April, when "Heartbreak Hotel" began its eight-week run at number one, to the year's end, he held the top spot on the pop chart for twenty-five of the remaining thirty-seven weeks. After "Heartbreak Hotel" came "I Want You, I Need You, I Love You," "Hound Dog," "Don't Be Cruel," and "Love Me Tender," the title song from his motion-picture debut.

In Eisenhower's America, however, Elvis didn't ascend his throne unchallenged. The truth of his power wasn't lost on parents, teachers, critics and other self-appointed guardians of adolescent morals. The controversy Elvis ignited covered every aspect of his performance from his

appearance to his singing. But what Elvis caught the most
flak for was his dancing. Looking back we see the raw
sexual aspect of Elvis clearly, but to my friends and me it
was neither simple nor obvious. The girls were going
crazy, but I'm not even sure that they understood why.
Certainly Elvis didn't believe he was doing anything
wrong. To my teenaged mind, Elvis expressed a passion
for living.

Many years later, whenever we'd reminisce about these
days, Elvis would exclaim, "Man, all I did is what came
natural! I guess if you have a dirty ol' mind, that's exactly
what you're gonna see in others." I think that even if Elvis
had lived to be a hundred years old, he'd always have found
the big fuss incomprehensible. Not that he didn't understand the effect he had on kids; he did. But his intent was
innocent. He just didn't see what was wrong with it.

Contrary to the myth, not every American adult found
Elvis shocking. I recall my parents watching him sing on
television and enjoying it quite a bit. In fact, when Elvis
appeared on *Ed Sullivan* the last time, in early 1957, my
parents were outraged that the cameras caught him only
from the waist up.

What drove us crazy about Elvis wasn't necessarily the
sexual freedom his critics claimed he was unleashing, but
freedom, period. Freedom to be yourself, to express yourself, to wear what you wanted to wear, to look the way
you wanted to look, to have your own style, your own talk.
My love of Elvis and his music inspired me beyond the
bounds of most fans. I'm sure that thousands of my peers
stood before their bedroom mirrors, perfecting the sneer
and the moves, but I had gone that extra step, imperson-
ating him. Despite my musical and theatrical ambitions, I
considered myself basically a quiet, shy person. Still, that
didn't prevent me from taking my conga drums to friends'
parties and entertaining them with my lip-synced impressions of Elvis. I suppose that qualified me as a pioneer in
the art of Elvis impersonation. And, following my idol, I
was sporting the longest hair and sideburns of any kid at
Fairfax High, quite a distinction during those conservative
times. I would play Elvis' records over and over, too. I

just felt the part, and I loved the music. And, like so many kids, I loved Elvis, because he made rock and roll bigger than anyone might have dreamed, and so he united my generation in their love for him and the music he was the symbol of.

The hottest news to hit Los Angeles in 1957 was that Elvis would be in town in October to do two shows at the Pan Pacific Auditorium, a huge arena usually used for large trade and auto shows. My friends Christian Dome, Chuck Lederman, a couple other friends and I tried to get tickets, but the show was sold out, so we knew there was no way we'd be getting in. At least, not legally. From my experience collecting stray baseballs at Hollywood Stars games and selling newspapers at Gilmore Field, I knew all about sneaking into places, an art I'd perfected at movie theaters all over town. Figuring the Pan Pacific would be as easy to crack, my friends and I vowed that we'd be seeing Elvis there, one way or another.

Christian, the only kid in our crowd to own a car, lived across from the venue, and I lived just a few blocks from there. The evening of the twenty-eighth, we saw crowds of people yelling and screaming outside, and the more we saw, the more determined we became to get in. After all, this was the happening of happenings, the city's first big rock-and-roll concert, and history in the making. Decades later John Lennon expressed everything we felt: "Before there was Elvis, there was nothing." There was no way we could *not* see him.

Christian parked the car, and we got out and started methodically casing the back and sides of the auditorium, trying the doors, checking things out. It was soon obvious the security was much tighter than usual, and we were all ready to give up when we happened to wander into a small parking area near a door. We realized this was the stage door, and our commitment to getting in was renewed. Pacing back and forth anxiously, we waited for some careless person to leave the door ajar. It was all so close, yet so far away.

Suddenly one of the guys called out, "Hey, look! There he is!"

I turned, and there, standing casually, with his foot propped on the bumper of a car, was Elvis Presley, re- splendent in his famous gold lamé jacket. A couple of other guys (his bodyguards, we assumed) stood nearby but made no move to disperse us. My friends stood gaping, but I was so thrilled that whatever barriers stood between me and my idol disappeared.

"Come on, you guys," I said, but nobody moved. They seemed petrified. "Come on!"

They didn't reply except to stare at me when I an- nounced. "Hey, I'm gonna go up and say hello."

I walked up to Elvis, and, much to my amazement, no one bothered me. When I was just a couple feet away from him, I said, "Hi."

"Hi," he replied, extending his hand to me as if we were neighbors, "I'm Elvis Presley."

"Hi, I'm Larry Geller. Nice to meet you."

I still recall how impressed I was by Elvis at that meet- ing. That he looked unlike anyone else was obvious from his photographs, but to see him in the flesh was something else. He had an innate energy that made him appear to be glowing from inside, something that he would never lose. As we shook hands, I just stared up at this guy with side- burns who was, from where I stood then, very tall.

"Well," he said politely in his Southern drawl as he nodded toward the stage door, "they want me in there now." It would have been easy for a star like Elvis to make up some excuse to escape a pesky kid, but I honestly didn't think that that was what he was doing. Then he walked away.

Stunned, I turned to face my friends and started walking back to them. From inside the auditorium I heard what I'll always think of as my first rock-and-roll screams. The shrieking and foot-stomping made it sound as if the Pan Pacific were about to explode. Elvis was on the stage.

As everyone read in the papers the next day, Elvis gave a performance so uninhibited and provocative, rolling around on the floor with a replica of Nipper the dog, RCA Records' mascot, while singing "Hound Dog," that the Los Angeles Police Department filmed the next night's

concert and let it be known they'd happily stop the show
at the first sign of anything "objectionable." The general
consensus was that Elvis' behavior the first night had been
somewhat suggestive.

Back in the lot my friends bombarded me with the obvious questions: "What was he like?" "What happened?" "What did he say?"

All I could do was keep repeating over and over again,
"Man, I shook Elvis' hand! I shook Elvis' hand!" The
other guys took turns examining my hand, looking for who
knows what. I guess we all expected that it would have
changed or somehow shown evidence of my remarkable
experience, but no such luck.

After that, we just couldn't leave, so we hung out near
the stage door, straining to hear whatever we could. When
the show ended, we hopped into Christian's car and were
in the vicinity of the stage door. Being wise guys, we
thought we'd cause a little commotion of our own, so I
pulled my jacket up over my head, and, with a friend on
either side of me acting the part of harried bodyguards,
we cruised around the parking lot. Someone in the crowd
yelled, "There he is! There's Elvis!" and all hell broke
loose. People chased our car, jumped on the running
board, and pounded on the trunk. We sped off down Beverly Boulevard, cracking up.

Elvis' impact on my generation was enormous, and,
looking back, I find it hard to believe that just over two
years after he burst on the national scene he was gone,
drafted for a two-year hitch in the Army. All of his fans
were shocked. The day Elvis reported for duty, it was
front-page news, dominating the headlines. Lots of adults
didn't like Elvis, but by going into the regular corps and
specifically requesting no special treatment, he won over
former critics. Maybe they still didn't care for the music,
but Elvis—he was okay. In his absence, the Presley mystique continued to grow.

Life went on. My old buddy Phil Spector, along with
two other kids, formed the Teddy Bears and had a number-
one hit in December 1958 with a song Phil wrote called

"To Know Him Is to Love Him." Phil still lived across the street, but we were no longer close. I graduated high school that February, my sights set on an acting career. In the midfifties I'd studied acting with, among others, Cory Allen, who had appeared as the unlucky "Chicken" driver in *Rebel Without a Cause*. On the advice of my friend Christian I decided to study cosmetology, a field that would allow me to earn a decent living within a relatively short time and would be my "something to fall back on" between acting jobs. By then my father owned a women's-apparel store, and after holding several low-level summer and afterschool jobs in the garment industry, I knew that I'd never follow in his footsteps.

I was nineteen and nearing the completion of my cosmetology studies when I happened to walk past a new salon on Fairfax Avenue. It was 1959, and the first thing about the place that struck me as unusual was a large stained-glass ankh, the Egyptian symbol of life, on the front door. Intrigued, I walked in and there met the shop's owner, Jay Sebring. Although I hadn't completed my formal training, he hired me immediately, and I soon became his first assistant, managing the shop and training other employees.

Jay (whose real name was Thomas Kummer) was a diminutive man with big ambitions. Some people viewed him as an egotist, and, indeed, he was driven and very proud. In August 1969, when I heard that Jay was among those murdered along with Roman Polanski's wife, actress Sharon Tate (a former love of Jay's), in one of the most brutal crimes of the century, I remembered something Jay liked to say, even before he was famous. "When I die, Larry," Jay had said, "everybody will know about it. My death will be one of the biggest stories ever to come out of Hollywood." I'm certain, however, that dying at the hands of Charles Manson's gang was not the kind of death he had in mind.

Jay became famous for developing a revolutionary, almost foolproof system of cutting and styling men's hair, which he called "hair architecture." He was also the first stylist in America to use hand-held blow dryers and to perfect a technique for styling with them. Though Sebring charged a then unheard-of five dollars per cut (the going rate was $1.50), in just a few months our clientele grew to include Frank Sinatra, Steve McQueen, Robert Wagner, Peter Sellers, George Peppard, George Hamilton, Robert Conrad, Henry Fonda, Cliff Robertson, Milton Berle, Glen Campbell, Steve Allen, Robert Vaughan, Tony Franciosa, Robert Culp and many others. Sebring's was without question the hottest salon in Hollywood. We put in eighteen-hour days, and even the biggest stars would patiently wait their turns.

Despite my early exposure to unorthodox ideas and philosophies, what I've termed my spiritual quest didn't begin in earnest until August 1960. I had just turned twenty-one and decided to journey to the sacred mountains of the Hopi Indians in Arizona. I was driving east on Route 66, just twenty-five miles from the Grand Canyon. Suddenly I experienced something so powerful that the only thing I can compare it to is being struck by lightning. In a few moments there in the desert, I was reborn and experienced a remarkable awakening that changed the course of my life.

Rather than being shocked or surprised, I was comforted and impressed to continue my quest. Although the wider flowering of interest in other religions, philosophies and teachings was several years away, there were massive amounts of material to be read and many, many people seeking the same things. Reading voraciously, I took in all I could, studying the Bible, Yogi Paramahansa Yogananda's best-selling works, including his *Autobiography of a Yogi,* and a wide range of metaphysical and spiritual works—the books often erroneously shelved in bookstores under the heading "Occult." Among them I had my favorites, those that I felt spoke more clearly to me than others: the works of the Lebanese poet/philosopher Kahlil Gibran, the inspirational works of Vera Stanley Alder, Nikos Kazantzakis, Gurdjieff, Paul Brunton and Krishnamurti.

Along with works of religion and philosophy, I began exploring the means of achieving perfect-balance harmony between the mind and the body. I studied various techniques and systems, many of which came into vogue years later: yoga, Tai Chi, meditation, vegetarianism. This led me to several teachers, all direct disciples of those who had founded the great religions and philosophic and metaphysical systems through which men may inquire into the character and implications of the human experience. By exploring our innate potential, we fulfill the Socratic injunction, to know thyself, and so find personal fulfillment.

My adventure took me through the portals of theosophy, Masonry, study of the Cabala, Taoism, Buddhism, Judaism and Christianity. I studied all the great world scriptures, from the widely accepted to the obscure. That some of these works, subjects and teachers have been in and out of fashion at different times or totally misunderstood by the world at large never concerned me, just as it hadn't bothered my parents. I've found through my studies and disciplines the source of strength and peace, and though I never sought to proselytize, I welcomed any opportunity to share ideas with like-minded people. To clarify the meaning of "spiritual" here, I must say that none of the paths I—and, later, Elvis—explored led to table-tapping mediums, séances or fortune-tellers.

Perhaps the single most important idea to come from my studies was that not everything in life is predetermined. We each have free will and are gifted with a lifetime of choices from which we mold our futures and ourselves. There are always fate and chance to contend with, creating conditions beyond our control, but we all have the power to reshape our thoughts and responses and so learn to attain anything the mind can conceive. I sincerely believe in these ideas, as did Elvis.

In 1963 I married my first wife, Stephanie (Stevie) Wolfberg. She was a year and a half younger than I, and we had much in common in terms of our backgrounds and spiritual interests. By then I was comfortably settled in at Sebring's.

On April 30, 1964, I was working in my booth at Sebring's, cutting and styling the hair of my close friend the singer Johnny Rivers, when my phone rang. The caller identified himself as Alan Fortas, a member of Elvis Presley's entourage. He explained that Elvis' current stylist, Sal Orifice, wouldn't be working with him anymore and that Sal had recommended me to Elvis.

"Elvis would like you to come over here to his house in Bel Air 'round four this afternoon and fix his hair. Can you make it?" Fortas asked.

At twenty-four years old, I had met and worked on a virtual Hollywood *Who's Who* and never felt nervous or out of place. Of course, some clients were friendlier than others, but after a while I felt comfortable with anyone. Elvis, however, was something else. For one thing, he was Elvis. Besides being a fan, I felt a close connection to him. Millions of others surely felt that way, too, and it was clear that Elvis' incredible charisma inspired that reaction. In my case, though, ever since the night we shook hands, I believed we shared a bond. I had never ventured to guess how that bond would manifest itself—that was up to fate—but it existed.

Though Elvis would always be the King of Rock and Roll, times had changed. I still loved rock and roll, and Elvis, but the spark of his earlier work was gone. Unfortunately, since his return from the service in 1960, his career had taken a different turn, characterized by mediocre movies, largely dismissable sound-track albums, and uneven singles. It was disappointing, to be sure, but hardly surprising. Elvis had blazed a trail to Hollywood that few, if any, other fifties rockers even dreamed possible. After Elvis' first four movies—*Love Me Tender, Loving You, Jailhouse Rock* and *King Creole*—and 1960's *Flaming Star*, many fans and critics and even Elvis himself thought he had the potential to be a real actor. That had been Elvis' dream, too, but something went wrong.

Of course I said yes to Alan's request, finished up my appointments, and drove over. At four, I met another of Elvis' employees, Jim Kingsley, inside Bel Air's eastern gates. Actually, I'd gone to Elvis' house once in 1960, when my sister and my stepsister asked me to drop them off there. They never got in, but they seemed to like just hanging out with the other fans. Still naive for my age, I didn't realize they had other things in mind. As we went up the drive leading to the home Elvis rented on Perugia Way, I glimpsed the excited fans who held their continuous vigil outside the gates wherever Elvis was. Except for their hairstyles and their clothes, the fans looked the same in 1964 as they had in 1956, and as they would look in 1977. They all radiated a mixture of frenzied anticipation and pure love. Over the years that sight would become as common as the sky. It was always there.

Entering the large modern house, I heard someone say, "Hey, man, I'll be right with you," in a familiar soft Southern drawl. I turned and saw Elvis sitting at a table with a few members of his entourage, the so-called Memphis Mafia. He was wearing a dark-blue peaked cap like the one Marlon Brando had worn in *The Wild One*. At twenty-eight Elvis exuded the same air of vitality and youthfulness he did in the fifties. Though I'd grown several inches taller since we last met, Elvis still seemed larger than life—more animated, more powerful in some way than any of the hundreds of stars I knew. The word "charisma" falls short of describing his magnetism and charm. It was as if he possessed some inexhaustible supply of energy he was compelled to burn.

Alan led me into the den, where Elvis joined us a few minutes later. Elvis walked up to me, offered his hand and said, "Hi, I'm Elvis Presley." We shook hands as I introduced myself, feeling a strange sense of déjà vu tinged with embarrassment. If only he knew we've met before, I thought, then laughed to myself. It would have sounded foolish.

Elvis then said, "I've heard good things about you from Sal. Tell you what: why don't we go into my bathroom. You can fix my hair, and we'll talk." When he opened the door to his bathroom, I expected to find a luxurious reclining barber chair at the basin, but was disappointed. As I looked around at the large, beautiful mirrored room, Elvis seemed to read my mind.

"Hey!" he exclaimed, grabbing a towel with which to

cover his face, then bending over to dunk his head in the marble basin. "Just shampoo it this way."

As I rinsed out the last traces of shampoo, the water drenched the towel, ran down his neck and soaked his shirt. Elvis lifted his head, and I handed him a fresh towel as we both patted his face and neck dry. He stood there, with his damp, soiled shirt and wet head, grinned, shrugged his shoulders and said, "What the hell—at least it's clean."

Elvis' nonchalance and easy informality impressed me. He was very down-to-earth and obviously concerned with making me feel comfortable. This was a courtesy Elvis extended to virtually everyone he met, no matter who they were.

Elvis explained that he was just completing work on his sixteenth film, *Roustabout,* which costarred Barbara Stanwyck. Several weeks had elapsed since the start of filming, and Elvis' hair needed to be dyed and styled to match the way it looked in the completed scenes. He'd been dyeing his normally sandy-brown hair jet black for many years because he believed that black hair gave him a stronger appearance and brought out his eyes.

For the next half hour I trimmed his hair. As I worked, occasionally glancing at Elvis' reflection in the mirror, he sat quietly watching me, concentrating on something, his steel-blue eyes following my every move. The interesting thing about Elvis was that, unlike most famous people, he looked and moved and spoke exactly as he did on television or in the movies. It struck me that Elvis didn't "develop" an image for public consumption: on some levels, he *was* his image. On the other hand, his low-key manner and friendly demeanor seemed incongruous, as if he were trying to tell you, yes, he was Elvis Presley, but he was someone else too. Over the years I would come to see how wide a line divided the public Elvis, the man we all thought we knew, from the private Elvis, the man he wanted us all to understand.

For the first hour or so, neither of us spoke. When I finished spraying and shaping his hair, Elvis nodded his approval and said, "Beautiful. That's perfect." Then, in a shy, cautious tone, he said, "Larry, let me ask you something. I mean, obviously you're an expert hair stylist and all, but Sal told me you're an interesting guy. What are you into?"

I thought I knew what Elvis was referring to, but this was 1964, and while there were other people into the same things I was, I didn't expect Elvis Presley to be one of them. What did Elvis know of subjects such as Scientology, yoga, mysticism and the like? Discussing these topics with strangers, you always ran the risk of being misunderstood or written off as a nut.

"Well," I replied somewhat self-consciously, "outside of my vocation, my main interest, which I am dedicated to, is my search for God and a greater understanding of myself. I've read and studied a lot of spiritual and metaphysical books, and I've learned how to meditate through practicing yoga. To put it simply, I'm seeking out my purpose in living. I don't want to sound corny, but—"

"No, man, no!" Elvis cut in, visibly excited, "that's not corny at all. Just go on talking; I really need to hear this. You have no idea what this means to me."

I talked about how, five years before, I had begun to wonder about life. Why? Is there a purpose to all this, or are the materialists and atheists right? Is the universe and all of life a mere accident? How did the products of the "big bang" evolve and differentiate into an animal kingdom, a vegetable kingdom, a mineral kingdom and a human kingdom, all incredibly related, all moving forward together on this mud ball called Earth? And what was *my* purpose?

Engrossed, Elvis hung onto every word. "What *is* your purpose?" he asked, looking into my eyes.

"If there is a purpose—if there is a grand design, a Creator, God—then my purpose is to discover my purpose. It doesn't matter to me if that takes years or a lifetime. That's what we're born to do. In fact, the very act of perceiving life from that perspective only enhances the quality of all aspects of our lives—our relationships with others, with ourselves, our careers, everything."

Elvis looked as if he'd been slapped. As he shook his

head from side to side, he said, "Whoa, whoa, man. Larry, I don't believe it. I mean, what you're talkin' about is what I secretly think about *all the time,* especially at night when I'm in bed. I've always known that there had to be a purpose for my life. I've always felt an unseen hand behind me, guiding my life. I mean, there *has* to be a purpose."

He suddenly leaned forward in his chair, his eyes shining as he pantomimed a plucking motion with his fingers. "Why was I plucked?" he asked as he gingerly grasped the invisible object that was himself and slowly lifted it into the air. "From millions and millions of lives, why me? Why was I picked out to be Elvis? I mean, there's gotta be a reason, a purpose, why I was chosen to be Elvis Presley."

"Without sounding corny, Elvis, you know that your life, your career—the fact that you became a legend at twenty or twenty-one—was no 'coincidence.' The way I see it, God's handiwork was behind it."

Elvis gave me a penetrating look, grinned and chuckled. "Listen, Larry, you don't have to feel you're being corny with me. That's why I could never get into the Hollywood scene. I mean, everyone's afraid of just bein' themselves. When I first came out here I went to a few showbiz parties. Man, everyone acted like they were my best friend. They really laid it on me, but that's tinseltown stuff. You know, the whole place seems like a damn movie set, and everyone's actin' and kissin' your butt. That's why when I finish a movie, I hit it. I get my butt back to Memphis. At least it's real, and I'm in touch with where I came from. Man, I always remember my mom's words: 'Elvis, don't forget where you came from. When you're on top, everyone will love you, everyone will want something, but if you slip, they'll all be gone.'

"Man, Larry," he said, his voice lowered almost to a whisper, "I swear to God, no one knows how lonely I get. And how empty I really feel."

Elvis studied my face as he spoke, and tears streamed down his cheeks. I was taken aback by this display and, to be honest, a little suspicious. Did he do this with anyone who would listen? Was Elvis just an emotional wreck, like so many celebrities? Why was he coming unglued? After another two hours of intense conversation, however, I realized there was something else going on. He was an extremely private person who did not share his inner life with even those who traveled and lived with him. As much as I felt we had truly hit it off, and as flattered as I was to be so confided in, it all seemed unreal and strange. Why me?

Elvis went on talking for some time, recalling his mother and his stillborn twin brother, Jesse Garon, whose existence and death he regarded as a precious mystery.

"Larry, I'll tell you, man, I really feel that meeting like this, and what we're talking about is, like you said, no coincidence. Hey, I'll tell you what. I never believed that anything was a coincidence. There's a meaning for everything. There's gotta be. Man, I always knew there was a *real* spiritual life, not the way the church dishes it out, you know, with hellfire and damnation and using fear.

"Man, I just can't believe this is happening. I've heard about metaphysics and the things you're talking about, only I have no one to talk about it with and learn from. I mean, if the guys"—and he stole a glance toward the den where the entourage sat—"heard us talking like this, they would think we should be locked up or something. That's why I told you what we're talking about is what goes on inside me. These are the things that really matter."

After we'd been talking in the bathroom for about three hours, someone knocked on the door. "Are you all right, Elvis?"

"Yeah, of course I'm all right," he shouted impatiently. "Leave us alone! I'll be out soon enough." Elvis then looked at me, took a deep breath and said, "Well, at any rate, Larry, my folks sacrificed their whole life for me. And it's so imbedded in my brain that I'll never forget. Never. My mama was so beautiful, and at night, when I close my eyes, I can feel her presence. And when I'm home back at Graceland, I know she's there. I can feel it. You'll see."

It was around eight in the evening. We never got around

CHAPTER

2

All things considered, what were the chances that Elvis and I would ever meet, even that once in the Pan Pacific parking lot, let alone twice? And how was it that two people from such seemingly different worlds would become close friends, brothers? Over the years, there would arise other questions that Elvis or I would ponder and always come to the same inconclusive "conclusion." As Elvis said so often, "You know, there are no coincidences, Larry. There's more to this than meets the eye." I always loved that expression, because it summed up so much about Elvis so well. He existed in two realms: that of the obvious (what meets the eye) and that of the "more," the other, the unknown. Rather than seeing our second meeting as the unlikely one-in-a-billion occurrence that it was, I've come to view Elvis and me meeting as the intersecting point of two separate forces that, while emanating from two entirely different sources, moved toward the same goal.

Just barely twenty-one in January 1956, Elvis appeared to many of us to have materialized suddenly, an unlikely but perfect idol for postwar America, sprung fully formed from the ether. Between 1956 and 1958, practically every one of his accomplishments was preceded by the words "phenomenal" and "record-breaking." Through overuse, terms like "phenomenon," "superstar" and "original" lose their potency. But no matter who follows in his wake, Elvis will remain rock and roll's first phenomenon,

27

its first superstar, and, despite the heavy traces of all his influences left on his work, an original.

And Elvis' power—what one book called "the shock of Elvis"—isn't always easy to appreciate or understand out of chronological context. For much of Elvis' awesome appeal and the love people have for him transcends and probably has little to do with his talent. Then, as now, what drew us to Elvis wasn't just what he sang, even how he looked; for me and for countless others, it was who he was. To paraphrase musician Robbie Robertson, Elvis stood on the highest mountain, holding the brightest torch. Discovering Elvis today is not—cannot be—like hearing "Heartbreak Hotel" or seeing him on television in 1956. Three decades have changed the meaning of almost everything Elvis was, or seemed to be, about: adolescence, freedom, sex, rock and roll. It's nearly impossible to see Elvis' playful, overtly sexual finish to "Hound Dog" from *The Milton Berle Show* in 1956 and truly comprehend the depth of his innocence, and the world's. Elvis is forever, but he's also of a special time and place. When asked about the reason for his success in these early days, he told one reporter, "Because God let me come along at this time."

To all outside appearances, fame had blown Elvis light-years away from his roots. In fact, however, Elvis' past loomed, alternately comforting and tormenting, his whole life. The past held meanings for Elvis that he alone could appreciate. At the very least, it was his true center, the one part of his life that he truly understood, the one time when he really knew who he was. His remarks about these years were rare and usually expressed his emotional reactions to events rather than detailing the facts of his earlier life. Elvis said that the years before he began singing professionally were "like a dream."

Elvis Aron (later corrected to Aaron) Presley was born on January 8, 1935, to Gladys Love Smith Presley and Vernon Elvis Presley, in East Tupelo, Mississippi. Half an hour before Elvis' birth, a midwife and a doctor delivered a stillborn boy, Jesse (named after Vernon's father, Jessie D.

McClowell, or J.D., Presley) Garon Presley. Though the family never knew Jesse, he lived on in their hearts. "They say when one twin dies," Elvis remarked once, "the other grows up with all the qualities of the other, too. . . . If I did, I'm lucky."

When serious complications developed, Gladys and baby Elvis were moved from the family's little two-room shack to a hospital. They remained in a charity ward for three weeks. Gladys' health, baby Jesse's death and the weakened condition of his surviving brother became three more items in a litany of problems the Presleys faced.

Gladys and Vernon, who just a year and a half earlier had eloped after a very brief courtship, were both children of sharecroppers. Vernon's father, J.D., was one of ten illegitimate children. J.D. was handsome, mean and a drinker. His wife, Minnie Mae, was the family's backbone, and she doted on her son Vernon as Gladys would dote on Elvis.

When Gladys married Vernon, he had no specific trade and, except for some knowledge of carpentry, no skills. Until Elvis became successful and appointed his father his personal business manager, Vernon's earnings would come from menial jobs.

Gladys, twenty-one on their wedding day, was four years older than Vernon. Like her husband, she had come from hard times. She adored her father, Bob Smith, a failed farmer and moonshine-maker who died when she was nineteen, leaving her to help support four younger siblings still at home and her invalid mother, Doll. Despite health problems during her pregnancy, Gladys continued to work, but after Elvis was born she stayed home to care for him. He was, would always be, the center of her life. Elvis and Gladys each had her father's sensuous eyes, finely shaped mouth and good looks.

Gladys and Vernon's place in the world as hard-working poor seemed secure, if unpromising. In the spring of 1938, however, whatever stability they enjoyed collapsed when Vernon was sentenced to three years in Parchman Prison for forging a check. Gladys was forced to go on welfare, a humiliating ordeal for her, so that she could remain home with Elvis. The degradation of poverty was difficult enough to endure when they were all together. Vernon's crime added an element of shame to their lives from which they never really recovered. His father's prosecution was one episode that Elvis almost never spoke of. Vernon served only a fraction of his sentence and was released on good behavior in early 1939.

Through it all, Gladys devoted herself to Elvis, preparing his favorite meals, taking him to church, walking him to school, teaching him to be respectful, responsible, hard-working and loving. Elvis said, "I was an only child—a very protected and spoiled only child." Despite hardships which might have driven other families apart, the Presleys remained close. They were also cautious and fearful, as if some great disaster lay around every corner. Unable to afford even minimal medical care, Vernon and Gladys dreaded the most minor illness or injury, fearing that Elvis might be taken from them. They cured Elvis' childhood illnesses, including frequent bouts of asthma, through prayer, but never stopped believing that with prenatal care or a hospital delivery Jesse Garon might have lived.

Elvis saw very early the power of poverty to keep people down, and as he grew older and could afford to he tried to banish from his world anything that he associated with the penury of his youth. For example, Elvis didn't like to see anyone around him in blue jeans. "Man, I don't want to wear those things, and I don't want to see them. I had to wear them. When I was growing up, they were the only pants I had," he said many times. "What do you think I worked so hard for? To get the hell out of those ugly ol' overalls. It's embarrassing for me to even see them." He had a similar abhorrence of any item of clothing that was brown, associating the color with the rough khaki work clothes his father and other poor men wore to work.

Gladys and Vernon wanted to see Elvis go beyond them in life. The first step out of their world was education, and so Gladys escorted Elvis to and from school, as much to ensure that he actually attended classes as to protect him. Elvis enjoyed certain aspects of school, especially music

and English. But because he was from among the poorest
of the poor, many children snubbed him, reinforcing his
feelings of being different. He often said, "Man, I was
misunderstood even when I was a kid back in Tupelo."

Elvis always loved music, and when he was nine or ten
his parents bought him his first guitar. He had learned
something about singing from listening to the radio and
records, and from singing in church. Elvis' first and deepest love was the music of his church. "Man, the very first
thing I could remember in my life was sittin' on my mama's lap in church. What did I know when I was two years
old? But all I wanted to do was run down the aisle and go
sing with the choir. I knew it then; I had to sing.

"I'll tell you something else too," he said several times.
"Those people [in church] might be whacked out, but they
know how to move. They're free. They're not afraid to
move their bodies, and that's where I got it. When I started
singing, I just did what came natural, what they taught
me. God is natural."

Elvis always read, and he especially liked comic books,
particularly action stories with larger-than-life heroes, such
as Captain Marvel. Though he was in many ways quiet
and shy, he pursued his passions. I was always struck by
his ability to concentrate all of his energies on whatever
was important to him or whatever had to be done. I witnessed his total absorption in a number of things over the
years, and while for some people that ability is developed
over time, it was part of Elvis' very nature. He surely
approached music—even as a child—with the same single-
minded sense of purpose. Around this time he struck up
a friendship with a local country-music star named Mississippi Slim, who allowed him to appear on a few of his
local radio broadcasts. From the day he first got his guitar,
Elvis often carried it to school, probably to impress the
other kids; sometimes that worked, sometimes it didn't.
But that didn't stop him. Even if he couldn't articulate it,
Elvis sensed that singing was the thing for him to do.

"I knew," he once told me, "in my own way, I knew.
I don't know how I got out of school. I used to sit there,
and all I did was look out the window and dream."

He took other steps toward his dream. In 1945 he won second prize in a children's talent competition at the Mississippi-Alabama Fair and Dairy Show for singing "Old Shep," a melodramatic song about a boy and his dead dog. Part of his prize was free admission to all the rides at the fairground, which he loved all his life.

When Elvis was around ten, Vernon left Tupelo, and for the next two years Vernon worked in Memphis factories. Again it was Gladys and Elvis—joined now by Vernon's mother, Minnie Mae, who moved in with them after J.D. abandoned her. Minnie Mae would live with the family for the rest of her life.

While Vernon was in Memphis Gladys was forced back to work. Vernon's father, who apparently maintained some control over the house he'd helped his son build, had sold the house Elvis was born in, and after a series of moves that began with Vernon's imprisonment the family was living on the edge of Shakerag, Tupelo's black section. Despite Vernon's and Gladys' efforts, life seemed to be getting rougher instead of better. One fall evening in 1948, for a reason no one really knows, the Presleys packed all that they owned into their car and headed for Memphis.

Elvis had felt early on that he had to get out of Tupelo— maybe because he realized he was different and could never fit in there, or because everyone knew of Vernon's stint in jail. Or, like so many people with great dreams, he knew his could come true only someplace far from home. Regardless of what caused his family to leave in the night (some biographers believe that Vernon had lost his latest job after being involved in some questionable business activity; Elvis never discussed it), Elvis was happy to go. Memphis was the big city, with a population of nearly 300,000. Work was easier to find, and people lived better, more "modern" lives. Memphis also boasted Beale Street, the legendary home of the blues.

They first lived in North Memphis, an undesirable area near downtown, in a cramped renovated house. Later the Presleys moved into a government-subsidized housing project, Lauderdale Courts. Elvis entered Humes High School in his sophomore year, and he graduated in 1953.

During those years Gladys worked as a seamstress, a waitress, a nurse's aide, and Vernon loaded trucks at a paint factory until his back gave out. Elvis worked part-time jobs, including as a movie usher, and spent some of his earnings on the flashy clothes he found at Lansky Brothers, a haberdasher catering to musicians and other aficionados of black pegged slacks and shiny, colorful shirts. The very sight of Elvis, with his long hair and sideburns, inspired more than a few attacks, some verbal, some physical. In his senior year, Elvis was rescued from a hostile gang by Bobby "Red" West, who became a friend and sometime bodyguard until 1976. Another sympathetic classmate and lifelong friend was the class president, George Klein, who became a well-known Memphis disc jockey.

Though Elvis pursued music, playing with local musicians, singing with a gospel group, he also kept a day job, driving a truck for Crown Electric. Sometime in the early fifties he met bass player Bill Black and guitarist Scotty Moore, members of a local country-and-western group called Doug Poindexter's Starlite Wranglers. The three wouldn't begin working together profesionally until 1954, and maybe Elvis was toying with the idea of devoting his attention to becoming a singer, but not yet.

Finally, on a Saturday afternoon in July 1953, Elvis took the decisive step, committing his voice to acetate at Sam Phillips' Memphis Recording Service, where for four dollars anyone could make a record. He recorded "My Happiness" and "That's When Your Heartaches Begin," songs made popular by the black quartet the Ink Spots. Sam Phillips' chief assistant, Marion Keisker, was there that day. Elvis is often quoted as having said when she asked him whom he sang like, "I don't sound like nobody." Apparently Marion agreed, because for several weeks after hearing Elvis sing she encouraged her boss to call him.

Despite Keisker's urging, Sam didn't call. Sam had launched his Sun Records label just two years before, and was known locally for recording black rhythm-and-blues artists (among them Bobby Bland, B. B. King and Junior Parker) and the occasional country act. Marion remembered Sam saying something to the effect that if he could find a white man who sang with the feel of a black man, he'd make a million dollars, and she felt that perhaps Elvis might be the man Sam was looking for. Elvis didn't finally meet Sam until he returned to the studio to record "Casual Love Affair" and "I'll Never Stand in Your Way," neither of which impressed Sam, either. In May, though, when Sam needed someone to rerecord a song he wanted to release, he did call Elvis.

Elvis came, of course, but the record, "Without You," was never released. He didn't feel he had sung it well, but the opportunity wasn't wasted. He spent the next couple hours singing everything he knew, and this time Sam heard something. He suggested that Elvis rehearse with Bill Black and Scotty Moore in the studio. Finally, on July 5, 1954, Elvis recorded his first hit, a cover of the Arthur Crudup blues "That's All Right." Five days later, on a Saturday night, the record caused a local sensation when it debuted on Dewey Phillips' (no relation to Sam) *Red Hot and Blue* show on radio station WHBQ. It was an overnight smash. Knowing that the record would be played that evening, Elvis had hidden in a movie theater. It was there, sitting in the dark, that he was found by his parents and told that Dewey wanted him down at the radio station studio for his first interview.

Following quickly came a series of firsts: first interviews, first press, first concerts. From the very start it was clear that Elvis had something—dark, potent, strange and irresistible. One Memphis paper headlined a piece on the new local star "He's Sex!" With a few exceptions, Elvis' early performances were as exciting as and possibly even more raw and suggestive than what the nation finally saw in 1956.

There were a few disappointments: a couple of failures to conquer the Grand Ole Opry (after the first of which an Opry manager advised Elvis to go back to truck driving), an unsuccessful audition for the national television program *Arthur Godfrey's Talent Scouts*. But there were far more triumphs as Elvis, Scotty and Bill (now known as the Blue Moon Boys) made news and fans wherever they played throughout the South. Before long the other established country acts Elvis often shared the bill with were requesting that he be put on last; no one could follow him. For the next year or so, Elvis was primarily a country phenomenon, riding country and blues charts with a series of rockabilly-style Sun releases (''Good Rockin' Tonight,'' ''Baby, Let's Play House''), culminating in September 1955 when ''Mystery Train'' b/w ''I Forgot to Remember to Forget Her'' hit number one on *Billboard*'s national country chart.

The constant travel from show to show kept Elvis away from home much of the time. The Presleys left the Lauderdale Courts in early 1953 and had moved four times since. Gladys worried about Elvis whenever he was out of her sight, and had premonitions of disasters. That she had correctly envisioned a car fire as it occurred near Texarkana, Texas (Elvis told her of it when he called sometime later), only increased her worries. She knew that Elvis made girls scream, which incited more than a few young men to challenge him. In May 1955 fans at a concert in Jacksonville, Florida, rioted. It was the first time the emotions Elvis inspired in his audience reached such a dangerous pitch. Soon these demonstrations of uncontrollable fans became the norm. He would be threatened, chased, hounded; his clothes would be torn from his body. But Elvis' dream was coming true, and there was no stopping him, a fact not missed by an ex-carny turned music-business manager named Colonel Tom Parker.

Elvis had been managed for several months by Scotty Moore, then by a local disc jockey named Bob Neal. Parker connected with Neal when he helped him procure a booking for Elvis, and within a short time Parker was managing Elvis. Gladys never liked Parker. Because Elvis was a minor, Parker had to convince not only his client-to-be but Vernon and Gladys that he would protect their son and make him rich. On August 15, 1955, with his father co-signing as his legal guardian, Elvis signed his first management agreement with Parker.

Though Elvis' career will certainly go down in show-business history as one of the worst-managed ever, Parker started off with a bang, convincing RCA Records to give the young singer the richest recording contract ever granted a new talent. For just $40,000 RCA bought Elvis' contract from Sun and the publishing rights to his records. And Elvis received $5,000, part of which he used to buy his mother a car, a pink Ford.

In January 1956 Elvis released the first of a long line of hits and made his national television debut on *The Dorsey Brothers Stage Show,* a normally sedate variety program. Over the next two months he would make six appearances, each more exciting than the one before it. Watching old tapes of Elvis then, one is struck by not only his talent and presence, but his pure joy. A playful sneer, a flirtatious glance, a shrug, a bump—each little gesture was tested, incorporated, expanded, refined, until by early 1958, when Elvis made his last television appearances of that decade, his mastery of his style was complete.

From early 1956 until March 1958, when he entered the Army, Elvis could do no wrong. Except for a miscalculated attempt to conquer Las Vegas, everything he turned his hand to was a success. His records sold in the millions, his television appearances guaranteed the highest ratings, his movies drew crowds all across the country. He was a star and, to fans and critics alike, sex personified. The public was surprised to learn that he was a soft-spoken, well-mannered boy. He played with his image just as he had tinkered with his performance, always trying things out. To one female interviewer who asked what he did with all the girls who threw themselves at him, he replied, "I usually take them." Elvis seemed a great bundle of contradictions, and yet all of it was true. That was part of his mystique.

It all happened so quickly that Elvis didn't always absorb it all, but some things stuck in his mind. One event he described was his first appearance on Ed Sullivan's show.

"I didn't even know where I was," he said. "I knew that going to New York meant that I was in the major leagues, but I was so scared I didn't know what I was doing. My shaking wasn't even natural, but thank God I moved, because that got rid of some of my nervousness.

"When I went on, I heard people screaming, but it all happened so fast. I just went with it. All I knew was, the only way to do it, the only way to make it, what got me to this point, was to just be natural and let it happen. And don't stop. Don't stop anything, don't think. The minute I started thinking, it would turn off. So, you don't think. Just do. Just be it."

Whatever it was, it was enough to inspire girls to carve his name into their skin with penknives and demolish his cars with their bare hands. It changed the way millions of kids viewed themselves and their world. It made Elvis a millionaire within nine months. Elvis was it.

In February 1957 he went to Hollywood to make his second film, *Loving You*, and took along his parents (who can be seen in the audience during one scene). The next month he bought Graceland, a twenty-three-room mansion that, though it was not even twenty years old, had fallen into disrepair. Originally Elvis and his parents had talked of getting a farm, but Gladys and Vernon had fallen in love with Graceland. It wasn't a farm, though it did sit on more than thirteen acres in Whitehaven, a suburb of Memphis that was still open and somewhat rural.

It should have been the happiest time in Gladys' life, but ill health, abuse of prescription diet pills, and tremendous anxiety over Elvis, who now couldn't venture out of the house without being besieged by fans, were wearing her down. According to family members, Gladys had refused medical treatment for gallstones, and by the time the family moved to Graceland that May she was depressed, apathetic and tired. She took any public criticism of Elvis personally. She resented his success for giving the family everything they wanted except him. Of this time, Elvis remarked that he felt he was working to give his mother everything—everything she deserved, to make up for all she'd suffered. Some people have also suggested that Gladys drank then, but if Elvis knew, it was his secret. He occasionally remarked about "the drinkers" in his extended family, and he detested drunks. Elvis did say that Gladys would have an occasional beer, but that was all.

In late 1957 Elvis' draft notice arrived. After getting a deferment so that he could complete filming his fourth movie, *King Creole* (one of Elvis' favorites of his films), he was inducted into the Army in late March 1958. Following basic training at Fort Hood, Texas, he rented a house where he could live off base with his parents, his grandmother and his friend Lamar Fike. Weeks after the move to Texas Gladys became very ill, and on August 8 she and Vernon returned to Memphis, where she was admitted to the hospital. Doctors found that she had hepatitis, but despite the fact that they weren't sure what caused it, their initial prognosis was promising. Inexplicably, though, she began failing the next day, and by the twelfth she was on the critical list. Elvis rushed home, and two days later, very early on August 14, Gladys died of a heart attack.

Her body was returned to Graceland, where she lay in state until Colonel Parker decided to move Gladys' body to a funeral home so that Elvis' fans could pay their last respects. With Parker in control, the national press had full access to Elvis and Vernon during the days before the funeral. Knowing Elvis, I find it hard to read his statements from those days without feeling like an intruder. That his private grief was so crassly laid out for public consumption helps explain why Elvis pretty much kept a distance from the press for the rest of his life. He remarked several times over the years that he preferred dealing with the press as infrequently as he did, and usually in press conferences—which he and Parker could easily control—rather than one-on-one interviews, because he felt it heightened his mystique. But it's hard to look at the events surrounding Gladys' death and not see another reason.

At her gravesite Elvis cried, "I love you so much. I lived my whole life for you. Oh, God, everything I have is gone." Elvis went back to Graceland and shut himself up in his room until he had to return to Texas. In the fall he traveled with his unit to West Germany and there served out his term of duty.

When he returned to civilian life in the spring of 1960, he was twenty-five. RCA had continued releasing singles, so he had had hits in absentia, and Parker already had some new movie deals cooking. But it wasn't as though he had never gone away. Many of the other early rockers who had come up with him were either dead or tamed. Their replacements, the so-called teen idols, were made of softer stuff. They were cuddly, shorn of sideburns, and gutless. Elvis wasn't sure that the fans would want him again, and in the back of his mind was the fear that, like most pop stars, he had had his moment of fame. Maybe it really was over. For fans like me, even if he had disappeared from the face of the earth in March 1958, he would always be the King.

In his personal life, things were also different. He was going back to Memphis, where he'd be surrounded by a smaller, close-knit group of friends and family. He had a girlfriend, fourteen-year-old Priscilla Beaulieu, whom he had met in Germany. Vernon was in love with his wife-to-be, Davada "Dee" Stanley, a divorced mother of three boys. Graceland was there, but, while it always would be home, it never would be the same. And neither would Elvis.

Less than six hours after I arrived at Elvis' home, I was driving through Beverly Hills, heading back to Sebring's to resign my position. Despite the shop's phenomenal success, the staff stayed small, consisting of Jay, me and only a couple of others. Jay had appointed me his chief assistant and spent quite a bit of time training me, so he was understandably upset to hear that I was leaving to work with Elvis. Only a few weeks earlier I had declined a similar offer from Peter Sellers. Words were exchanged; Jay said that he felt entitled to a percentage of my future earnings, which I flatly refused to agree to. Though we had not been close friends, I was disappointed that we parted on less than amicable terms.

At that moment, however, what Jay thought was not

really important to me. Personally and professionally, working for Elvis was obviously a tremendous opportunity, one I'm not ashamed to say I jumped at. I was so excited that in my haste to get out of the shop I tripped over my case and fell on my right forearm. As the pain tore through me, I knew that the injury was serious, but, although I realized how much having a broken arm—and I am right-handed—would hinder me, I made a conscious effort to put it out of my mind.

Stevie was happy about Elvis, too, but she also worried about my arm. Although we both believed in meditation and self-healing, Stevie said, "Larry, this is really beyond anything you can heal yourself." I knew she was correct; my arm had swollen to three times its normal size. "You've got to go to the hospital, honey. You've got to."

"Yes, but if I go," I replied, "they're going to put me in a cast, and I won't be able to work." It wasn't just the prospect of working with Elvis that was on my mind. I had just walked away from a secure, well-paying job, and Stevie and I had our two small children, son Jova and baby daughter Kabrel, to think about. Sitting up all night, wide-awake and in pain, I kept telling myself that this was nothing more serious than a sprain or a bruise. Years later, when I was X-rayed for another injury, doctors discovered that this had been a hairline fracture.

The next morning my arm looked worse, and the pain was nearly unbearable, but I had an appointment to be on the Paramount lot at 8 A.M. I was going to be there, no matter what. I wore a long-sleeved shirt to hide the swelling.

Elvis arrived about five minutes after me. Nervous and in pain, I focused all my attention on just doing my job. The pain made me awkward, and Elvis added to my difficulty by just being Elvis. He was always full of kinetic energy and literally never sat still. Every few seconds he'd be turning his head in a different direction, leaning one way, then the next, just constantly in motion. At several points that morning I was sure I'd black out from pain, but I didn't.

Along with the usual hair-care items, I had packed several books for Elvis, including *The Impersonal Life, Autobiography of a Yogi, The Initiation of the World* and *Beyond the Himalayas.* Elvis accepted the books happily and seemed anxious to read them. As soon as he finished one, he'd ask me to bring him another. So began a pattern that continued for years. Although it hardly fit his public image as the King of Rock and Roll, Elvis was a voracious and careful reader. The books we shared offered ideas about religion, God and man vastly different from anything Elvis might encounter in Tupelo or Memphis, areas where such books were denounced as evil, even satanic. Almost all of the works dealt with abstract metaphysical concepts, and some were written in an archaic, convoluted style that can be difficult to follow. He impressed me with his diligence and determination to understand each word he read. Before long you rarely saw Elvis when he wasn't carrying his newest book and a dictionary. Inquisitive by nature and eager to learn, he displayed no compunction about interrupting someone in midsentence to ask the meaning of an unfamiliar word. For someone like Elvis, who was desperately self-conscious about appearing ignorant, this was a big concession.

The first work Elvis read was *The Impersonal Life,* a very small, pocket-sized book of less than two hundred pages. A man named Joseph Benner, acting as a channel, "received" the book's message sometime around 1914 from his higher divine self, or God. *The Impersonal Life* appealed to Elvis for several reasons: it speaks of purpose, of an intelligence—God, if you will—guiding seekers to the knowledge of the god within us all. An early passage reads: "In one of My other Revelations, called the Bible, you are told much about 'The Word,' but very few, even the most learned Bible students, comprehend My meaning."

Elvis grew up in the First Assembly of God Church, an evangelical, fundamentalist Pentecostal denomination. The small wooden First Assembly of God church Elvis attended as a child had been built by the preacher, Elvis' Great-Uncle Gains Mansell, the husband of Gladys' Aunt Ada. In church Elvis learned the basic tenets of his faith:

that the Bible was infallible, that Jesus would return and the good would be rewarded and the evil punished. True believers were commanded to live in the world but not be of it. This explains why when Vernon, who was never a religious person, took Elvis to see his first motion picture at the age of thirteen, he warned his son not to let Gladys know. In Elvis' church, all movies, including such innocuous fare as *Abbott and Costello Meet Frankenstein,* were forbidden. Interestingly, it wasn't long after Elvis discovered the movies that he began to drift from the church. Part of it was his age, but another part had to do with learning for the first time that maybe the preachers weren't always right. Were the Abbott and Costello movies really evil? Was he no longer a good person for having seen one?

There's a tendency to think of all Protestants, particularly Southern Protestants, as the same, but they are not. The point where the First Assembly of God parts company with many other denominations is in its recognition of the supernatural and its acceptance of such phenomena as speaking in tongues and divine healing as the work of God. In early interviews Elvis made it a point to distinguish between the church he attended and the Holy Rollers. There was some "dancing," but it was nothing like what Elvis would later become notorious for. Elvis took from the church dancing its naturalness and unself-consciousness, its spirit of freedom and release, not its specific movements. Though Elvis loved many things about church—the singing and dancing, the stories and sermons, the ceremony, the community—he often said what the church taught about God ("hellfire and brimstone," Elvis called it) was wrong, because it inspired fear of rather than love for God.

Elvis described feeling, even at a very early age, that there had to be more to spirituality than what organized religion presented. I think this shows that he instinctively perceived a difference between Christianity's exoteric and esoteric aspects. Rather than taking the Bible literally, as many of his fellow parishioners did, Elvis sensed that the words and stories were mere symbols and myths that held deeper significance and meaning for those who sought to discover them. It's important to remember that although he was less than satisfied with his church's literal-minded exoteric teachings, he never rejected them out of hand. His dissatisfaction wasn't with Christianity or the Bible, but with man's interpretations, though he believed that differences in interpretation served a purpose. Some people could grasp God only as He was presented in Bible stories.

For the first time he came to believe in the universal Christ, or the light of Jesus and his teachings, which some of us believe is embodied within everyone. This idea goes much deeper than what Elvis had been taught as a youngster: basically, believe in Jesus and you will be saved.

"I always knew there was a truth to my religion," he often said. "Somehow I never lost faith in God, despite those old preachers tryin' to make people feel guilty for things they never done. I always knew that deep inside me there were answers that went beyond their rigid old closed minds."

Guided by the readings, Elvis made that truth a foundation onto which he added ideas from other teachings. The process was progressive, and Elvis moved from one level of study to the next just as a child graduates through consecutive grades in school. The widespread misconception about Elvis' spiritual life is that he was some kind of faddist, jumping from one philosophy to the next on whim, embracing anything and everything just because it was "weird." While it is true that Elvis lacked the patience and discipline to stick to certain practices, it wasn't out of fickleness. In fact, he remained a Christian his whole life, but not a Christian to the exclusion of anything else. He was open to other beliefs and teachings, and even then he realized that no one has all the answers.

He wondered about everything, and didn't see where having faith automatically precluded having questions and doubts. "I mean, what was Jesus doing, where was he during those 'missing' years?" Elvis would say, joining a centuries-old debate. "What's so strange about the idea that he might have been traveling to Egypt or India? Didn't Jesus himself say, 'Ye are gods'? And what about reincarnation? It sure does explain a lot of things. And even if it isn't true, why shouldn't we be able to read and talk about it, and decide for ourselves?''

In Elvis' mind, all of these things enhanced and complemented his earliest beliefs and illuminated ''the truth'' of his religion.

What touched off Elvis' spiritual crisis and made his search so all-consuming was his life. From just the few hours I had spent with him that first day in April, it was apparent that he felt stranded by both his disenchantment with his religious education and the vacuousness of the lifestyle that fame had thrust upon him. Neither offered anything of value that he could use to offset the emptiness of the other. Particularly in Hollywood, Elvis realized that he needed something more substantial and nourishing in his life. Naturally, he turned to the spiritual, because he was a deeply spiritual person. He lived in constant pursuit of that elusive ''something else'' that gives life real, true meaning.

The seeming inequity and paradoxical nature of his past never lost their power to confound him. The years of degrading poverty suddenly ending in a grand flush of fame and wealth; Gladys' dying and leaving her son at the most frightening, vulnerable moment in his life. Elvis' inability to reconcile the ostensibly contradictory nature of a personal God who blessed his parents with only two children, yet took one away at birth; one who bestowed on Elvis riches beyond his wildest dreams but stole away his mother. To someone with a fundamentalist turn of mind, Elvis' life could be seen as a series of blessings and punishments in which one hand gave while another took away. Elvis yearned to know why, and if the why was unknowable, he wanted to know what other people had thought, written and said through the ages. He hungered for understanding. He needed to know that in his quest for understanding he was not alone, that seeking these answers didn't set him further apart from other people but instead brought him into an ages-old community that includes some of the greatest minds who have ever lived.

The Impersonal Life offered an interpretation of God and His purpose different from any Elvis had encountered, one that struck a chord in him, articulating things he had long felt but could barely conceive of, let alone express. *The Impersonal Life* spoke of man and the universe as manifestations, or reflections, of a Creator's idea, and all part of a single entity.

> *The Key is*
> *To Think is to Create, or*
> *As you Think in Your Heart, so it is with you. . . .*
> *You have within you all possibilities.*

To begin understanding his life, Elvis had to go beyond his childhood teachings. Among his relatives were people who believed that any book but the Bible was sinful, so it's easy to see how without some guidance Elvis might never have discovered the words that changed his life. *The Impersonal Life,* which stated that all knowledge served some purpose, that even people of flawed character have something to teach, opened the door for him, removing the restrictions imposed by organized religion. He saw that one didn't have to be a preacher or other religious authority to teach, and that the Bible wasn't the only book that recorded God's word or offered hope for man; in fact, it wasn't even the oldest.

For someone like Elvis, who had wondered where he fit into the scheme of things, what his purpose might be, what meaning lay behind the improbable and extraordinary events in his life, a passage such as this spoke very clearly: "When you have found The Kingdom, you will likewise find your place in It, realizing . . . that your work was all laid out for you from the beginning, and that all that has gone before has been but a preparation and a fitting of your human personality for that work."

In other words, knowledge promised an understanding that Elvis' life wasn't a fluke or an accident, and despite whatever doubts he felt about his deservedness, all of his life was in fact a preparation for the present and the future. Elvis suddenly came to believe that he had a purpose.

In the years to come, Elvis always kept a copy of *The*

Impersonal Life with him wherever he went and gave away hundreds of copies to others.

Since 1960, Elvis' movie commitments had required him to spend several months a year in Hollywood. Despite his initial enthusiasm for making films, Hollywood held no charm for him, and he remained something of an outsider there, even though he was probably one of the most sought-after stars. For one thing, Elvis never felt comfortable around strangers no matter where they were from. And "Hollywood types," phonies and users repelled him. Unlike most public figures, though, Elvis lacked the self-confidence to dismiss insincerity and rejection. He took these things personally. To a certain extent, Elvis was out of his element, partly because he was in an element uniquely his own. He was the star who eclipsed all other stars, so he couldn't possibly "fit." He was part of a crowd that only he belonged to, a crowd that didn't exist.

Perhaps it was because he longed to be regarded not as a star, not as Elvis, but as a person, that he rejected Hollywood, where his stardom was all he had to offer most people he met. Gladys, a wise but unsophisticated woman, set foot in Hollywood only once in her life, but that was enough. She was naturally suspicious of strangers and outsiders, as were Vernon and Elvis, but, unlike them, she had the confidence and the good judgment to voice her views. She had warned Elvis about these people, and her warnings rang in his ears until the day he died. That, combined with the insecurity he experienced outside the confines of his family and entourage, made a semireclusive lifestyle all the more attractive to him. He knew the pain of humiliation and ridicule. He saw no reason to go out of his way to be with people who didn't understand him, and who might laugh at him or criticize his unworldliness. Why would he? Why would any of us if we didn't have to? The source of Elvis' uneasiness wasn't always obvious, but after only a few days with him I learned that comfort, or avoidance of discomfort—physical and emotional—was the axis on which everything else revolved.

The glaring indication of Elvis' need for familiarity and

companionship was his entourage, a group of young men known collectively as "the guys," "the group" or the "Memphis Mafia." Before my first days on the set of *Roustabout*, I knew little of Elvis or the guys: he was a star, these were his people. Only after I had become a permanent part of his life did I realize how firmly entrenched Elvis and everyone around him were in their ways. They surrounded and protected Elvis; they thought in terms of "us" and "them." They seemed consumed by a mild case of bunker mentality.

Some people in Hollywood assumed that all that the guys did was hang around Elvis, but in fact Elvis was a demanding boss, and there was a lot to do. Though a guy's job description could change over the years, or he might be called on to do anything, in fact he had only one job, and that was to "take care of business"—which meant taking care of Elvis. That entailed driving him, arranging for a private movie screening, procuring a favorite type of fireworks, attending to his wardrobe, making sure that the stranger whose plight moved Elvis got the money or the new car.

Time would reveal some of the guys as less than loyal, but that was all years ahead. In the early and middle sixties, the guys were just the guys. They wanted to work for Elvis, and, it should be remembered, Elvis wanted them working for him. They provided him with a sense of security and familiarity wherever he was. They grounded him and helped keep him relatively sane during these years. His reasons for hiring them ran the gamut from their having been close friends at Humes High School (Red West, Marty Lacker), cousins (Billy Smith, Gene Smith), Army buddies (Joe Esposito, Charlie Hodge), or people he had met along the way that he liked having around (Lamar Fike, Alan Fortas).

The group's configuration changed many times through the years, as guys either tired of living Elvis' upside-down, hurry-up-and-wait lifestyle or struck out to earn their livings in saner, less disruptive ways. But with very few exceptions, anyone who held an important position and left Elvis eventually found his way back. Even if (or, I should

say, especially if) Elvis fired them. Regardless of what
transgression prompted the dismissal, Elvis nearly always
found a way to forgive, and before long—maybe the next
day, maybe six months later—the ex-employee was back.
Once Elvis befriended you, he might see your flaws, but
he worked around them. He found the good in each person
and turned a blind eye to everything else.

Most public figures maintain something of an entourage, but few have anything like the Memphis Mafia. There
was something about them that Hollywood people found
off-putting, to say the least, and from my first impressions
it was easy to see why. The group invariably arrived on
the set en masse, all decked out in variations of the styles
Elvis wore: flashy suits, brightly colored shirts from Fred
Segel's, black Continental boots. Elvis with his guys was
a lot like a frat-house road show. Between takes movie
sets became the scenes of water-balloon fights and other
juvenile practical jokes. Even Hollywood regulars who believed they had seen everything were taken aback by the
Mafia's behavior, and probably more than a little surprised
that Elvis—who was generally considered a polite, soft-
spoken, dedicated young man—seemed oblivious of the
impression his guys made. Before too long the Memphis
Mafia had earned themselves a reputation as some of the
wildest guys in town. Those who worked with Elvis knew
that the entourage was part of the deal and had to be tol-
erated. Early on, it was hard to tell if Elvis was aware of
how the Mafia was perceived, or whether or not he even
cared.

To outsiders, a twenty-four-hour, seven-days-a-week job
was anything but glamorous. But for many of the guys,
working for Elvis was fun and exciting. And to each of
them in his own way Elvis was a friend and always acces-
sible; he never set himself apart. If you wanted to be with
him, you could. Many believed they were Elvis' best
friend, not because they deluded themselves but because
Elvis made people feel that way. He was gracious and gave
you his full attention, whether you were the President or
his gardener. With Elvis, you traveled to places you would
never have seen otherwise and met people the folks back

home only read about in the papers. If your wife wanted plastic surgery, or you needed a down payment on a new house, you could count on Elvis. To guys whose alternatives ran the gamut from pumping gas to holding down a ho-hum white-collar job, there was no reason to leave Elvis.

An incident on the *Roustabout* set a couple of days after I started revealed a lot about Elvis and the guys. As long as Elvis worked in Hollywood, we always had very early calls, so we'd be on the set and ready to go at around six in the morning. Elvis never wore a watch and rarely cared about the time except when he was following a work schedule. Then he was strict about punctuality and never late if he could help it. This day, the director, the makeup person, a studio executive and I were waiting for Elvis in his dressing room and beginning to worry that something might have happened to him. Just then Elvis strode in, followed by a group of guys, ignoring our questions and concerns and acting as if nothing were wrong. After a few moments, he sprang up out of his chair, grabbed at his chest, gasped loudly and fell to the floor. Everyone ran to where he lay motionless, all fearing the worst. After several seconds had passed and Elvis' little practical joke had proved a success, he got up, laughing heartily. He could be wild. His nickname for himself, which he later had inscribed on a bracelet, was Crazy.

If you didn't know Elvis, this was a very childish, stupid little prank worthy of a ten-year-old. Yet, as I would see, play—in the form of wisecracks, practical jokes, outrageous behavior—was very important to Elvis. It alleviated boredom, broke tension, distracted attention from other issues; but, most of all, by acting the way he had acted when he was younger, he could pretend—even for a few minutes—that he was still the same person he had always been.

Elvis liked some of his employees better than others, naturally, but basically he liked each enough to keep him around. That didn't mean, however, he didn't see room for improvement. Elvis wanted very much for the guys to make a good impression. Over time he became increasingly sensitive to outsiders' reactions to them, and he felt, and rightfully so, that their antics reflected on him.

Whenever we worked on any movie at MGM an older gentleman named Alex was assigned to act as Elvis' designated chauffeur. Years before, Alex had driven for other stars, including Clark Gable. While Elvis was filming, I'd hang around with Alex, who had a trove of great stories about Gable (whose dressing room at MGM was used by Elvis), Spencer Tracy and Montgomery Clift. Of course, few of the guys cared about Alex's stories, but they did enjoy playing cards with him, either hearts or poker, and in those games the sky was the limit.

A bunch of guys were playing hearts on the set. Elvis was on a break, and as he and I walked back to his trailer dressing room he caught sight of the card game. At first he said nothing, and I stepped into the trailer, thinking he was behind me, but he suddenly turned and strode back to the table. He stopped and stood silently glaring for at least a minute. When he knew he had everyone's attention, he said in a low, angry voice, "I told you guys." He walked away, furious and humiliated, and the guys knew it.

Elvis believed that if he could uplift himself—financially, emotionally, intellectually—anyone could. All it took was putting your mind to it, doing what you had to do. Contrary to the Mafia's image, some of the guys were bright and sensitive, such as Jerry Schilling and Charlie Hodge, two I liked especially. For the most part, though, regardless of Elvis' efforts or good intentions, the battle to reform some of the group's lesser lights was going to be uphill all the way.

A few weeks later, after shooting for *Roustabout* ended, Elvis invited me to come back with him to Memphis. Like most fans, up until then I knew nothing of Elvis' personal life except what I'd read. Gossip columnists dutifully reported the studio publicity mills' rumors linking Elvis with his female costar of the moment. And he was the country's most famous bachelor. Probably the most scandalous rumor circulating then was that Elvis kept a young girl back at Graceland. Less than six years before, another Memphis rocker, Sun Records star Jerry Lee Lewis, saw his career ruined within days of the press exposing his marriage to his thirteen-year-old second cousin, Myra. Suggestions that Elvis had something equally unsavory cooking back in Memphis raised a few eyebrows, even in Hollywood, where someone in his position was expected to be promiscuous. While people in show business might be allowed their eccentricities, the very idea of Elvis living in sin with such a young woman was shocking. Only Elvis' all-American image, extremely private lifestyle, and the fact that Priscilla rarely left Memphis explain the story's staying so tightly under wraps.

So I knew of Priscilla, as did practically anyone who could read a newspaper in March 1960 when Elvis completed his tour of duty and headed home from West Germany. Priscilla was "the girl he left behind," or so the stories went. Despite the fact that Priscilla didn't meet Elvis until August 1959, approximately six months before he returned to the States, and that, at fourteen, she was ten years his junior, the press served up a fairy-tale romance, and the American public gobbled it down. Between the time Elvis left the service and May 1962, when Priscilla moved to Memphis, they communicated sporadically; sometimes several months elapsed between transatlantic phone calls. But in the end, true love, and, more to the point, Elvis, won out. Following their daughter's extended visits to see Elvis in Los Angeles and Graceland, Priscilla's parents finally capitulated to Elvis' and Vernon's pleas and permitted Priscilla to move to Memphis. As Vernon and Elvis promised Mr. and Mrs. Beaulieu, she did complete her schooling and, as far as the public knew, lived with Vernon, Dee and Dee's three little boys, Rick, David and Billy Stanley, in a separate house on a lot adjoining Graceland.

Elvis' situation with Priscilla was risky. The most obvious question—which hardly anyone bothered to ask—was, despite Elvis' honorable intentions, what kind of parents send their sixteen-year-old daughter thousands of miles from home to live, if not with, then certainly within dangerous proximity to the sex symbol of a generation? That the arrangement aroused suspicion didn't escape Elvis. He knew Jerry Lee Lewis personally. Before we left Memphis that May, he made it a point to say, ''It's not like you think. It's not one of the Jerry Lee Lewis deals. I'm not a pervert, man. It's just that Priscilla is my girlfriend, and I bring her to California once in a while. I control the situation. I'm independent and I have my freedom.''

One evening in late May 1964 we set out for Memphis: Elvis, I, his bodyguards Alan Fortas, Red West and Sonny West, his cousin Billy Smith, the Mafia foreman Joe Esposito, Jim Kingsley, a general assistant, and Richard Davis, who was also a general assistant as well as Elvis' valet. We boarded Elvis' large customized bus. Elvis loved to drive anything, and, because he still feared flying, during the sixties we traveled between Memphis and the West Coast by bus. The routine was to drive from Los Angeles after completing a film, then drive back a few days before Elvis was needed for the next movie. The bus was accompanied by a caravan of cars and station wagons, all packed with luggage. If we were lucky enough to leave on schedule, the trip stretched over four or five days, because we'd stop for sleep in motels during the day and travel only at night. Elvis' bus was quite luxurious by the day's standards, equipped with stereo, television and eight-track tape deck.

This being my first trip back to Memphis, Elvis took it upon himself to stick by me and show me the ropes, so to speak. We sat together during the whole journey, talking and getting to know each other.

Less than an hour after we left Beverly Hills, we were approaching San Bernardino. Suddenly Elvis extended his hand toward me.

''Here,'' he said, opening his palm to reveal a couple of triangular-shaped tablets that I later learned were Dexedrine, a potent amphetamine commonly prescribed for weight reduction, narcolepsy and, in children, abnormal behavior syndrome. To the general public amphetamines seemed a wonder drug: they kept you slim and awake.

General knowledge of their adverse effects and potential for abuse were years away. Elvis had been using amphetamines in various amounts since his Army days. They were legal, they came from a doctor, so how could they not be good for you? He honestly could not see any danger.

"Take these," Elvis implored, "because we're going to be up and we'll be driving. We want to be alert." I'd been smoking marijuana since the early sixties, but had never ingested pills of any kind. For some reason, though, the hundreds of miles that lay ahead and the fact that Elvis and I had so much to talk about weakened my resistance. I popped the pills into my mouth and settled back for the long ride ahead.

And what a trip it was. As Elvis sat listening intently, I talked, and talked, and talked, and talked. I literally could not shut up, and while Elvis enjoyed hearing me ramble on and on about every spiritual book I'd ever read, every idea I'd investigated, by the next day my jaw was killing me. Only later did I learn that Elvis didn't want me to "loosen up," as he so delicately put it, for his benefit alone, but for the guys'. From the moment Elvis embarked on his spiritual studies, he never totally relinquished the idea that he could teach others by his example. He believed that everyone had the potential to improve one's life, one's attitude, one's disposition, and could do so by taking time each day to read and meditate. That he had some inkling of the guys' reactions was obvious. And just as Elvis set me up as the mouthpiece, to say to the guys things he wanted to say himself, many of them answered him by making me a sort of walking effigy of the spiritual Elvis, the guy they didn't like. The wisecracks and insults they didn't dare hurl at their boss were aimed squarely at me.

The next day we stopped in Williams, Arizona, to get some food, stretch our legs and gas up. The speed had worn off, leaving me exhausted. I found myself chatting with Richard Davis. He too had stayed up the night before, listening to Elvis and me talk. All he had to say about it was, "I'll bet you took psychology in college, didn't you?"

I paused for a minute. Psychology? Who had mentioned psychology?''

"No," I replied naively. "I went to college for a while, but I didn't take psychology."

What a strange thing to say, I thought. Only later did it dawn on me that to many around Elvis the spiritual studies weren't about God, or religion, or faith, or philosophy as they understood them. Rather, this was strange, foreign and somehow sinister. In Richard's mind—and he wasn't alone—it was inconceivable that Elvis would eschew football magazines and water-balloon fights willingly to read *The Initiation of the World* or *The Prophet*. Something— or someone—must have "influenced" him, they reasoned. This wouldn't be the last time I'd be accused of using "psychology" with Elvis.

Everyone seemed to perk up as we approached Memphis. Never having traveled to the South, I looked on my initial trip as an adventure, and not just because of Elvis. The South was so different from the rest of the country, and worlds away from my southern-California home. The leisurely pace, the verdant landscape, people's soft accents and old-fashioned hospitality charmed me. Eventually I even got to enjoy the humidity. I often remarked that I felt like a palm tree among the magnolias, and it wasn't long before Memphis became my second home.

Before we left Los Angeles Elvis had invited me to be his guest. There have been few sights as unforgettable to me as my first look at Graceland. As we approached, I was surprised at how little it was. From the front Graceland appeared to be a small-scale model of a grand mansion. If you removed the four white columns and the front portico, it would resemble the average large shuttered stone house found in any upper-class suburb. On either side of the front steps stood large white stone lions.

Judging from the outside, Graceland might have belonged to anyone, but once I got an eyeful of the interior there was no mistaking that this was Elvis'. Though he redecorated the interior several times, his taste remained faithful to certain basic "principles." The colors he chose reflected him: intense blues, shameless reds, midnight black and creamy, rich golds contrasted sharply with the predominantly white walls. The furnishings were always spanking new. The rarity, age, value or superior craftsmanship of antiques was lost on Elvis. "When I was growing up," he often said, "everything we had was old. I don't want any old stuff around me now." Between the time Elvis died and June 1982, when Graceland was opened to the public, its interior and furnishings were again changed, so what people see today isn't necessarily Elvis' work. For all its decorating faux pas, it was Elvis all the way—dramatic, extreme, personal, conceived and executed without regard to anyone's opinion but his own. After all, it was his home.

His grandmother, Minnie Mae, or Dodger, as everyone called her, had a ground-floor room off a hallway that ran under the staircase leading to the second floor. I can't remember it well enough to describe now, but later, after Stevie had visited Graceland we agreed that Dodger's blue room looked like a kitschy backwoods vision of heaven. Dodger loved it and thought it the most beautiful place in the world. It made her happy, and, as I quickly learned, that made Elvis happy, and that was really all that mattered at Graceland.

In Hollywood Elvis often spoke at length about his family. Whenever he did, his devotion to and love for them was apparent. Part of growing up is leaving your childhood home and family, but not for Elvis. Though a symbol of teenage rebellion, Elvis was very old-fashioned in most respects. His father and his grandmother meant the world to him, and even though his relationship with Gladys was clearly special, you never got the sense that he loved the other two any less. Elvis' family provided his center, and he felt responsible for them. As the bus sped up the drive and through the famous Music Gates, we saw the entire household standing on Graceland's steps, waving and smiling, thrilled to have their Elvis safe at home again.

Vernon was in many ways the quintessential Southerner, or, more specifically, a Northerner's idea of a Southerner. Just nineteen when Elvis was born, Vernon was in his midforties when I met him. He rarely said much. He spoke softly and never pronounced the *l* in his son's name; it was always "Evis." Trim and handsome, Vernon was the picture of a modern-day Southerner made good, far removed from the hard work and disgrace of his earlier years. That it was his son who had made good and lifted the family up from despair, not he, never seemed to bother Vernon, or, for that matter, Elvis. They loved each other deeply.

As I got to know Vernon, I saw that beneath his low-key cordiality, like the guys around Elvis, he suspected and feared anyone or anything he didn't understand, Vernon's poor background, limited education and strict religious upbringing made him uncomfortable with Elvis' unorthodox studies. Vernon rarely had occasion to take charge of anything, nor did he particularly care to. The sole exception was when his familial sense of loyalty overrode his own basic inclination to leave well enough alone. Because Elvis never developed any concept of how to handle money or cared what things cost—matters Vernon was acutely aware of—I'm sure Vernon saw me not as his son's employee or friend, but as another weekly expense. Later Vernon would voice his objections to Elvis' spiritual pursuits, but at the time he was friendly but distant.

Except for the occasional blowup, Elvis treated his father with respect and love. When Elvis spoke of how Gladys had slaved to earn a decent wage, he never blamed his father, even though Vernon's casual attitude toward responsibility was at least partially to blame. When Vernon and Dee married in 1960, a few months after Elvis left the Army, Elvis didn't attend the ceremony. While he tried to make the best of things, he always felt that Vernon's rush to find another woman showed a lack of respect for Gladys. Typically, Elvis was torn between wanting to accept whatever made his daddy happy and his own ambivalence toward Dee.

Priscilla was also there to greet us. Elvis hadn't lied: she was very pretty, upbeat, and sophisticated beyond her years. With her hair dyed the same shade of black as Elvis', they made a striking impression. Despite all his talk in Los Angeles of having his "freedom" to play the field, Elvis obviously cared about her very much. One reason he loved Priscilla was that she was so different from other girls he'd known, especially the starlets he'd met in L.A. He knew she wanted to get married someday, and he believed that staying home in Memphis, running his household and raising their children would satisfy her. Despite the wide disparity in their ages, Priscilla gave Elvis stability, and, their living arrangements aside, he viewed her as a person of extraordinarily high moral standards. Wishful thinking and projection convinced Elvis beyond a doubt that Priscilla and his mother were similar, in that both were faithful, honest and true. At her tender age, Priscilla hadn't yet formed her adult personality. In her efforts to please Elvis, she more or less went along and tried to conform to his image of her, as so many people in love do. When and if he settled down, Priscilla would be there. She didn't put herself first, she expressed no interest in going into show business or having any other career. Elvis would be the focus of her life as he'd been the focus of his mother's; that was good enough for him.

Between that first day Elvis and I spoke and when we arrived at Graceland, Elvis kept Priscilla posted through their phone conversations on me and our discussions. Having endured the guys' response to Elvis' new interests, I wondered about Priscilla's reaction. Did she regard her boyfriend's new passion as his next distraction, something to fill his time between making movies, riding motorcycles and playing football? Or did she believe him when he told her that this was the most important thing in his life? There was no way to know. That I found Elvis' enthusiasm encouraging and, to be honest, flattering, didn't blind me to the fact that almost everyone else in his "family"—Priscilla, the guys, his blood relations—was confused by this change in Elvis.

As much as Elvis wanted everyone in his life to share in his quest, there was no one he tried harder to inspire than Priscilla. Although there'd been no formal announcement, and Elvis occasionally hinted that he didn't see any reason to marry anyone, everyone assumed that a marriage would take place, someday. Elvis didn't go out; there was

CHAPTER

3

In those first few weeks I worked for him, Elvis and I had countless discussions about the different teachings and traditions. Elvis loved discovering connections, regardless of the subject. He wanted to know how beliefs, ideas, words, symbols, names and concepts originated and how they were interrelated. Elvis was also fascinated by numerology, and with good reason. On the most basic level, he was a perfect 8, someone concerned with the material and the spiritual, intense, ambitious, lonely and misunderstood.

He and I explored the world of numbers, poring over every book we could find. Elvis acted like a kid let loose in a toy store.

"Good Lord!" he exclaimed several times. "I probably would never have left my church if they taught this material."

The deeper Elvis delved, the more connections he made between his discoveries and his religious upbringing. The science of numbers, letters, symbols and cycles appealed to him, because it imposed a system on the universe. The world as we understood it, then, was the conscious creation of God, complete with its own patterns and meanings. There was no such thing as coincidence; nothing happened at random. We traced numerology's roots back to antiquity and to the Biblical Hebrews, the Chinese, the Egyptians and other early cultures. We read numerous accounts of the life of the sixth-century B.C. Greek philosopher Pythagoras, whose legendary university curriculum included mathematics, astronomy, philosophy and music, all disciplines derived from the esoteric wisdom of numbers. Following the ancient axiom ''God geometrizes,'' we examined the countless similarities among Islamic art, Gothic architecture, complex Oriental mandala patterns and the Chinese *I Ching*.

Studying literature, we learned how, during the medieval and Renaissance periods, cryptograms and other enigmatic words, phrases and numbers were hidden in literary works. Shakespeare, Milton, Spenser and other writers resorted to these methods to convey forbidden information. We saw how the ancient Hebrews incorporated numbers and letters, and with this knowledge obfuscation gave way to revelation. The Old Testament's books of Genesis, Numbers, Ezekiel and Enoch, to name but a few, are laden with mystical revelations to those who can understand. The ancient Cabalists knew how to decode these secret messages and hidden meanings. Elvis looked for the true meaning of everything. With that goal in mind, we set about drawing up charts for each person around Elvis; he continued doing this until the end of his life. The two charts he came back to most often were Colonel Parker's and Priscilla's. He was uncertain about the essential influence those two had over his life.

When it came to the Bible, Elvis would say, ''Lawrence, to me this is how I'm giving praise to glory to my Creator. To finally get a mere glimpse of what it's all about. I mean, to look behind the veils, man. Now the teachings of the Bible begin to make real sense. I'll tell you what: I think all those prophets and the ones that wrote the Bible are much wiser and greater than I ever imagined.'' For example, after reading the Book of Ezekiel and sketching out the figures and objects it describes, Elvis concluded that it concerns a sighting of unidentified flying objects.

Words fascinated Elvis. Though he knew that his name had been given to him because it was his father's middle name, he still wondered where it originally came from. ''How does anyone name their kid Elvis?'' he asked one day, scratching his head. Then he said something I would hear countless times: "There had to be an Elvis, and there's a definite reason for that name."

Study revealed that *El* is synonymous with El-Ohim, God as He is referred to by the Jews. And *Vis* is spoken of as power, as the force of God. We also found that *El* was used in a number of faiths when referring to the Divine in the highest aspect. It meant the sun, the preserver and savior. For example, Beth-El (which so many Jewish temples have adopted around the world today) means "house of the sun," or, in present-day terms, "house of God." Long before we met, Elvis was aware that Aaron, his middle name, was the name of Moses' brother, a high priest of Israel. And, of course, Elvis is an anagram for "lives."

"In Judaism," I explained, "rabbis change people's names according to numerological principles. The science of numerology comes from the Cabala, the ancient Jewish mystical work, and specifically from a part of the Cabala called the Gematria. The Gematria deals with numbers and uses the twenty-two characters of the Hebrew alphabet and their corresponding numbers to obtain information about a person's character and fate. Today, if you were to go to a numerologist, he or she would first assign a numerical value to each letter of your name, add and/or reduce these, and then interpret the resulting numbers or combination of numbers."

Then I told Elvis a story about my childhood to illustrate the point. When I was just a few days old, I started coughing up my food and turning blue. Frightened, my parents rushed me back to the hospital, where doctors determined that I had a closed valve in my digestive tract. In those days my chances of surviving were somewhere around fifty-fifty. My mother refused to accept that her baby might die, and so she ran to the rabbi and told him what was happening. He replied, "Relax. Don't worry. We'll change his name from Laib to Chaim."

My parents had given me the Hebrew name Laib, but on the rabbi's advice they renamed me Chaim, from *chai,* which means life. And I lived.

Elvis loved this story. When I told him that a chai symbolized life, that it had a specific numerical value, and drew it for him on a piece of paper, he recognized it immediately.

"Wow!" he exclaimed. "I've got to get one of those. I've noticed that a lot of guys in Hollywood wear that."

Shortly afterward he purchased a chai made of gold and wore it always. He's been widely quoted as saying that he wore both the chai and the cross so that he wouldn't be kept out of heaven "on a technicality," a remark that suggests Elvis took Judaism lightly. Nothing could be farther from the truth. Though he wouldn't reveal it to me until 1977, Elvis was part Jewish and he viewed his Jewishness as something precious and sacred, another thing that set him apart from other people and accounted for his being different and misunderstood. At one point he seriously considered studying Hebrew so that he could read religious texts in their original language. As he learned more about Judaism, he realized how little most of those around him, especially Vernon, knew about it, and how much their views were shaped by prejudice and ignorance. This was Elvis' secret, one he kept largely out of shame.

Elvis' confusion and secrecy about Judaism came from his upbringing. When he was quite young Gladys told him that her maternal grandmother, Martha Tackett Mansell, was Jewish. Once Gladys imparted this fascinating information, however, she warned sternly, "Don't you tell. Don't you mention this to the relatives or your daddy." It was never clear how Vernon felt about there being Jewish blood on the Smith side; he didn't talk about it, and that may have said as much as any words.

"You know, when you think about it," he remarked years later, "our whole modern civilization is built on Jewish thinkers. Look at the Jewish religion. Jesus was a Jewish boy. In psychology, there was Sigmund Freud. All of our science is Albert Einstein. And look what's going on in Communist Russia. That was all started by Karl Marx's writings.

"Listen, man, if we went back into everyone's family tree, if we went back one hundred, five hundred years, a thousand years, if we could do that, I'll bet we'd find that everybody living today has some Jewish blood and that we all come from the same place.''

Elvis truly believed this, yet retained a vague, unspoken fear of revealing it or letting anyone know just how much it meant to him. He wanted to tell someone, but couldn't.

It's impossible to determine how that ignorance was manifested in the forties and fifties, but if what I'd witnessed in midsixties Memphis was any indication, Gladys' fears were well founded. Three men in the entourage, Alan Fortas, Marty Lacker and George Klein, were Jewish, but most of the other guys understood it in terms of their not attending church, celebrating different holidays and not being Christians. Some of them *still* believed that Jews had horns. This was the atmosphere in which Elvis kept his secret.

This good Southern-Christian-boy-made-good considering himself at least part Jew? How would the public react? What would Vernon or Colonel Parker say? Thinking like this probably did more to keep Elvis in check than anything else.

It was typical of Elvis to try to communicate important things without actually saying them outright. Considering how careful he was not to reveal his Jewish heritage, something that occurred just a few days after I made that first trip to Memphis is very interesting.

One day Elvis said, ''Come on, we're going to go somewhere. I want to show you something.''

We got into the backseat of one of the many cars he kept at Graceland, and, with Alan Fortas driving, Elvis, I and a couple of the other guys took off. For Elvis, this was considered an intimate outing. It seemed that he didn't feel the need to surround himself with so many people when he was at home. Alan pulled out of the Music Gates, and we traveled down Highway 51, which is now Elvis Presley Boulevard. After a few minutes, Elvis said, ''We're going to visit my mother. I wanted you to go with me. I want you to see this.'' For most of the seven-mile drive to Forest Hill Cemetery we rode in silence.

Elvis loved his mother and missed her very much, but little about his reaction to her death was bizarre or abnormal, except perhaps that every word he uttered between her death and her funeral was broadcast to the world. Certainly Elvis was very sensitive about certain things, maybe even hypersensitive. Watching a news report about abused children or seeing a film on the Holocaust, Elvis would clench his fist and curse, "God damn them!" with tears rolling down his cheeks. His identification with victims—of poverty, bad luck, Hitler, anything—was complete and consuming. It was his nature. Some consider this an over-reaction on Elvis' part, a sign of instability, to which all I can say is that if more of us reacted that way, the world might be a better place. Elvis was sensitive and extremely emotional to begin with. If two people weren't getting along, he'd sense it and try to help them work it out. While he could mask his deepest private thoughts and bury the most painful memories, his emotions ran close to the surface.

Considering all this, he impressed me as having accepted Gladys' death. When he spoke of her, his tone wasn't morbid. He believed in God, and God's will. He didn't say a lot about the day she died, or what caused her death, or how it changed his life, though it certainly did. If Elvis was "obsessed" with Gladys, it was with her life and their love for each other, what she taught him, things she had warned him about, and the irony of her having died when she did.

When I'd known Elvis a few days, he said, "Can you imagine? Here I am; our whole life struggling. I'm on the scene about three years, and my mother dies! She didn't really get to taste the fruits of my success. She missed it. But thank God she got to see some of it, thank God she was there for that moment of time. God gave her to me, God let her stay. But there was a reason she left, Larry. There was a reason. Maybe she's guiding and helping me from the other side."

We got out of the car, and Elvis led me to his mother's grave. At one end stood a marble statue of Jesus standing with his back to a cross, his arms extended in a gesture of comfort and welcome. The base, which bore the name PRESLEY, was flanked by a pair of small winged angels whose hands were clasped in prayer. Several feet away lay the memorial stone, a large dark rectangle. On its light marble face was inscribed "GLADYS LOVE PRESLEY, APR. 25, 1912—AUG. 14, 1958," and on the side, "NOT MINE BUT THY WILL BE DONE."

I accompanied Elvis to Gladys' grave several times over the years, and each time he would do exactly the same things he did the first time. He never brought to the grave flowers or any other tokens, only himself. He'd grow quiet as we approached the site, then stand before the grave in silence for maybe fifteen minutes.

After several moments Elvis looked down at the cross on the marker's left side and said, "I want to have a Star of David put on here. I'll see somebody about it in the next day or two."

When we got back to Graceland, Elvis told Vernon of his plan. Vernon made a valiant effort to keep cool, but the very idea—a Star of David on a good Christian woman's memorial stone—vexed him. Why would Elvis want to do such a thing? Although Vernon never came right out and expressed his objections, from the way he referred to the star—not even calling it a Jewish star but a "Jewish sign," and saying it as if it were the mark of the Beast—you knew he wasn't pleased. But that was what Elvis wanted, and that's how it would be. Elvis knew that it distressed Vernon, and, while he was determined to have it done, he was sensitive enough not to make an issue of it. Once it was engraved on the stone, the star was never mentioned again.

Through the sixties Elvis made at least three movies a year, so the time spent away from Hollywood was precious. A routine of sorts had been established. Following each long drive back from Hollywood, Elvis holed up in his room for a few days to sleep and eat. His appetite was tremendous, and only youth, regular karate workouts, crash diets and amphetamines kept him in shape for the cameras. Many of his later health problems surely began with his diet: multiple helpings of the few foods that he loved, most of them high in sugar, salt, fat, cholesterol and spices, and low in fiber, complex carbohydrates and vitamins. In fact, Elvis' daily diet was a textbook example of how not to eat. An extremely health-conscious eater since 1960, I couldn't imagine eating some of the things Elvis consumed. The first few times we ate together I had to remind myself not to stare as he coated his dishes with what looked like ounces of black pepper or gorged himself on multiple helpings of lardy fried meats, greasy french fries and sugary pies.

Given how physically beautiful Elvis was and the pride he took in his appearance, it's surprising that vanity didn't arouse a greater awareness of and respect for his body. Many of his books (including the Bible) said, in so many words, that the body is a temple, to be nourished and cared for, but Elvis overlooked those parts. Intellectually, he knew it was correct, but he figured, what the hell. Anything concerning health invariably fell into one of Elvis' blind spots, and it's easy to understand why. For all the abuse his mortal being endured, for the most part Elvis remained an incredibly good-looking man. Part of this was certainly genetic. Vernon was a dashing guy, even in his last years, and photographs of Elvis' forefathers, especially on his mother's side, show them to have been beautiful in a timeless, almost unearthyly way. Whether the cause lay in his family's having wanted for food in the past or in Elvis simply doing what he wanted to do, or some deeper reason, Elvis loved to eat. And like anything that Elvis enjoyed—with the exception of promiscuous sex—he did it to excess. It was shortly after I joined him that he began embarking on car-buying sprees and giving away lavish gifts to friends, family, fans and unsuspecting strangers.

Elvis' family extended beyond his relatives to include all his employees, their wives or girlfriends, and their kids. Elvis loved the idea of families, and he understood and identified with children. He delighted in giving gifts to his three younger stepbrothers, Rick, David and Billy. Shortly after getting to Memphis, I phoned my wife, Stevie, and arranged for her to fly to Memphis with the kids. I was staying in one of the downstairs rooms. Elvis was happy to have the rest of my family around, too.

The morning after Stevie arrived, I was upstairs doing Elvis' hair, as I did almost every day. During the three weeks I was with Elvis before we came back to Memphis, there hadn't been a good time for him to meet Stevie. I felt uncomfortable about imposing on him, and I knew they'd meet eventually. He knew a little about Stevie from our talks, and this was certainly no big deal. Still, Elvis became a little nervous about meeting her. I had to laugh: Elvis Presley nervous about meeting anyone. The idea seemed ludicrous, but there he was, jiggling his leg and tapping his fingers, asking me questions about her, honestly anxious about making a good impression on my wife. After we finished I went downstairs, where Stevie and I waited in the gold record room for Elvis to come down.

He entered, sharply dressed in a black bolero shirt, black pants and a shoulder holster, complete with gun.

"Elvis," I said, "this is my wife, Stevie. Stevie, this is Elvis Presley."

For several seconds Stevie stood staring at Elvis, speechless. When she snapped out of it, she said, "Elvis, I have to be honest with you. I don't know what to say."

"Stevie," he replied softly, "I don't know what to say to *you*."

After seeing thousands of people fumble for words and strive to maintain some semblance of dignity around him, Elvis found Stevie's candor charming, and he loved her from that moment on.

As everyone knows, Elvis loved cars and kept a fleet at Graceland or wherever he was, for the group's use. We each had a special car we considered "ours," usually one Elvis offered to you or the one you liked best. Any Elvis fan from the fifties knew all about Elvis' famous pink Cadillac. Long before Elvis became a star, Gladys had mentioned seeing a gorgeous, gleaming pink Caddy, and in the fall of 1956 he presented to his mother a brand-new candy-pink Cadillac. The fact that Gladys didn't drive didn't bother Elvis. Practicality wasn't always one of his main considerations when it came to anything. Though over the years hundreds of cars passed through his hands, her car remained at Graceland, more or less cared for but rarely driven.

One day Joe Esposito, who was essentially the Memphis Mafia's de-facto foreman and chief liaison between Elvis and the Colonel, said, "Larry, you drive the pink Cadillac." Judging from Joe's tone when he gave me the keys, I was getting stuck with the low car on the automotive totem pole. To the others, the newer the better, and this was just an old car. But I was thrilled to have it. This was the classic, the antique, *the* pink Cadillac. Probably no one but Elvis felt the same way as I did about the Caddy. He also had a great '57 white Continental, another classic that I drove now and then.

In Memphis I drove that pink Cadillac everywhere. Elvis and I were about the same height, with roughly the same build, and wore our dark hair in the same style, and we both drove the pink Caddy. As I'd be driving down a street with Stevie and the kids, people would turn and stare. Many people, after taking a quick glance, automatically assumed it was Elvis behind the wheel. (My career as an Elvis impersonator revived!) Initially the confusion and commotion amused me, but after a few people tried pulling me off the road it ceased being funny. It quickly reached the point where people didn't seem to mind that it was me driving the car and not Elvis. People around Memphis knew that this was Elvis' car, and whoever drove Elvis' car had to know Elvis.

I'll never forget driving down Winchester Road one day when a guy pulled alongside me and began yelling. I rolled down my window, thinking something was wrong with my car, and the guy tossed a yellow envelope through the window and into my lap.

"Give this to Elvis!" he shouted.

Stunned, I replied, "Okay, man. I'll give it to him." I started to ask what it was, but he roared off down the road. A split second later I realized how stupid this was. I didn't know what was in the package. It could have been a bomb. As it turned out, it was a demo record of a song the guy wanted Elvis to hear.

One day Elvis asked me to do something for him. We'd spent hours talking about our lives and getting to know each other, and it seemed strange that most of the "heavy" conversation inevitably led Elvis to his past, particularly his childhood in Tupelo. What Elvis asked me to do sounded odd: take the pink Cadillac and drive to Tupelo. He wanted me to see with my own eyes what he was talking about.

Looking back, I see now how ignorant I was. My idea of what being poor meant had been neatly limited by my good fortune; few poor people lived where I grew up. Being poor means not having much money, or nice clothes, or a nice home. For those who've been spared living with poverty, it's impossible to truly understand the psychological toll it extracts. What did I expect to find in Tupelo? I now wonder. Little houses, maybe run-down and weathered but picturesque, people wearing plain but decent clothes, their features chiseled into what some euphemistically call "character." I was so wrong.

Tupelo was very old, so old you could envision the Civil War happening right before your eyes. The area inhabited by blacks was shamefully dilapidated. The little houses didn't even have foundations; most sat unevenly atop cinderblocks. Few had indoor toilets. I pulled up to one place, and when I got out of the car people standing nearby stared at me. In my hand was the new camera I had picked up, thinking that a journey to what I expected to be a quaint little old-fashioned town would yield some nice photographs. I was getting ready to record the scene when I stopped cold. No one spoke a word, but it was impossible to look into their eyes and not feel that I was going to take something from them, maybe not their souls, but certainly their dignity. My God, I thought, what am I doing? These are people I don't even know.

I got back into the car and drove on to the house Elvis was born in. When he asked me to go there, I had wondered how I'd ever find that one little house, but, as it turned out, once you were in Tupelo there was no way you could miss it. Signs posted everywhere directed one and all to Old Saltillo Road and the birthplace of the town's beloved son. Within minutes I was there.

Years after my visit local organizations renovated and "improved" the two-room shack Vernon built before Elvis' birth, transforming it into the charming little country cottage Elvis should have been born in. At the sight of the house's old, worn whitewashed wood, its outhouse and outdoor pump, its dirt "lawn," I realized that a person living in twentieth-century America couldn't possibly sink any lower. The shack was so tiny, three people fitting inside it, much less living there, seemed impossible. From then on, whenever Elvis mentioned his past, I'd recall that little house as it stood then and what it symbolized.

I drove back to Memphis with at least a reference point from which to measure how far Elvis had come and why his past held him. Children raised in poverty never fully escape its grasp. Certainly there were other children as deprived as Elvis, but it's typical of most of us to compare ourselves to those who have more rather than less than we do. Even the youngest child compares what he lacks to what other children have and measures his worth by the results. The next question is always, Why? More specifically, Why me? In most children's minds, the answer inevitably leads to the child himself.

Despite Elvis' dramatic, occasionally blustery style and hair-trigger temper, he actually felt entitled to or deserving of very little. God had blessed him, so the good things he had were "gifts," of which he was a passive recipient. Perhaps Elvis thought that they might have been bestowed on anyone. If anyone had asked Elvis to list reasons why God picked him, he would never dare to suggest it was because he was deserving. Sure, he was Elvis Presley, but in his mind somebody had to be, and that still didn't grant him a license to stand up for himself. It didn't take a degree in psychology to understand these things about Elvis. He rarely found the words for them, but he felt them keenly and acted accordingly. That's why he sent me on this "mission."

My first few weeks in Memphis were an intensive crash course by Elvis on Elvis, an experience that was both wonderful and bizarre. Overall, though, life at Graceland was mostly fun. Despite my differences with some of the guys, we had good times. Though Elvis was leaning toward the spiritual, he still enjoyed many of the same reckless, silly things he'd been into for years.

Usually around midnight we all headed for the Memphian Theater, where we watched the latest movies without being hassled by fans. Elvis loved films, and he studied them carefully. One evening during that first visit Elvis announced, "We're going to the Fairgrounds tonight!" The Fairgrounds Amusement Park, now called Libertyland, was one of Elvis' favorite places. As a child, he had snuck into the fair to avoid paying the admission fee. For a couple of thousand dollars, they'd open the park for us, and we'd stay there until six in the morning. Deep inside, Elvis was a big kid at heart, and he thrived on this stuff. The first time Stevie and I went to the Fairgrounds, we boarded a roller coaster with Elvis and ended up riding it continuously for about an hour—up and down and up and down. It wasn't my idea of fun, but Elvis loved the whole experience, especially seeing how much good-hearted torture we could endure.

Next we headed for Elvis' favorite ride, the bumper cars. As a kid I had liked riding the bumper cars, because they were miniature versions of the things grown-ups drove and because no matter how much you bumped, no one got hurt. Or so I thought.

Elvis played rough, and one rough game he liked was a sort of bumper-car war. We'd split up into two teams, and our goal was to ram the hell out of one another. I didn't know that rule, nor had I been apprised of the group's unspoken rule: all new guys must be "initiated." I was the new guy, so I was it. Initiation consisted of being constantly rammed in a game of Memphis Mafia-style bumper cars. Their technique was brutally simple: You started the attack by beginning your run from the farthest side of the rink. As you approached your target, you stood on the seat, then, at the moment of impact, you jumped down hard on the car, using all your weight to "bump" your opponent if not to death then certainly in that general direction.

Elvis was no saint in any of this: he was into it as much as anybody else, but he wasn't malicious. If you got hurt, he would be the first to see how you were and recommend that you take time out or get help. His cousin Billy Smith and most of the others were like that, too. They all had a rowdy streak, but they weren't out to hurt anyone, at least not deliberately.

Red West and his cousin Sonny West were the glaring exceptions, however. Red, who had befriended Elvis back at Humes High School, did many things for him, but primarily he was a bodyguard, as was Sonny. These guys took their jobs very seriously, which is commendable. But when it came to protecting Elvis or engaging in any kind of macho activity, Red's zeal became excessive, sometimes frighteningly so. Though it would become a familiar sight over the years, I got my first look at Red in action during the bumper-car game. He came at me as if he were protecting Elvis from me. Maybe in his mind he was.

"I'm going to kill you, you motherfucker!" he screamed. "I'm going to get you!"

And he did. By the time I crawled out of my car, swollen purple bruises covered my spine. When I finally got back to my chiropractor in Los Angeles, he took X rays and informed me that I had suffered a whiplash. In a bumper car?

Now that I was seeing the guys daily, our differences became more apparent. During this period Elvis and most of the guys were serious students of karate. Elvis first took up the martial arts while he was in the service. He eventually became an accomplished practitioner of karate and earned a black belt. In his prime he was quite good, the personification of his karate nickname, Tiger Man.

Elvis enjoyed the physical aspects of the art and appreciated its spiritual roots. Sometimes he attended karate class with a bunch of the guys. In the seventies, Elvis decreed that each class, no matter where it was held, would begin with a period of silent meditation. The guys obediently sat on the floor and meditated, but only because the Boss said to.

I had studied and practiced Tai Chi for several years. Tai Chi is both an integrated exercise art and a living philosophy. The movements of Tai Chi are executed at a slow, even pace, utilizing deep diaphragmic breathing and intense mental concentration. For these reasons, it is also referred to as "moving meditation." To someone unfamiliar with Tai Chi, it might resemble a very passive, Oriental dance done in slow motion.

Every evening Stevie and I would go out into Graceland's backyard or under the carport and practice for forty-five minutes to an hour. Because Elvis understood and respected all of the martial arts, he appreciated Tai Chi, though he didn't practice it. But many of the guys thought this was the funniest thing they'd ever seen. To them, Tai Chi was wimpy, sissy and worthless, since it was neither violent nor aggressive. A critical number of guys measured their power and their self-respect by how quickly they could knock someone out.

Stevie and I enjoyed our time in Memphis, but there were numerous little indications that, much as Elvis wanted us to be there, we'd never really fit in. Stevie always sensed that we were resented by some of the other guys and their wives. When Priscilla asked Stevie and me what we did to relax, we told her that we liked to read, talk, meditate, practice Tai Chi and do other things. Priscilla found very odd the fact that we hadn't mentioned watching hours of television daily. She couldn't fathom what people would do with their free time if they weren't being hypnotized by the tube. Our relationship with Priscilla remained cordial but distant, even though Stevie, Priscilla, Elvis and I did things together without the others. Priscilla really didn't know what to make of us, and Elvis was clearly changing, moving in a direction she wasn't naturally inclined to follow.

In June 1964 Elvis returned to Hollywood, where he began recording the soundtrack to his seventeenth film, *Girl Happy*. These sessions yielded two hits, "Do the

Clam'' and ''Puppet on a String,'' typically dopy sound-track tunes. By then Elvis was beyond being bored with the movies; he was disgusted. He knew that the sound-track material was trash, and this made him angry. After a record-breaking string of sixteen chart-toppers, Elvis' records sales had slipped noticeably. Of course, judgments like that are relative; several of the worst sound-track albums sold a million copies each and hit the Top Ten. But after ''Good Luck Charm'' in spring 1962, over seven years would pass before his next number-one single.

There's no question that Elvis possessed one of the greatest voices of the century. As to whether or not he could have been an accomplished actor, we'll never know. But he had a burning desire to try, and he gave impressive performances in several pictures. Several important directors recognized his potential, and there was no denying that Elvis had charisma and presence, in real life, on records and on the screen. If you consider all this, and then look at most of his movies, the pieces don't fit. Elvis regarded making the movies as doing his job. He came on the set, did his work and went home.

When *Girl Happy* was just a few days into production Ann-Margret came to visit Elvis on the set. They'd met the year before when she costarred with him in *Viva Las Vegas*. Gossip had it that things between them were serious, and though Elvis dismissed the stories as studio publicity, they were true. Priscilla made her displeasure known to Elvis, and though he pleaded his innocence, she didn't really buy it. Neither did anyone else who knew him.

Ann-Margret's visit came approximately a year after their affair began, and though their relationship was waning, they appeared very happy to see each other. Elvis and Ann-Margret were beautiful together; not only were they each very attractive, but they shared an energy and enthusiasm for life that made you feel happy for them. Elvis was very fond of her and loved to make her laugh.

They seemed to have all the elements for an enduring relationship, but Elvis confided that she intimidated him. A serious woman, Ann-Margret wanted a definite commitment from Elvis. She had her own career, which she wasn't about to throw off for anyone, and, more important, she was independent and wouldn't take orders. Few women Elvis became involved with had that kind of resolve and sense of self, at least initially. With a few significant exceptions, women who stuck with Elvis took orders, never talked back and didn't mind being treated like slaves. More than once I wondered why any woman would accept those terms, but Elvis never lacked for women willing to oblige him.

Ann-Margret wasn't that type, and Elvis recognized that he'd never exert the control over her that he had then over Priscilla. It inevitably came down to a choice between Priscilla, someone Elvis believed he could sequester a couple of thousand miles away whenever he wanted to enjoy his "freedom," and Ann-Margret, who challenged him, if only because her life didn't revolve around his. It was a challenge he never rose to with any woman, which is unfortunate. Years later Elvis explained what he believed was the main obstacle to continuing with Ann. "Two egos, two careers—it didn't seem like a lasting thing. Women should be at home to raise a family. That's how I was raised. It's the only way to go."

In the wilds of Hollywood Elvis' attitudes toward women were almost quaint. He eschewed promiscuity, although he had certainly gone through some wild periods. "I realized that sex wasn't the answer," he said, "that you can go too far with it." It's interesting that while Elvis went too far with almost everything else in his life, sex was different. He never fully understood his effect on women. He recognized it and knew how to use it; he just didn't get it.

Elvis often talked about the lives of other great entertainers. Anyone whose experiences resembled his own fascinated him. Enrico Caruso, whom Elvis fell in love with after seeing Mario Lanza in *The Great Caruso*, and whose records he collected, was one. Elvis wanted to learn everything about how men like Caruso handled their fame and how it changed them. In show business, few had flown as deeply into fame's uncharted territory as Elvis; he grabbed at all the information he could get.

Elvis was also intrigued by the life and death of Hank Williams. One of the preeminent talents in contemporary country music, Williams died of a heart attack, brought on by excessive alcohol and drug consumption, on New Year's Eve 1953, just weeks before Elvis got his first breaks. Like Elvis, Williams was born to a sharecropper's family and struggled in poverty, and Elvis in his early career traced Williams' steps on the regional country-music circuit. Williams was just twenty-nine and riding in the back of his Cadillac to another show when he succumbed after years of drinking and dependency on prescription painkillers. It seemed that whenever we were in Nashville we met people who had known or worked with Williams, and Elvis could never hear of him without remarking on his death.

"Can you imagine that? He OD'ed on drugs. Drugs! Can you imagine that? What a tragedy, and now his little son has to live with it," Elvis said.

Another star who interested Elvis was Rudolph Valentino, the silent-screen star of the 1920s and the century's first male sex symbol. Elvis saw parallels between himself and Valentino's most famous character, the Sheik. There was a vague physical resemblance between the two, as we saw in the otherwise worthless *Harum Scarum,* where Elvis wore the Sheik's trademark costume and heavy, dark eye makeup. Elvis' curiosity centered on Valentino's legendary power over women and the cult that arose after the actor's death.

One day when we were talking about Valentino and other sex symbols, I noticed Elvis sort of shying away whenever I'd refer to him as being in the same category. He'd sort of shrug his shoulders and look away, embarrassed. Finally I casually remarked, "Elvis, you've got to be the leading sex symbol in the world."

He shook his head. "Are you nuts?" he asked, incredulous, as if this had never been suggested to him before. "Are you crazy, Larry?"

"Elvis, come on, man."

"No, no, no," he replied.

"Get with it. You're *Elvis.*"

But he still demurred, clearly embarrassed that women, millions of them, everywhere, would gladly give anything to have him. Elvis, consciously or not, had courted that sort of attention in the midfifties and gotten it with a vengeance. He quickly learned that it had to be controlled, because it was overwhelming and dangerous.

After I had finished dyeing his hair, Elvis said, "Come on. Let's go look at some mail."

Now, Elvis rarely perused the fan mail that arrived by the sackful every day of his life. Earlier that day he had retrieved a pile from the office downstairs. He surely had some idea of what to expect, because the tone of his voice was so funny, so conspiratorial and guilty at the same time, as if to say, "Let's be dirty, let's do something naughty. Let's look at Elvis' mail." And he was Elvis!

He opened the first envelope, which contained a lengthy, graphic obscene message written on toilet paper. A woman wrote, "I want to do this to you, I want to do that to you," and so on. Elvis was reading and had just gotten through the second or third paragraph when he stopped and said, "Whoa, whoa! Is anyone watching! This is bad. We can't do that." His mischievous grin barely concealed his shame.

He tossed the tissue missive aside, regained his composure and eagerly said, "Let's do another one."

The second letter contained a note and some pictures. When Elvis showed me the photos, I marveled at the woman's nerve. She was so homely and the poses were so lewd, it was unbelievable.

Elvis eyed the display, then quipped, "Well, I guess she's just advertising."

The next envelope contained a regular loving fan letter, which Elvis seemed relieved to find. For Elvis, theoretically, sex was everywhere, and had been since he was twenty-one. Although he might deny it to me and anyone else who asked, subconsciously he had to know, or at least sense, that women—probably millions—could be his. But Elvis knew that things weren't always what they seemed. Sexually, could he live up to Elvis' public image? Could any man? These things, combined with his moral upbring-

ing, made wholesale sex less appealing to him than it might
have been to most other young men in his spot. He knew
that women were drawn to his image, not to him, and in
his mind they were two separate entities. He didn't need
to be worshiped or made love to by just anyone. Elvis
wanted something rarer and more precious: to be loved.

As others who knew Elvis will attest, his immersion in
spiritual studies was dramatic and instantaneous. Diving
head first and drinking deep, Elvis lost interest in many
other things. His life consisted of scenes that never
changed. It was either living in Memphis in seclusion or
living in Beverly Hills in seclusion. Even the previously
liberating shuttles between Memphis and L.A. got to be a
bore. Once Elvis got into reading and discussing his books,
this period was clearly demarcated: there was Before
Geller and After Geller, and everyone noticed. Especially
Colonel Tom Parker.

Though I knew of Parker and had heard everyone in the
entourage refer to him at one time or another, I hadn't had
the pleasure of meeting him. One day that summer, after
one of his typically brief phone conversations with his
manager, Elvis said, "The Colonel wants to talk to me.
He wants to have a meeting."

This was highly unusual, since Elvis and Parker rarely
spoke longer than five minutes once a week and only occasionally met in person. We got into Elvis' Rolls-Royce
and were driven to the MGM lot in Culver City. The car
stopped outside a door bearing a sign that read "Elvis
Exploitations." This was the place: the office suite pa-
pered with Elvis' image and filled with the Colonel's collection of all forms of elephant stuff—statues, trinkets,
pictures. From here Parker barked the orders, signed the
papers, collected the checks, and otherwise managed "his
boy."

I waited in the Rolls while Elvis went inside. Some of
the guys who had come along congregated around the car.
The back door was open, and we were chatting, when
Henry Fonda approached. At this, all the guys straight-

ened up, put on big smiles, and loudly greeted him. "Hi, Mr. Fonda! Hi, Mr. Fonda! Hi, Mr.—"

Fonda nodded politely, then came up to the car and, looking in, exclaimed, "Larry! How are you doing?"

In 1962 I had been involved in a car accident and for some weeks afterward was pretty heavily bandaged up. Whenever Henry came into Sebring's he had always been so kind, asking how I felt and how things were, and he clearly remembered that now.

As he climbed into the car to visit, the guys stood with their mouths open. About five minutes later Fonda left. As soon as he was out of earshot, they asked, "Do you *really* know him?"

After another ten minutes or so, the door of Elvis Exploitations burst open and Elvis emerged, his face red and his jaw clenched in anger. He quickly stepped into the car, and after one of the guys slammed the door behind him he started screaming.

"How dare that son of a bitch!" Elvis shouted. "He doesn't know the first thing about my life. He doesn't know anything about me. He said I'm on a kick, a religious kick. It's not a kick, it's my life. And my life is not a kick!"

Elvis had a volatile temper, and anger built up inside him until he exploded in rage. Once he got started on something, he'd rant and carry on for hours. He needed to blow off steam, and all anyone could do at those times was sit and listen. Many around Elvis feared these outbursts, though I don't know why, since people were safe; only inanimate objects were in danger. Elvis knew that his temper was a problem. "I realize something about myself," he said once. "I have the power of heaven or hell in me, and that's what I've got to learn to balance. Because they're dangerous. I've got to learn how to conquer that hell."

To hear Elvis shouting in the Rolls you'd think he hated the Colonel. As long as I knew Elvis he always resented Parker. He understood and appreciated what his manager had done for his career in the early days, and never begrudged him his due for that. Elvis realized how easily he could have been the King of Rock and Roll for a day. At the same time, though, he hated Parker's meddling into his private life and was growing impatient with the career course his manager had charted for him. Even more than that, though, Parker's single-minded obsession with his client's earnings to the exclusion of all else—artistic value, Elvis' feelings about what he had to do—hurt Elvis. It sullied his career and his reputation, and effectively ensured that through the sixties no serious, substantial project would ever be offered to Elvis.

Parker was a master deal-maker who made Elvis the highest-paid actor in Hollywood. While other actors may have commanded per-picture fees in excess of the $1 million Elvis got, he often made double that again because he received an unprecedented 50 percent of all profits. It didn't matter to Parker that the films were, for the most part, garbage. Who knows how much more Elvis might have earned or, more important, how his life might have differed, had he done fewer but better films and records. Parker and Elvis were both flamboyant personalities, and they shared a single dangerous trait: a need to see every endeavor produce instant, dramatic, grand results. Parker proved his worth, moneywise.

One story Elvis related to some of the guys with a good deal of laughter was how Parker once negotiated his contract with a major movie studio. Several studio attorneys were anxiously awaiting Parker's arrival when he finally blew in, deliberately late, of course. Accompanied by his chief assistant, Tom Diskin, Parker sat down as one of the studio people began talking about the new film contract.

Parker abruptly cut him off, calling out, "Diskin, let me have the ball!"

From the bag he carried, Diskin produced a crystal ball, which Parker placed before him and gazed into. "Let's see what the ball says," Parker proclaimed, rubbing the ball and uttering an occasional "uh-uh." "Let me see," he finally said. "That will be one million dollars for Elvis Presley and [he named a figure] for Colonel Parker. Mr. Diskin, does the crystal ball ever lie?"

"No, sir," Diskin replied.

"Gentlemen," Parker said, "that's the deal!"

With that, he left as quickly as he'd come in, with Diskin—carrying the crystal ball—trailing behind.

Elvis got a big kick out of this story. He also believed that the Colonel's business advice was basically sound. For example, Elvis agreed with Parker's edict that none of us who were with Elvis could take personal snapshots of him at any time. He and Parker each loved and hated the other, sometimes simultaneously. But they both loved power even more.

Despite what the Colonel said, when it came to his work in the sixties Elvis would have gladly slowed the pace, even dropped his earnings, to explore his potential and recapture his public's respect. Parker couldn't see or understand his client's need to make a picture that he could bear to watch or cut a record that didn't make him cringe. Parker refused to allow Elvis the one thing he craved and needed: recognition as a serious artist. Elvis was unsure of himself in many ways, but he knew that he was good— or that he could be good or better—at anything he tried, if only given the chance. Parker stood between Elvis and those chances. Chances require taking risks, something Parker wasn't about to do with his only client. More than once Elvis said he was being betrayed. If only he had known.

Did Elvis ever suspect that Colonel Tom Parker of Huntington, West Virginia, wasn't who or what he claimed? Gladys had viewed with suspicion the fact that Parker's title was honorary, not earned in service but granted by a crony. What would she, Vernon and Elvis have thought if they had lived to learn what the world discovered in 1981: that Colonel Tom Parker, besides not being a real colonel, wasn't really Tom Parker either, but an illegal immigrant from Holland named Andreas Cornelis van Kuijk? Through shrewd salesmanship, self-promotion and dogged attention to detail, Parker rose above whatever, or whomever, he left behind to become one of the least understood, most powerful and most feared managers in show business.

Every now and then Parker would sit down with several of the guys and me and start lecturing us in a friendly, avuncular way about how to succeed in business, in life, in anything. He had all the answers.

"First, I get up early in the morning," he'd say, his big fat blue eyes surveying us. Then he'd ramble on about how you've got to stay ahead of things, take care of details, watch your step.

Between the time he is believed to have arrived in the United States, 1929, and 1953, Parker had served two years in the U.S. Army, toured the country with several carnivals and been Tampa, Florida's, dogcatcher and top pet-funeral director. Then he moved into the music business, first as a free-lance concert promoter, then as advance man for the Grand Ole Opry, and as singer Eddy Arnold's manager.

In 1953 Eddy fired Parker, but within a year Parker was back in the game, having signed Hank Snow to a management contract. By the time Parker crossed Elvis' path he was heading Hank Snow Jamboree Attractions, a major country booking agency with an impressive roster including the Carter Family, Minnie Pearl and Ferlin Husky. From this respectable position, and with the help of business partner Snow (one of Gladys' favorite singers), Parker worked on the Presleys. Vernon was a pushover for the old carny's promises and claims; he'd have signed a pact with the devil. Even Elvis later said as much. And maybe Vernon did. Elvis was still a kid, but an anxious, restless kid understandably eager to test his newfound powers and see how far they might take him. Gladys tried to hold out, but her dislike of Parker was so unspecific, based on feelings and hunches, she finally gave in. Elvis never forgot that she'd done so against her better judgment.

Beginning with the first vaguely worded, open-ended contract, Elvis was snared. Elvis' feelings of indebtedness to Parker waned with time, but the obligation due, because he'd made a deal and his word was his bond, didn't. The Colonel devised other means of holding his prize, but he didn't need to. By the sixties Elvis had already forged his own chains out of loyalty, trust, honor and fear.

Parker's real strength wasn't what he did, but what he

knew, and he knew these things about Elvis. He knew that until the day Elvis changed his thinking about his life and his career, until he became an essentially different man, his own man, he'd never be in control. The "religious kick" threatened just about everyone around Elvis to one degree or another, but none so much as Parker. The Colonel recognized and respected power, and throughout the years he had been able to keep one step ahead of his client. The only thing that would surely blow the whole game for them both would be if Elvis simply decided not to play Parker's game.

December 1964 found us all in Memphis for the Christmas holidays. Between Christmas shopping, going to the Memphian each night and working, it was hectic, but we were young and having the time of our lives. Christmas was Elvis' favorite holiday, and each year he ordered Graceland festooned with colored lights and other decorations. Inside stood an exceptionally large, lush tree covered with ornaments and lights and surrounded by great piles of beautifully wrapped gifts.

Except for the relatives who lived at or near Graceland or who worked for Elvis, few of his kin came around much. But there were many of them this Christmas. "They're all going to come now," Elvis said wearily. "They all want something."

Elvis came from a very large extended family, so there was always a relative—or someone claiming to be a relative—with his hand out. Elvis was usually happy to help anyone in need, but he disliked feeling obligated to do something or unappreciated after he did. The main reason he was less than thrilled with seeing some of them this year was his studies. He knew what they'd think and was especially wary of his Aunt Lillian, Gladys' eldest sister. Lillian had been particularly close to Elvis' mother and was extremely religious.

"My aunt's coming over today," Elvis said to me. "Oh, boy, you'd better get ready, 'cause now you're gonna see the narrow-mindedness." He expected her to lay the fundamentalist line on him, and he wasn't in the mood.

You could tell by looking at Lillian that she was a Smith. She had Gladys' dark coloring and hair, as well as her sister's full, round cheeks. At one point in their conversation, Elvis started talking to her about fundamentalism. He could have kept his new ideas to himself, but for some reason he felt compelled to make his aunt understand them. As he predicted, his explanations of the cosmology of the universe fell on deaf ears. She didn't like hearing this kind of talk from her nephew, but Elvis didn't back down. He expected as much, and he was ready.

She seemed concerned about the books he was reading; she didn't think anyone should read anything on God or religion except the Bible and a few other Christian texts. Everything else, she informed Elvis, was demonic.

Elvis then handed her a copy of *The Impersonal Life*. She opened it and gave it a cold cursory glance, passing it back to Elvis with a look of indignation. She didn't know just what about it she objected to, because she didn't read a word of it. But she knew what it wasn't, which was enough for her. Aunt Lillian was definitely a tough customer, but Elvis didn't give up on anyone, not even her.

Whenever Elvis returned to Memphis between films, I came along. Stevie and I brought Jova and Kabrel with us to Memphis. We never stayed at Graceland together, though whenever I was in Memphis without my family I had a room there. Generally, our family either stayed at the Howard Johnson's motel near Graceland or rented an apartment for the two or three months we were in town.

Because we knew we'd be staying in Memphis during Elvis' customary three-month hiatus after the holidays, Stevie and I arranged for a friend to get us a pound of Acapulco Gold. I couldn't risk carrying drugs, especially not while I was with Elvis or traveling across state lines, so Stevie was to bring the grass with her when she flew to Memphis, where we'd meet. When I got back to Memphis Stevie regretfully informed me that our pot had gone up in smoke when she tried to dry it in our kitchen oven. We wrote to her friend, in code, asking her to mail us another brick. We enclosed a check and waited for a reply.

About three weeks later, our friend's sister called to tell us that our friend had been busted by the police. During the raid, a cop had picked up our letter, which also stated that we were enjoying our stay in Memphis with Elvis, quickly perused it, then threw it away. Our friend's sister's assurance that the police couldn't possibly have read and deciphered our letter smacked of wishful thinking. How I wanted to believe her, only a sick feeling in the pit of my stomach told me it wasn't so. That was it, I resolved, no more grass. We flushed our last couple of joints and tried to forget about our close call.

Late one afternoon, about a week later, Stevie, the kids and I were in the pink Cadillac, going from our hotel to Graceland. As we turned onto Highway 51, Stevie remarked that the car behind us seemed to be tailing us. In the rearview mirror I saw two men in a vehicle with Arkansas plates. As we turned left, toward the Music Gates, the other car swerved sharply right, crossing the dividing line and stopping directly across from Graceland, in what was then a vacant lot.

Instinctively, I quickly pulled back from the gates and sped across the highway, hoping to confront the two strangers. When they saw us approaching, they sped off. Desperate to know what the hell was going on, I followed. Our game of cat-and-mouse escalated into a high-speed chase, with both cars reaching speeds of over eighty miles per hour. Trying to lose me, the other car careened through shopping centers, tires skidding and screeching as pedestrians frantically jumped out of its path. Risking the lives of my family and those innocent bystanders, I pursued the car, my only thought to stop them and find out what they wanted. When I braked to keep from running over an elderly couple, I lost the other car. All the while Stevie screamed at me to stop.

"Forget it, Larry! Let them go! This is too crazy. Let's just go to Graceland."

I wasn't listening. I cruised around the parking lots, hoping to see the car. I was ready to give up, when it reappeared. The chase resumed. Stevie was hysterical; I'd lost my mind. Racing down the streets at even higher speeds, they eluded me again. I tried to find them, but before I did Stevie's pleas finally brought me to my senses.

Shaken, we headed for Graceland, where we sat in the den with Elvis, Vernon, Priscilla and all the guys and their families. I tried to relax, but my thoughts kept returning to our bizarre ordeal. I couldn't shake the feeling that there was more to come.

Within the hour, the telephone rang, and I knew. Marty Lacker answered and gave the caller a series of monosyllabic answers before he said, "Elvis, you better take this."

Elvis walked over, took the receiver and answered the caller with short, terse replies. His face was blank, but I knew that the call concerned me. Elvis put down the receiver and announced, "Y'all better come down to the front gate with me. There's trouble." Looking at me, he added, "Larry, you better wait here."

Everyone in the house, including my wife and children, followed Elvis outside. Sitting motionless in the den, I wondered what was going on. What had I done? For the next ten to fifteen minutes time stopped, then the phone rang.

"Larry," Elvis said. "You better come down here now. I'm in the guardhouse, and I'll explain it to you when you get here."

I went out the back door and, turning toward the Music Gates, saw the commotion on the street. There stood well over a hundred fans, some snapping pictures, about twenty police cars, reporters, and several plainclothes cops trying to round up everyone. Elvis broke from the crowd at the guardhouse and hurried toward me. When he got close enough, he whispered, "Just tell me one thing. Are you clean?" I assured him I was. He put his hand on my shoulder and said, "Listen, Larry, here's what's going on. The police think you're smuggling marijuana. I explained to them there's some kind of mistake, but they need to take you downtown. Look, just cooperate with them, and I promise you they won't lay a finger on you." Trying to shore up his claims, he added defiantly, "I'll call the damn mayor, and if he's not there I'll call the governor of Tennessee."

Vernon walked up, and once he was in earshot Elvis said, "Daddy, if they get out of line with Larry, we're pullin' out of Memphis, and I mean it. I put this fuckin' city on the map, and if we have to sell Graceland we will. Now, I told Larry that they just have to do their jobs, they're just going to question him. But I'm telling you, if they lay one hand on him or treat him wrong, that's it. Larry's my brother, and I'm going to stand by him no matter what."

Vernon replied, "Well, son, whatever you say."

The three of us walked toward the guardhouse, which sat just inside the open Music Gates. Elvis led me to the officer in charge, who explained I would have to be handcuffed. It was procedure. I asked to speak to Stevie and, with Elvis and Vernon standing near, told my wife the little I knew.

"Stevie, there's nothing to worry about," Elvis said, trying to reassure her. "I've arranged everything. They just want to talk with Larry downtown, then he's comin' right back. I'll watch after you and the kids, and I'll get you home myself later."

They handcuffed me and led me to the police car. I turned to look at Elvis and Stevie. Elvis winked and nodded. I knew he was with me and was relieved that he'd be back at Graceland making calls on my behalf and, most important, looking out for Stevie and the kids. Still the humiliation and shock were devastating. Instead of taking me downtown for questioning, as they'd assured everyone at Graceland they would, the police drove me to my motel, where I was roughly escorted into the manager's office. The manager glared at me as if I'd just murdered someone.

The next thing I knew I was standing handcuffed in the middle of my room as policemen overturned drawers and pulled out lighting fixtures. Elvis' assurances and vows of revenge meant nothing to these guys. I knew that if they found so much as a single seed, it would be over for me.

After their meticulous search yielded nothing, we were back in the cars and headed downtown. At police headquarters I was taken into a large room, where a couple of dozen men were leaning against the walls. They were a mix of uniformed and plainclothes cops, and all faced a desk at the far end of the room, where sat the sheriff. He instructed someone to remove my handcuffs, then peered over his glasses, occasionally glancing at some papers on his desk.

"Larry, tell me the truth," he said. "Does Elvis know you're transporting drugs across state lines?"

I was stunned. Did they really think Elvis and I were involved in drug trafficking? Or were they trying to fabricate something to make a case because of Elvis' name? Like "When did you stop beating your wife?" this question had no good answer.

A skinny young officer standing to my right roughly elbowed me and said, "You better speak up in a hurry, boy." When I didn't answer, he "nudged" me again, even harder. "You better answer the question," he repeated.

"Tell him not to talk to me that way," I said to the sheriff. "If he touches me again like that, you're all going to hear about it, and I won't talk to anyone."

The sheriff reprimanded the officer, which was small comfort, since next he recounted in some detail the surveillance that had been carried out. They had monitored me and tapped my phones.

"We know every move you've made, Larry," the sheriff said. "And we know all about Steve McQueen and Jay Sebring too." After he rattled off a list of other acquaintances, I knew he wasn't bluffing. Sebring and McQueen were part of a Hollywood clique I hung out with occasionally. Among this group it was common knowledge that Sebring supplied most of the drugs. It was also known that Sebring was wild when it came to drugs and women, though these were secrets to the rest of the world. When the police mentioned those two names, I knew they were onto something and this wasn't a local fishing expedition but a federal investigation. Upon my return to L.A. several weeks later various friends told me of being arrested and jailed. In one case, police planted drugs in a friend's home, then charged him with possession.

The picture was darkening, and Elvis' threats to call the

mayor and the governor paled, but, trusting Elvis as I did, I felt no need to call an attorney. Looking back, though, it's easy to see how law-enforcement officials abused their power. The historic Supreme Court *Miranda* v. *Arizona* decision, which established that no suspect could be questioned without first being advised of his rights, including that of obtaining legal counsel, didn't come down until 1966. Needless to say, I wasn't advised of my rights.

I was taken to booking, where I was fingerprinted and photographed, then locked in a jail cell. The scene had all the elements of a movie cliché: the ominous clank of the iron doors, the freezing-cold concrete floor, the hostile expressions of my seven or eight cellmates. For the next few hours I kept to myself, nervously hoping no one would bother me. As the night wore on, I sat shivering on the floor. I tried to distract myself by recalling the stories of various mystics and philosophers who in their "dark nights" gained illumination. I told myself that this was just another test, another experience "along the path."

I don't know how long I was in the cell before I became ill. Breaking into a fevered sweat, I called out to the jailer and told him I felt sick. A few moments later they had me back in handcuffs, sitting in a paddy wagon en route to Baptist Memorial Hospital. There, cuffed to a bed, I was examined by a doctor, who proclaimed that, my 102-degree fever aside, I was fit to go back to jail.

Sometime in the darkness of morning the jailer called my name. He opened the cell door, led me out and deposited me back in the sheriff's room. It was after four A.M.; still, I was surprised to see my tormentor, the local sheriff, sitting behind his desk in his pajamas.

"Larry," he said apologetically, "I'm very sorry all this happened. None of this will be on your record, I assure you. I had to keep you here because I was pressured by the federal narcotics agents. I received a call at home about you and so I came right down. You just tell me where you want to go, and I'll have one of my men drive you."

It was still dark when the policeman dropped me off at Graceland. I got into the pink Cadillac and drove right to the motel, where Stevie was waiting for me. No surprise, the management asked us to leave, so we packed up and checked into another motel. While I was in jail, Elvis had made sure that Stevie and the kids were all right. He had driven them around town, constantly reassuring Stevie that he wouldn't let anything happen to me. I also learned that at the very moment I was being led away from Graceland in handcuffs, Elvis had instructed one of the guys to jump over a back wall, find a pay phone, and call our friend in Los Angeles and tell her what was going on and not to send us anything else in the mail.

The next afternoon was Christmas Eve. Elvis, Vernon and I were sitting in the den, talking about my ordeal.

"Man, I'll tell you," Elvis said, "it's a good thing Larry's here. I told you I'd get you out with no problem, and if they ever tried to do anything to you, I swear to God we all would have pulled up stakes and left Memphis for good."

Elvis was very pleased about the outcome but still angry. My little scrape made for a real adventure and gave him a chance to be a hero, to demonstrate his loyalty and love. He just wouldn't let go of it.

"Last night," he continued, "I called the mayor up and told him what was goin' on, and he told me not to worry, that he'd take care of everything. And he did." Elvis gave me his famous smile and winked.

Not a week later, my family and I were asleep in our motel room. Because we stayed up until dawn with Elvis we rarely woke before noon. Around eleven-thirty we heard a knock at the door. We had arranged to have a bellboy deliver our mail and, assuming it was he, Stevie opened the door a crack and reached out for the mail. Without warning, the door flew open and smashed against the wall. Half asleep, I jumped out of bed and found myself staring into the faces of two plainclothes cops, their guns drawn and aimed at me.

"Put your hands up and sit down," one said, tossing a search warrant onto the bed. My heart stopped as I read the words "suspicion of smuggling heroin and marijuana."

Handing me a large manila envelope, one of them barked, "Okay, open this now. We got you, Larry. We've been waiting for this to arrive."

I quickly thought, This is a setup, and the envelope's a plant. Then I saw the return address. It was from a friend who probably hadn't heard about the last fiasco, and, worse, a friend who often sent us "gifts." I kept glancing at Stevie and the envelope.

"Don't stall. Open it now!"

Slowly I tore open the envelope and apprehensively looked inside. Trembling, I extracted the contents. When the cops realized what it was, their faces blanched, then reddened with embarrassment. Inside were two pictures— one for me, and one for Elvis—of Jesus.

Later, when I told Elvis of our "visit," he was enthralled by every detail, his eyes gleaming. He slowly arched his eyebrows as I took the picture of Jesus from its envelope. When he saw it, he was almost as relieved as we had been.

"Larry, I love it! I love it! A masterful stroke!" he exclaimed, laughing. "Larry, I think that really seals it, man. They won't bother us again. You never know: that picture surprised those guys just as much as it surprised you and Stevie. For a different reason, but, hey, that picture has power. All the masters have that look. That image has been branded into those cops. Someday it might even help them wake up."

For years after, Elvis kept his copy of Jesus' picture next to his bed.

CHAPTER

4

By the time we left Graceland for Hollywood in early 1965, Elvis and I had spent hundreds of hours together. Looking back, I'd say these were probably the happiest years of Elvis' life after his mother's death. At thirty, he was in his prime, a millionaire countless times over, and still the King of Rock and Roll, though to judge from the movies and the recent spate of record releases a king in exile. While those things certainly bothered Elvis, he dealt with them by not dealing with them. He felt powerless to make substantial changes in his life, so he coped by ignoring what displeased him and focusing on Priscilla, his family and his friends to the exclusion of all else. There he did find happiness. Behind the Music Gates was no Colonel, no Hollywood, no commitments, and no Elvis as the world knew him.

Whenever my thoughts turn to those times in the midsixties, I see Elvis and all of us living an enchanted life, free from care and always laughing. I always recall the laughter. Elvis was one of the funniest people I ever met, not in the sense that he told great stories or jokes, but his wry sense of humor and funny way of looking at things had us cracking up most of the time. He might respond to a remark with a certain smile or look, and it would be funny. He seemed to be always doing something to make Priscilla laugh. Years later I would come to know the kind of forced, almost timed laughter of the sycophant, but not then. Despite this, there were still tensions.

In 1966 I became interested in the classical guitarist Segovia and took lessons with Virginia De Santos. She was a woman in Los Angeles who had studied with Segovia and, interestingly enough, was also into metaphysics. Shortly before that I met a fascinating man in Memphis, a guitar-maker whose family had been crafting fine Gómez guitars in Seville, Spain, for generations. I purchased one of his instruments and dedicated whatever free time I had between my family, working for Elvis and attending the American School of Religion to learning the instrument. Moviemaking involves a lot of hurry-up-and-wait, so I brought my guitar, my sheet music and a stand with me each day. Whenever I wasn't needed, I'd practice in Elvis' trailer.

One day when I was running through a beautiful Bach exercise one of the guys burst in, looking for something. Hearing the music, he stopped dead in his tracks and said, "What the hell's that damn Hong Kong shit you're playing?"

Aghast, I replied, "This is Bach. Johann Sebastian Bach."

"Never heard of the son of a bitch," he answered with a smirk, obviously pleased with himself.

Of course, everyone who worked with Elvis got certain perks, though understandably some were a lot more attractive than others. One of the best fringe benefits was the women.

The spiritual studies seem to be inconsistent with the party atmosphere in Hollywood, but even this aspect of life took on a typical Elvis twist. Almost every night that he was in Hollywood, about a hundred young women would congregate outside the house. Now, there being only one Elvis, that left ninety-nine other possible dates for everyone else to choose from. The guys got spruced up in fancy shirts and fine black leather boots, trying to look their best. Of course, most girls wanted Elvis, but there were plenty who, knowing the slim odds of connecting with him, would take their chances on the "filtering system." Party time was heralded by one or two guys standing near the open front door. "You, you, you, you, you, you!" they'd call out, pointing to their choices. Minutes later fifteen or more girls were inside, each wondering if this was her lucky night.

Every night was a party, but never with any alcohol or drugs. These bashes reminded me of the chaperoned high-school parties I used to attend with Ricky Nelson: strictly soda pop, potato chips and dip. Very straight, especially considering what went on at other Hollywood parties in this period. Some of the girls might even go into the kitchen and cook a little. There was nothing wild, no orgies. Elvis was too straight and too intimidated by anything overtly sexual for that. Besides, although he was no longer the subject of scandal he'd been in the fifties, he respected the ever-present threat of bad press. And he had to consider Priscilla, waiting so patiently back home. Years later, when I read ridiculous stories about orgies and things like two-way mirrors, I laughed. I never saw anything of the sort back then, and if it had existed I'd have seen it.

Also keeping these get-togethers low-key was the type of girl who came by: predominantly Goody Two Shoes, sweet, wholesome and just nice. Naturally a few came in with the express purpose of bedding the King, but to the trained eye their intentions were transparent. Elvis' instinctive revulsion at a brazen, aggressive woman couldn't be disguised, and after a while it became known that certain behavior wasn't welcome. This isn't to say that nothing unsavory ever happened at Elvis' house, just that it rarely happened with Elvis.

Every evening Elvis sat on a big couch in the den, playing his guitar and singing, or philosophizing and talking about his books. He spoke of life, life after death, and, predictably, women loved it. I wouldn't suggest there were more than a few with an enduring interest in these subjects, but the mere idea of Elvis—the King, the alleged great womanizer, the sex symbol of our time—being so open and sensitive was a turn-on in itself. They ate it right up. Countless times one of the guys sarcastically quipped to me, "Yeah, we know, that's your thing—getting the

chicks. You got into all this for chicks." It did "work,"
but that wasn't why we were into it.

As time passed, the people around Elvis began to get a
clearer idea of what spiritual studies entailed and their effect on Elvis' behavior. Some, including Priscilla, believed that Elvis "changed" his attitude about sex because
of the teachings, but in fact his feelings about sex—
especially sex outside marriage, and promiscuity—remained
pretty much the same. The difference was in how Elvis
expressed those feelings after the teachings articulated
them for him. Sex and sexual behavior are discussed very
frankly in many of the books Elvis read, and their values
concurred with those he had grown up with, the values of
his mother. In his heart Elvis desperately wanted to live
up to his ideal of a moral person. He realized and accepted
that being that good wasn't always possible. Though Elvis
had transcended most of the limitations of his background
and lived with fewer restrictions than the rest of us, he
fought temptation. It was always there, and he was human.
Still, he felt compelled to live a moral life, even if most
people didn't expect it of him.

Many Memphis Mafiosi saw it differently. The wildest
and least discriminating among them thought that Elvis
was crazy. After all, if *they* had been Elvis . . . Elvis
understood where they were coming from, but he still
didn't like it. Crude talk of conquests repelled Elvis. He'd
never preach about it or criticize the guys directly, though
he might let Red or another of them know what he thought.
But their forays onto the wild side were relatively tame.
You would never see two girls in bed with one guy, for
instance. For all their bad-ass swagger, they were too
straight for that.

When it came to women, Elvis operated under the pro-
verbial double standard. He adored a certain type: petite,
pretty, passive, demure. She had to be respectable and
willing to mother him. Elvis was a mama's boy, and he
sought women he could respect the same way he had respected his mother, women who possessed his mother's
values; in short, a very old-fashioned girl. "Man, when a
girl starts swearing, she loses me right there," he'd say.

The distance between the behavior he'd tolerate from women and what he'd take from men was a chasm. He didn't like women who were aggressive or outspoken, feeling that the man should dominate in any kind of relationship. Elvis also had very conservative taste in women's clothes and was turned off by too much cleavage or skirts that were too short. Interestingly, he liked seeing these things on television or in a movie, but not in real life. He was obsessed with women's feet. "The minute I see a woman's foot," he said, "I know if I like her or not."

After shooting for the day ended, at around six, I'd go to the house to style Elvis' hair. Invariably we stayed in our "study" (the bathroom) for hours, talking about everything. At this point Elvis was requesting a new book almost every other day. Within three weeks after our meeting, he had accumulated several dozen books, which he kept piled in tall stacks; by early 1965 he owned well over one hundred, among them *The Secret Doctrine, The Urantia Book, The Fourth Way, The Mystical Christ, Leaves of Morya's Garden, Adventure in Consciousness, Cheiro's Book of Numbers* and dozens more.

He devoured the books like a person studying for a college final. It was never enough for him to simply read a book; he had to absorb it, think about it, question it, link its thoughts and ideas with all he had read before and things he had heard people say. Elvis dog-eared pages, highlighted passages and jotted notes and questions on the endpapers and throughout the margins. For Elvis, reading wasn't a passive activity; each book promised a new adventure, a new way of viewing things. Very few of the books he owned exist today. I have some of them, because Elvis and I shared books. Most were given away, thrown out, lost or stolen. That so few have surfaced in the hands of collectors confirms my suspicion that, fearing public criticism of his son's "weird" ideas, Vernon, or perhaps someone else who shared Vernon's feelings, tossed them out. After Elvis' death Vernon told me on several occasions that he felt he "had to put the books away, because of what people might think."

It's too bad, because any intelligent person who examined one of Elvis' cherished books would see his dedication and intelligence. Of all the charges leveled against Elvis, the most ridiculous and unfair was that he was a stupid man. There weren't too many around Elvis equipped to judge his intelligence. Granted, his formal education was limited, and an innate shyness kept him from speaking at length to very many outside his circle. But Elvis was one of the brightest people I've known.

We saw a lot more of Colonel Parker in Hollywood. With Tinseltown's big money, hype, studio politics and deal-making, Parker was in his element, and his glory. People who knew, worked with or had dealings with Parker speak admiringly of his shrewdness, power, flamboyance and nerve. The Colonel commanded everyone's respect and usually got it, even if it was given begrudgingly. He wasn't one to temper his business relationships with sincerity or warmth, or even the illusion of them. He talked, you listened; he asked, you answered. That was the way the manager wanted it, so that's how it was.

By the midsixties Parker had positioned everyone around Elvis exactly where he wanted them. Vernon, by nature passive and reserved, turned his head as Parker usurped his authority over his son. Following Elvis' lead, the guys deferred to Parker. Some went beyond the call of duty, spying on Elvis and reporting back to the old man.

Certainly the Colonel wielded a great deal of influence over Elvis, but it was hard to witness this without wondering exactly its extent, why, and how. Even back then, it was obvious that Parker's "guidance" of Elvis' career was off course. Parker's boast of not reading or approving the movie scripts said it all: he really didn't care.

When he could no longer evade questions about the embarrassing caliber of Elvis' films, Parker replied, "How do you argue with his kind of success?" It was not that he didn't understand the criticism; he was too intelligent not to. But Parker's world lacked a moral center. Loyal and true, he gave his all to Elvis, in his fashion. The pair's common goal and their problem were Elvis' success. The lure of guaranteed success couldn't be denied. Had Elvis found himself drowning in a flood of commercial failures, Parker might have been forced to move. But who knows? Parker was proud of his carny days, back when he had made some chickens "dance" on a straw-covered hot-plate.

What was Parker's power over Elvis? There had to be more to it than ironclad contracts and seven-figure checks. Biographers have suggested everything from blackmail (supposedly about Vernon's past) to hypnotism to mutual affection and respect, but none of those things explains it. At the same time, though, I must say that nothing that's been revealed about the Colonel in the years since Elvis' death surprises me. Ultimately, Parker's power over Elvis was as strong as it was because Elvis gave it to him. Only Parker could convince Elvis to do what he wanted him to do every time he asked. How Parker managed to accomplish this and why he'd want to may never be know, but the fact is that Parker intimidated Elvis, and Elvis spoke of fearing him. Elvis kept his contact with Parker to the absolute minimum. Parker's report on the latest million-dollar deal could be dispatched over the telephone in less than five minutes.

Oddly, of all the people around Elvis, the one who went out of his way to make me feel comfortable and welcome was Parker. Like so many things he did, though, this demonstration of concern served other purposes. His real intent lay elsewhere.

The Colonel would come onto the movie set periodically, by which I mean once or twice during filming; actually quite infrequently, considering that his star was Elvis. I hadn't been around long when I saw him walk onto the set, stand and just stare at everyone. Rumors circulated among the guys that Parker knew a lot about hypnotism and mind control. These may or may not have been true. To judge from the guys' behavior in Parker's presence, it would appear that he had some ability. One time, a group of us were sitting in a grass hut on the set of *Paradise, Hawaiian Style* when Parker entered. He stared at Billy Smith, and Billy "became" a monkey. Parker made gestures—pulling his ear, tugging his nose, scratching his head—in Charlie Hodge's direction, and Charlie got down on the floor and acted like a dog. Parker turned to someone else, and that person behaved like another animal. What were the guys responding to? Hypnotic suggestion? Fear of the consequences if they didn't play along? The point is that Parker got people to do things they didn't necessarily want to do, a very powerful ability, regardless of its source.

"See," he said, his face cast in a grin while his eyes seemed to bore through my head, "they're all hypnotized. But no," he added, as if answering a question no one else could hear or talking to himself, "we won't do one on Larry, because Larry knows hypnotism."

With that he gave me a conspiratorial smile and said to no one in particular, "Where's a chair for the Colonel?"

Several guys rushed over with chairs for the Colonel.

"And get one for Larry," Parker added, knowing there was probably nothing the guys would rather do less.

Most times Parker came around, he had me sit beside him. He'd make small talk, ask some questions. One day he announced loudly enough for everyone to hear, "Larry, you missed your calling in life. You should have been on the stage. I'm telling you. I know. You should have been on the stage."

He paused and looked off as if envisioning my name on a distant marquee. "I can see it now. You look the part, you have the knowledge of psychology, and you know how to hypnotize people. You would make a great magician on the stage. People would follow you."

I said nothing, and Parker kept nodding and smiling at me as if we shared a secret. I understood exactly what he was saying, and he knew that I did. It was obvious: he was referring to my "influence" on Elvis. And who would know more about "influencing" Elvis than the master himself?

One day the Colonel came to the studio and said, "Larry, I want to talk to you. Sit down."

I took a chair beside him, and he reached into his pocket and took out a little white booklet, which he handed to me as if it were a rare and precious tome. On the cover was a picture of a melting snowman.

"Nobody else in the group has one of these," he said. "I'm making you a member of my club."

Parker's "club" was the American Snowmen's League, a strange and mysterious organization whose size and membership are unknown to all but Parker, the League's Imperial Potentate. The snowman represents the art of "snowing," or conning, people. A snowman, then, is a con artist.

I didn't even begin to understand what it was until later. All I could do was stare at it and say, "Okay, thanks, Colonel."

Opening the booklet, I found inside a table of contents listing several chapter titles, such as "Counteracting High Pressure Snowing: The Melt and Disappear Technique," followed by thirty or so blank pages.

I never attended a meeting of the group, and in fact it wasn't until years later, when Elvis' biographers wrote about the League, that I learned there ever were other members. According to several sources, Parker's colleagues included motion-picture and record-company executives, high-level corporate officials, perhaps even a United States President or two. Reportedly, membership if free, it's the getting out that costs you. On the other hand, even these facts could be the fallout from another snowing. Who else belonged to the club really didn't matter, though. Parker's actions always spoke louder than his words, and this gesture summed it up. In Parker's eyes, he and I were in the same league, so to speak, and I was a good enough snowman to earn his respect. I was working for Parker now.

Parker enjoyed playing with people's heads and would enlist even total strangers in practical jokes designed to keep them off balance. Once when I was visiting a spa the Colonel frequented in Palm Springs, a girl who worked there asked me my name.

"It's Larry Geller," I replied.

"Oh, *you're* Larry Geller!" she exclaimed, as if she had been looking for me.

"Yeah," I answered, confused.

"I heard about you," she said. "I understand that you're a magician. Colonel Parker told me so."

Just thinking of the lengths that man would go to in order to set up something like this made my head spin. Parker was an enigma, and early on I stopped trying to figure him out. The rules were clear; I just tried to stay out of his way.

Elvis' prescription-drug intake, which was confined to amphetamines for crash dieting and marathon drives, now included the barbiturates Seconal and Tuinal, and Percodan, a semisynthetic narcotic analgesic often prescribed for moderately severe pain, such as from injury or dental surgery. None of these drugs, when taken in its prescribed dosage, is considered high in potency, though all of them are addictive. Because prescription medicines were all Elvis took, and he obtained them legally, he wasn't involved in what we'd call "drug culture." No pusher lurked, though a licensed physician was but a phone call away. Elvis referred to his drugs as "medication," and, to a certain extent, he truly believed that medications were necessary and that doctors did only what was best for their patients. He had studied the *Physicians' Desk Reference*, an annually updated guide to prescription drugs, and was quite knowledgeable on the subject.

Elvis wasn't the only person in our group using drugs. Drinking went on, a couple of the group and I smoked pot, and several of the guys were psychologically, if not physically, dependent on stimulants. Looking back I see the seeds of the denial and enabling behavior of those around Elvis that would bloom in the next decade. Over the years it's been claimed that Elvis either was ignorant of his medications' potential for abuse or took them solely for their medicinal benefits. For the most part, I believe those statements are true, but occasionally Elvis said or did things that revealed another facet of his thinking. His attempts to enlist others in his drug-taking reminded me of the way guilty children act when they try to persuade their straight friends to share in their fun—and guilt. He knew that he was getting more from his pills than the doctor had ordered.

Elvis' drug problem had its roots in the complexities of his personality and the uniqueness of his life. It saddens me that over the years this aspect of Elvis had been so widely sensationalized, apparently without anyone's trying to understand why Elvis took his medications. In the current atmosphere of increased understanding about substance abuse and a more charitable attitude toward substance abusers, it's clear that in the eyes of Elvis' most heartless critics, his sin wasn't so much the abuse itself but his attempts to keep it a secret.

After our first speed session, Elvis didn't broach the subject with me again until one day when he offered me a Percodan tablet, saying, "Here, try this. It won't hurt you."

Again, like a fool, I relented, and felt strange for a few hours. That was one of the last times I ever took a psychoactive prescription drug. The experience suggested that while Elvis' wall of denial about drugs was strong, it wasn't impermeable.

One day in the spring of 1965 Elvis and I were upstairs at Graceland, getting ready to leave for L.A.

"I really don't want to go back to that town," Elvis said wearily. "I don't want to do another damn film. I just wanna stay here—study our books, meditate, far away from that craziness."

His anger was tempered with resignation. We both knew Elvis had no choice about going to Los Angeles. Typically, he had procrastinated, concocting excuses to stay longer in Memphis than we should have stayed, so that by the time we finally hit the road our schedule didn't allow for stops along the way for anything but gas and fast food. Right before we boarded the bus, Elvis said, "Look, when we're on the road, there's something I need you to do." He flashed me a conspiratorial grin. "Talk about God, just keep talkin' and explainin'. I want the guys to hear what you and I are into and what we do every day. It'll be good for them, and if they don't like it, it's too damn bad.

They need it. We all need it. Somehow it'll rub off on them, someday.''

Once we were just a few miles out of Memphis, Elvis said, ''Larry, let me ask you something. What's meditation all about? I mean, what does it accomplish, anyway?''

He winked and nodded, and I began speaking. By now I was hip to Elvis' ploys. He used my talking to the guys as a way to divert attention from himself. It didn't work: the guys knew what he was up to. For the next couple of hours, he kept me talking by asking new questions whenever I ran out of things to say in answer to the previous one. Elvis sat in silence with a disturbed, distracted expression, as if pondering some question that had no answer. The ''lecture'' ended, and after a while we settled into the usual routine, playing eight-track cassettes or listening to the radio. We were making pretty good time, which was a load off the guys who'd be answering to an angry Colonel if Elvis showed up late.

We weren't far from Amarillo, Texas, when Elvis, who had taken the wheel, pulled into a motel without saying a word to anyone.

Frowning, Joe Esposito said, ''Hey, Elvis, you said we're going straight through. We can't stop here. We've got to be in L.A. We're already late.''

Elvis looked up and shrugged, cutting Joe off. ''Don't worry, Joe. We're not staying here, we're just stopping to get cleaned up. Just get me a room and get the guys someplace to rest. Give me about ten minutes or so, then we'll hit it.''

We were in our room barely two minutes when the phone rang. Joe answered it and then handed me the receiver, sighing in exasperation.

''It's Elvis. He wants to see you. Hurry up, Larry, we gotta get the hell out of here. Don't get into one of your damn all-night discussions. That's all we need.''

I found Elvis in his room, sitting on the edge of the bed, looking worn and depressed. Without speaking, he rose and, while pacing back and forth, kept shaking his head in dismay. Finally he declared firmly, ''All right, all

right, Larry. Just tell me the damn truth, man. What am
I doin' wrong, huh? What's wrong with me? Maybe God
doesn't love me or something, because all I know is that
I read for hours every day, every night, ever since you got
me started. I haven't stopped. I've been like a damned
fiend or something.''

He paused, then pleaded, ''All I want is to know the
truth, to know and experience God. I'm a searcher, that's
what I'm all about. You woke that up in me, and ever since
I started I haven't had one experience—nothing. I really
believe in all the spiritual teachings. I believe, only nothing happens, and I want it to. Oh, man, I want it so bad.
What the hell is wrong?''

Elvis' pain and confusion surprised me, but I tried to
keep calm while explaining how each idea we had discussed over the past months had its place among the others, how each built upon the others and together they
formed something very beautiful. The spiritual readings,
the meditation, our conversations—all these contributed to
our development, but they were just parts, stages, of a
process that might continue for the rest of our lives. No
one knows when that moment of revelation may come; it's
not a ''prize'' one ''earns.'' For some, it never comes,
but that is all the more reason to continue working toward
God.

''Elvis,'' I said, ''the problem is that you've been jam-
ming too much information into your head too quickly.
Your whole experience so far has been cerebral. You're
not a computer, you cannot program yourself with data
and automatically produce a higher awareness.''

''Then why are you feeding it to me?'' he asked in a
challenging tone.

''You want to crash the gates of heaven, Elvis—instant
entrance, like you get everything. But it doesn't work that
way. Before God, you're no different from anybody else.
You're not favored because you're Elvis Presley. He doesn't
care about your millions of fans or the money you make.''

Elvis looked numb with shock. I couldn't tell if he was
reacting to what I'd said or to how I'd said it, or both. I
had never heard anyone speak to him like that, and I recall

briefly thinking that a display of his legendary temper might be in the offing. But Elvis' habitual quickness to anger and his often inscrutable gaze were masks. Beneath them he was a sincere, honest man. He wanted the truth, he was dying for the truth. For a long while we sat in silence.

"Talk about God!" he suddenly exclaimed, as if this were the solution. "Just keep talking and explaining."

"Elvis," I replied, ignoring his command, "there's an old Zen story that might be illuminating." I recounted a familiar tale that authors and teachers have repeated ad infinitum: A Japanese Zen master's student inquired, "Master, for years I have dutifully obeyed your instructions, following all the rules, meditating daily for years, but enlightenment has eluded me. Why, Master, after all the sacrifices and hard work have I remained in darkness?"

As he listened, the master poured tea into the student's cup and continued doing so until the cup overflowed. Out of respect, the student silently watched the tea run over the table and onto the floor.

"Master!" he exclaimed. "The cup is already full. Why do you keep pouring when no more tea will go in?"

The master smiled and replied, "Exactly. And like the cup, *you* are running over, and nothing more can come in. How can I show you Zen unless you first empty your cup?"

Elvis' expression showed me he'd gotten the point.

"You have to drop your ego, Elvis," I continued, "and make room for God. How could new 'tea,' or new knowledge, or new experience enter the 'cup' unless the student first gets rid of the old tea of ego? Or, as Jesus says in Matthew, 'Neither do men put new wine into old bottles.' The point is that for something new or revelatory to occur we must prepare ourselves, we must empty the old vessel for the new substance to take hold. We have to drop the ego for any enlightenment. Forget the books, Elvis. Let go of your knowledge. Become empty so God can have a place to enter."

Elvis looked down at the floor, then back at me, then

grinned. Nodding in agreement, he said softly, "Well, you're right." He chuckled softly to himself. "I guess I needed that. Let's hit it."

Relieved, everyone else gathered out by the vehicles, anxious to get moving, Jerry Schilling, Billy Smith, Red West, Elvis and I boarded the bus, while the other guys took the cars. Elvis drove, and I sat up front next to him; Jerry, Billy and Red were in back. Over the next twelve hours, we traveled through New Mexico and Arizona, a route we'd taken several times before. For some reason that we never really understood, the rest of our little caravan disappeared.

Since our talk in the motel room, Elvis had remained unusually quiet. Every once in a while he'd turn to me and nod, letting me know he was thinking about things. Eventually he said, "I'll bet there's a reason why we're lost from the rest of the guys, and I'll tell you, I'm glad. 'Cause now it's an adventure. Being alone like this in God's country . . ." his voice trailed off in midthought.

"Man, I needed this, to really shake the past and be alone like this with nature, away from everyone else."

We drove on through the desert in silence. In the distance mountains loomed in the fading light. An iridescent blue sky seemed to drape itself over the sacred mountains of the Hopi Indians and color everything in view with a peaceful, heavenly shade. As we were marveling at the sight, Elvis suddenly gasped and cried, "Whoa!"

When I turned to him, he was slumped back in his seat, slack-jawed, staring at the horizon. Following his gaze, I saw a cloud, a single white mass floating in the sky. From the cloud emerged a clear, definite, recognizable image.

"Do you see what I see?" Elvis asked in a whisper. I looked again. "That's Joseph Stalin's face up there!"

Try as I might to see it any other way, there was no denying that it was Stalin's face in the cloud.

"Why Stalin? Why Stalin?" Elvis asked, his voice breaking. "Of all people, what's he doin' up there?"

Before I could answer, the cloud slowly turned in on itself, changing form and dimension until the image faded and gradually disappeared. I knew we had witnessed

something extraordinary and turned to say so, but stopped
when I saw Elvis, staring into the cloud, his eyes open
wide and his face reflecting wonder. It's almost impossible
to describe how he looked then without sounding hokey,
but Elvis' expression was the one that you read of in the
Bible or other religious works: the look of the newly bap-
tized or the converted. He appeared so peaceful, so accepting, so open, so happy. It was something I had never
seen before and I would never see again.

I looked up at the glowing billowy mass, but saw only
a cloud. Elvis swung the bus over to the roadside and
brought it to a violent halt.

"Just follow me, Larry!" he shouted as he bolted out
the door and began running across the sand. I finally
caught up, and as we stood in the cool desert breeze Elvis'
face beamed with joy.

"It's God!" he cried. "It's God! It's love. God is love,
Larry."

Tears streamed down his face as he hugged me tightly
and said, "I love you, I love you.

"Oh, God is real. It's all true. I love God so much. I'm
filled with Divine Love. I've finally seen what you were
tryin' to tell me, and you were right. It's beyond words
and beyond the ego.

"Now I know, now I know. I'll never have to doubt
again. God loves me. God is love itself!"

Laughing and crying simultaneously, we smiled and
hugged.

"I thank you from the bottom of my heart. You got me
here. I'll never forget, never, man. It really happened. I
saw the face of Stalin and I thought to myself, Why Stalin?
Is it a projection of something that's inside of me? Is God
tryin' to show me what he thinks of me? Then your words
about getting rid of the ego and all that played in my head,
and I cried out to God, 'If that's really me, Lord, I want
to die. All I truly want is You. Please, God, fill me with
Yourself. Destroy me, if that's what it takes.'

"And then it happened! The face of Stalin turned right
into the face of Jesus, and he smiled at me, and every
fiber of my being felt it. For the first time in my life, God

and Christ are a living reality. Oh, God. Oh, God,'' Elvis
kept saying. Then he paused and added a peculiar aside.
''Can you imagine what the fans would think if they saw
me like this?''

''They'd only love you all the more,'' I replied.

''Yeah,'' he said, ''well, I hope that's true.''

Red West, who was standing by the road, shouted,
''Hey, Boss! What the hell's goin' on out there? Are you
all right?''

The sound of Red's voice jolted Elvis out of his bliss.
His hands dropped abruptly from my shoulders, and he
took a deep breath.

''I'm okay, I'm okay!'' Elvis shouted flatly.

Red stood still a second, scratched his head in confusion, then shrugged his shoulders before turning to re-
board the bus.

''Oh, man,'' Elvis sighed in frustration, ''how do you
possibly explain to a nonbeliever when you just had a
vision? I mean, a vision when Almighty God touches you
and reveals Himself? I saw the Christ and the anti-Christ!
Oh, Lord.''

Elvis shook his head; he was torn between exhilaration
and dread, knowing how this would go over with everyone
else. It was one more thing about him that no one else
would understand, one more thing for everyone around
him to laugh about behind his back. Emotionally and
physically drained, Elvis wrapped his arm around my
shoulder for support, and we made our way unsteadily
through the sand back to the road.

Once on the bus, Elvis tried acting as if nothing unusual
had occurred. ''Look, Red, maybe you better drive. I'm
going back to lay down for a while.''

Red nodded but kept staring. As if reading Red's mind,
Elvis added, ''And don't worry about me. I've never been
better, that's for sure.''

I was sitting in the back with Elvis, glancing out the
window, when it struck me that this very spot, where
Highway 66 nears the south rim of the Grand Canyon, was
where I'd had my first spiritual experience, something that
changed the course of my life.

Night fell, and Elvis' vision was hours old, but he couldn't get over it. It took me quite a while to tell him of my own experience, and he truly understood it.

"Holy Mother of God," Elvis said, glancing at the guys in the front of the bus, "I suppose they'd call this a co-incidence or something. But how do you explain this? How is it even remotely possible that we both had the same type of experience? Our first spiritual initiation from God in the very same state and on the exact same mountain? You know as well as I do that this is due to our karma. This goes way beyond, and much deeper than we're both probably aware of. We'd better keep this to ourselves, 'cause they'd try putting us both away if we tried to explain this one."

At three in the morning Elvis was still awake, wired from the vision and trying to absorb it all. He'd doze off a bit, then spring back to consciousness and exclaim, "Whew! It happened!"

He was totally disoriented, not only because something very important, spiritually speaking, had occurred, but because for once something unplanned and totally unprepared had taken him by surprise. Such things didn't happen too often in Elvis' world.

Suddenly someone screamed. "We're on fire! We're on fire!"

Elvis snapped to, and Red quickly stopped the bus on the shoulder. The back axles and the undercarriage were aflame. We managed to put the fire out, but the bus was a total wreck and couldn't be started. Luckily, we were only a few miles outside Needles, California, in the Mojave Desert. The five of us pushed the bus into town, where we checked into a motel.

"Let's just get some vehicles, Larry," Elvis said wearily. "I'll have Alan come back here later and get it repaired. I don't want to think about it. Just go hire some cars. Here's my wallet."

It was Elvis' wallet, all right, practically bursting at the seams from dozens of credit cards but without any currency inside. I pocketed the wallet and started walking in search of a car-rental agency. It was eight or so in the morning, I was running on virtually no sleep, needed a shower and a shave. I found myself standing at a counter and saying to a wary man behind it. "Yes, sir, I'd like to rent two cars. I'm with Elvis Presley. He's down the road at a motel."

The clerk wasn't buying this one, so, thinking it would help, I handed him the wallet. Flipping through the cards, he asked, "What are you telling me? *Elvis Presley?"*

"Yeah," I answered.

Flinging the wallet at me, he screamed, "Get out of here!"

While I was wondering what *his* problem was, it occurred to me that the easiest way to get from Needles to Los Angeles would be by cab. I phoned a taxi service, and the people there were only too happy to help. Within minutes, two cabs were at the motel, and we were ready to go.

We loaded all of Elvis' luggage into one cab, and then Jerry, Red, Billy, Elvis and I crawled into the second. Red and I sat in front, while the others sat in the backseat. As we rode down the highway, our driver couldn't stop himself from turning every few minutes to stare at Elvis. That was understandable, but when he hit a cruising speed of eighty miles per hour and still couldn't keep his eyes off his famous passenger, I yelled, "Hey, man, slow down! You're going to kill us. Yes, this is Elvis. Everything's okay. Just calm down."

But who could blame him for staring? Our transportation problem solved, Elvis resumed pondering the desert incident. Every few minutes, he'd stick his head and arms out the back window, fall back into his seat, take a deep breath, and say, "Whew!" or "Whoa!" or some other expression of total amazement. After his whole life of church upbringing, of reading and hearing about other people's experiences, he had something of his very own. Belief was no longer a matter of faith but one of knowledge. Now Elvis knew.

When we arrived in Los Angeles, four hours or so later, the other guys who'd been lost during the drive were lined up in front of the house, waiting.

"Where the hell you guys been?" Joe shouted impatiently. *"Where* have you been?"

"Oh, we're fine, fine," Elvis replied distractedly. "Everything's cool. Larry, come with me. See you guys in a bit."

"What the—"

Elvis didn't answer, seemingly oblivious of the commotion. Red tried to explain our little adventure, but from the look of things he wasn't getting too far.

Elvis walked directly into the den, and I followed.

"Close the doors," he said, taking a seat on the couch.

As I closed the wooden louver doors, the guys began congregating around them. Of course you could hear everything anyone in the den said, and the guys intended to do just that. I could hear their whispers through the doors, but Elvis didn't seem to notice them, or, if he did, he didn't care.

"All right, Larry, that's it," Elvis said firmly. "I'm not making another fucking film again. I'm not; I can't. How can I make a teenybopper movie now? I can't do this. I can't do it anymore. I know the difference. I know now. I know," he said solemnly. "I've got to do something real with my life. I want out. I want to become a monk and join a monastery. I want to be with God now. I don't want this bullshit anymore."

As he was saying this, I thought, I've created a monster. Elvis was an extremist in everything, and the spiritual studies were no exception. Rather than using this experience to help him correct and redirect his life, he embraced it as a perfect excuse to abandon his life altogether. He was running on a dangerous mixture of pure adrenaline and exhaustion. This couldn't happen.

"Elvis, Elvis," I said, "you must understand you've been given a talent and a gift from God that's unprecedented. You have more fans than anyone that's ever lived. They look to you, Elvis. They love you. They'll listen to you. You can make meaningful films. You can sing meaningful music. Now you can do things in a conscious way instead of being asleep. Now you can be your own man.

Now you can be independent. Now you don't have to be swayed by other people.''

Elvis knew whom I was referring to, and my point seemed to have hit its mark until he said, "Larry, I'm not making a move unless you tell me what to do.''

What? I thought. I had known Elvis only a little over a year, and I was just twenty-six, but even if I'd been one hundred this was ridiculous.

"I know you're going to tell me the truth,'' Elvis continued, ignoring the shock on my face. "You got me into that, and that's good, but I want to listen to what you have to say. I'm going on your advice, and I'm going to do what you tell me to do and no one else.''

I could hear shuffling on the other side of the doors. Elvis and I knew that Joe and Red told Parker things. Parker's angry face loomed in my mind. This was insane.

"Elvis, listen.'' I drew a deep breath. "You just had the experience of your life, and it's a wonderful experience; it's good. Even though we're all tired and we're out of it and you're out of it, you're going to rest and everything's going to be okay. But, Elvis, remember you're Elvis Presley. You have a responsibility to the world. They need you, and you need them. Now you can really do things in a conscious, wonderful way.''

Elvis sat looking straight at me, shaking his head no.

"Elvis, please listen to me. Get some rest. You need rest, Elvis. You'll have a different point of view when you have some rest. Trust me. You say you'll listen to what I say? Okay, so get some rest. We'll worry about this later.''

Finally succumbing to reason or exhaustion, Elvis said, "Okay. Yeah, right. Right, right, right.''

He went to his room, leaving me to worry about what would happen next. The most pressing problem was the guys tattling to the Colonel, but the most important issue was Elvis. He had come so far, and yet in one crucial way he was stuck. It was as if he couldn't exist without making someone else the authority over his life. The whole point of the studies was to liberate you from the prison of a life lived without knowing God or yourself. Making life richer, fuller, more meaningful—that's what the studies, the talks, the experiences were for. The goal wasn't to lead you from one master to the next, but to help you make your own decisions. Of course, Elvis could never stop being Elvis; no amount of knowledge or understanding would change the fact that he couldn't walk down a street alone without being accosted. But after seeing Elvis and the Colonel, then listening to him this afternoon, I found that things came into focus. There was a riddle about Elvis: How did a shy, deferential, insecure young boy become an aggressive, confident, secure man? He didn't. Fame certainly reduced the number of masters Elvis served, but there would always be one.

It was some time before Elvis calmed down and could contemplate his experience without being overwhelmed. Despite my panic, I believed that with time he would put it into its proper perspective.

Elvis' vision was probably one of the most significant experiences of his personal life. In terms of his spirituality and his studies, it was the key. In the early seventies Elvis said, ''It took me years to understand what that experience was all about. In fact, I'm still in the process of understanding it. Because the main thing is, that was my contact, my first real conscious contact with the divine, with God, with knowing that God *was,* not just believing and thinking and talking and reading. That was knowing. It's taken me years to understand, and it's the hardest thing in the world. I think it was easier making it [in show business] than learning to know myself.''

I don't know if Elvis ever told Parker what happened; I doubt it. The vision in the desert may have transformed Elvis' life, but it had no effect whatsoever on his schedule. Soon after returning to Los Angeles, we set to work on the film *Paradise, Hawaiian Style* and fell back into the Hollywood routine.

Though Elvis despised Hollywood and pretty much kept to himself, he did have occasion to meet other actors and entertainers whom he liked. By mid-1965, over four years had elapsed since his last live concert. Music was his life, so he kept up with all the new sounds. Between 1958 and

1964 rock and roll underwent so many changes—as an art, as a sound, as a business—that "Heartbreak Hotel," sideburns and gold lamé were considered artifacts. Elvis' midsixties recordings fell far behind the cutting edge, and he knew it. He had some concept of who he was and what he'd done, but as he looked forward what did he see? The next dozen stupid movies? Another vocal tour de force like "Song of the Shrimp"? At thirty, Elvis' days of glory, of immediate relevance, were stretching farther behind him with each passing year. He casually remarked on how it seemed that older performers such as Rudy Vallee and Bing Crosby had degenerated into self-caricatures doing the same things they'd done twenty or thirty years before.

"Oh, wow, man," Elvis said. "I would never let that happen to me. That's sad. It's pathetic, man, a poor old fifty-year-old guy. How could they do that? I'll never let that happen to me."

He observed the current scene with interest and, at times, amusement. Back in Memphis we had seen a feature-length documentary on the British rock scene. Elvis liked the Dave Clark Five a lot, but the group he couldn't stop talking about for the longest time was the Rolling Stones. The group's lead singer, Mick Jagger, had a way of dancing that was different and kind of peculiar. A white boy incorporating black rhythm and style, Jagger moved distinctively, jerking his head back à la Chuck Berry doing his duckwalk. The beauty of Jagger was in the eye of the beholder. Millions found him sexy; Elvis thought it was one of the funniest things he had ever seen.

"Damn, man," Elvis said between chuckles, "look at it! That guy looks like a crazed chicken on LSD!" For years Elvis retained that image of Jagger and couldn't think about the Stones without laughing.

He liked some of Bob Dylan's songs and often quoted lines of Dylan's lyrics in conversation. In 1966 he recorded "Tomorrow Is a Long Time," but he couldn't stand the sound of Dylan's voice. Elvis admired great singing more than anything else, and he was a fan. He told me of driving in Los Angeles and spotting Judy Garland. "Miss

Garland, I'm a big fan of yours!'' he screamed out the window.

"And I'm a fan of yours, Mr. Presley,'' she replied.

Elvis admired singers for their voices; he usually didn't care what style of music they sang. He said of Andy Williams, "He's got the greatest pipes of any white singer around.'' He admired Frank Sinatra's singing, though he wasn't particularly fond of Sinatra's material. Dean Martin, Tony Bennett (especially singing "Rags to Riches,'' a favorite of Elvis' that he recorded in 1971), Al Hibbler (of "Unchained Melody'' fame), Nat King Cole and Lou Rawls were others he praised. Elvis enjoyed singing ballads and gospel music the most; it was all that he sang at home. He must have had ten thousand songs in his head, and I vividly recall sitting around wherever we were, listening to Elvis sing for a couple of hours almost every night. Either Elvis or Charlie Hodge played piano. Driving in the bus, Elvis would sing along to a tape by Roy Orbison, another singer he greatly admired. He'd play the same tape over and over again, and we'd join in on "Pretty Woman,'' "Only the Lonely'' and "Candy Man.'' Though Roy didn't have his first big national hit until mid-1960 with "Only the Lonely,'' he had skirted the Top Fifty in 1956 with "Ooby Dooby,'' on Sun Records.

Once as we were walking to a sound stage Elvis was approached by an Englishman named Gordon Mills, who managed the Welsh singer Tom Jones. Tom had recently broken in the United States with "It's Not Unusual,'' which Elvis liked. Because both he and Tom came from lower-working-class backgrounds (Tom's father was a coal miner), and their singing styles were natural and untaught, Elvis felt an affinity with Tom. Over the years they kept in touch and frequently hung out together whenever they both happened to be in Las Vegas.

Of all Tom's sings, Elvis loved "Green, Green Grass of Home.'' He was on the road when he first heard it, and he instructed Alan Fortas to phone up a Memphis radio station and request it. Each time a disc jockey played it he'd say, "This is for Elvis.''

Elvis loved black music; in fact, probably the only kinds

of music he didn't care for were jazz and opera. (Though some experts have stated that Elvis had the range and technique to have sung opera.) Upstairs at Graceland, adjacent to Elvis' bedroom was his "office." There was a sofa, a great barber chair, mirrors, a stereo and a huge collection of black gospel and jubilee records. Some were 78s dating from as far back as the twenties. Never a gospel buff myself, I unfortunately cannot recall the titles or the artists who sang on the records Elvis cherished. But there was one gospel singer Elvis often spoke of and admired, a black reverend named Jimmy Jones. According to Elvis, Jones was tall and handsome and wore an immaculate white suit. He'd walk down a church aisle singing the Lord's praises as women fainted in the pews. Now, what's interesting is that very few people seem to have heard of Jones; he is not mentioned in any of the gospel books I've consulted. But Elvis had his records and was fascinated as much by his personality and legend as by his voice.

On the secular side, Elvis' passion was soul singing. He considered James Brown "the state of the art" in rock and soul. "No one moves like that man," Elvis often said in admiration. "They all copy him, but no one's got the soul of James Brown."

Probably the sole exception in Elvis' eyes was Jackie Wilson. One night in 1965 a bunch of us accompanied Elvis to Ciro's, on the Sunset Strip, to see Wilson, who was then at the peak of his career. A series of hits in the mid- to late fifties ("Lonely Teardrops," "Reet Petite," "That's Why [I Love You So]") brought Wilson to national attention. He was a graceful, handsome ex-boxer whose live performances and highly charged, sexual persona were legendary. Women loved him, and in his prime he had few peers.

Someone phoned ahead to the club and made arrangements for Elvis to see the show. When we arrived the place was already packed. Once people caught sight of Elvis, things got wild. They had roped off several tables in the front for Elvis and the rest of us. Elvis, Stevie, Priscilla and I sat together at one table.

Everyone was waiting for the show to start and had almost recovered from seeing Elvis when we heard some commotion behind us. We looked up to see James Brown coming in. Elvis waved him over and invited him to sit at our table, which he did. Midway through Wilson's phenomenal show, the singer stopped and introduced James Brown, which drew round upon round of applause. Brown sat down, then Wilson introduced Elvis. When Elvis stood, it sounded as though the roof was going to fall. Everyone was standing and cheering, screaming loudly, and clapping. Many minutes later, Wilson finally got back to his show.

Wilson't set was frenetic, and at one point Elvis leaned toward me and whispered, "Look at that guy sweat, man. Look at him sweat. Chicks dig it. They really dig it."

Afterward we went backstage. Wilson was very nice and gracious. After the usual compliments and small talk, Elvis remarked to Jackie about his profuse sweating.

"Man, I'll tell you, the chicks really dig that," Elvis said. "How do you do it?"

Wilson grinned and said, "Hey, that's simple." He showed us a large bottle of salt tablets and then revealed his secret. Each night before a show, he'd swallow a handful of tablets, guzzle a few quarts of water, then go onstage. Once he got moving, the sweat would wash off him like rain. Soon Elvis started incorporating this trick into his weight-loss regimen. It was dangerous, it depleted potassium and overtaxed the heart, but it produced one of Elvis' favorite things: an instant result with minimal effort.

Pop-music history is divided not solely by years but by the people who dominated or personified each era. In the forties it was Sinatra, in the fifties Elvis, of course, and in the sixties the Beatles. Elvis listened to their records and liked their music, but he wasn't as crazy about them as he was about, say, James Brown. When the Beatles first arrived in the United States, in February 1964, they received a congratulatory telegram which, though "signed" by Parker and Elvis, was sent without Elvis' knowledge. This has been interpreted as proof that Elvis resented or disliked the Beatles, when in truth he was just as ambivalent about them as he was about most other performers.

He knew that his recent records weren't big hits because they were inferior to not only the Beatles' work but his own best product. He honestly did not view the Fab Four as "rivals."

In August 1965 the Beatles were in Los Angeles to give their historic Hollywood Bowl concerts. Parker had met with the Beatles' manager, Brian Epstein, a few days earlier, and the two agreed that their clients would get together on the evening of August 27. We were all very excited about it. Everyone in town wanted to meet the Beatles, but the only American they expressed the vaguest interest in seeing was Elvis.

That evening I drove up to the house on Perugia Way in my steel-gray Mercedes. The meeting was to have been kept top secret, but fans have their ways of finding out all there is to know, and word had spread through Los Angeles like brushfire. The Beatles and Elvis were stars to the stars, so I wasn't surprised to find Elvis' house under siege. Hundreds of people were loitering about, carefully scrutinizing each car as it passed, craning their necks to see one of the Beatles. Everywhere you looked there were policemen, and it was obvious that the security had taken a great deal of planning. The cops apparently had lists containing the make, model, license-plate number and other information about who would be driving what and who should be admitted. I was waved right through and went inside.

I found Elvis sitting in the den, acting very relaxed even though he was, as always, fidgeting. He wore a very colorful bolero, with a high collar. (Elvis wore high-collared shirts and jumpsuits not because he believed that his neck was too long, but because he was inspired by drawings of various spiritual masters wearing high collars in David Anreas' *Through the Eyes of the Masters*, a favorite book.)

The Colonel was also there; it was the only time I had seen him at Elvis' home except for a birthday party. To the left of the living room where Elvis and the group were congregated was a den with a small roulette table. Brian Epstein played roulette and talked shop with Parker for most of the night.

Sitting around Elvis were the Beatles—John Lennon and Paul McCartney on one side, Ringo Starr on the other, and George Harrison cross-legged on the floor at Elvis' feet. You could see that the Beatles were awed by Elvis. All they did was stare at him, as if they couldn't believe their eyes. Introductions were made all around. Then we stared at the Beatles, the Beatles continued gaping at Elvis, and this might have gone on all night if Elvis hadn't said, "Look, guys, if you're just going to sit there and stare at me, I'm going to bed."

They chatted for a while, then stared watching the large color television. One of the first things Paul said was, "Whoa, I never saw this before!"

"You don't have this in England?" one of the guys asked, incredulous.

"Oh, no!" Paul replied, not taking his eyes off the screen.

No one could believe that with all their money, the Beatles didn't have color TVs.

Elvis and the Beatles played guitars for a while. Elvis was beginning to learn bass guitar, and Paul gave him a few pointers, which Elvis graciously accepted. Little by little, the tension eased and everyone relaxed. Ringo wandered off to the game room, where he spent most of the evening shooting pool with Billy Smith, Richard Davis, Alan Fortas and Marty Lacker. Ringo impressed me as a quiet, sort of goofy guy. You couldn't tell if he was bored or out of it. George was also pretty subdued. Paul, on the other hand, seemed very eager to discuss technical matters, asking Elvis about guitars and strings. Elvis expressed interest in how the Beatles' records were selling and asked about their experiences on the road.

"Elvis," one of the Beatles said, "these crowds, they get crazy and they run after you. Man, like what do you do? It's scary."

"Boys, let me tell you something," Elvis replied in his best down-home tone. "If you're really scared, you're in the wrong business."

Everyone laughed, and then Elvis recounted some incidents from the early days of his career, being mobbed

and chased, near-crashes in airplanes, and other hazards
of the life.

John said, "But you're on your own. At least we've got
each other. If somebody pushed me onstage and said,
'You're on your own,' I don't know how I'd cope."

Elvis' expression revealed that he wasn't exactly sure
how he'd done it, either, but he appreciated John's thoughts
and concern. Elvis had finally met someone who could
understand what he'd been through.

About an hour after everyone arrived, someone asked,
"Where's George?" He was missing, and I volunteered
to look for him. He couldn't have gone too far without
risking his life. I'd heard from some people that George
was an intelligent and interesting guy, and I wanted to
speak with him. I looked everywhere inside, but no
George. I found him standing outside in a dark area near
the pool, smoking a joint.

"Hey, what's going on?" I asked. "You all right?"

"Yeah," he replied and offered me the joint.

I took a drag, and we stood outside for about forty minutes, talking about various aspects of Hinduism. He was
very kind and soft-spoken, and obviously quite bright. I
liked him a lot.

It was getting late, and I knew that Stevie wanted to
meet the Beatles. Since our home was only five minutes
away, she'd never forgive me if I didn't pick her up. I
excused myself, called the house and said, "Just get the
kids, get ready. I'm coming to get you."

Within twenty minutes I had picked up Stevie, Jova and
Kabrel and was back at Elvis'. The kids, at three and one,
were oblivious of the occasion's historical significance and
sound asleep. We came in the front door, each carrying a
sleeping child. John Lennon happened to be standing right
inside the door.

"John," I said, "this is my wife, Stevie."

John immediately fell to his knees, took Stevie's hand
and kissed it.

"Glad to meet you, Mum," he said, hamming it up.
Elvis laughed.

John was a funny guy, very witty, and he had that dry,

sort of off-the-wall, Monty Python absurdist sense of humor that Elvis dug. Elvis liked all the Beatles, but John was his favorite.

Years later John had Elvis' hotline number, which very few people did. Elvis later told me that in the seventies, when the U.S. Immigration and Naturalization Service sought to deport John because of a 1968 British conviction for possession of marijuana, he phoned Elvis. John always claimed that the bust was a setup, but this cut no ice with the United States government. John was the target of FBI surveillance from 1970 until he finally won the right to stay here in 1975. Based on documents released under the Freedom of Information Act, some Lennon biographers have charged that the government considered him a very real danger because of his involvement in antiwar and leftist causes.

Elvis later told me that he advised John to make a public statement against drugs, which John did. Elvis also claimed that John asked him about people he could contact who might be able to help him.

John and I had a very interesting conversation about avant-garde art, and he took my telephone number and invited me to visit the group at the house they'd rented.

"We're partying. Do you know any girls?" he asked.

"Yeah, I do," I replied, thinking to myself, He's John Lennon. Why is he asking me to get him some girls? Within a couple of minutes, Paul was at my side, saying, "Hey, how about some girls?"

Toward the end of the night, Elvis wanted to show the Beatles his new black Rolls-Royce Phantom Five, which was parked in the garage. To get there you had to go outside, and the people standing up on the fence could see us. When we walked out, the shouts tore through the night air like thunder.

"Elvis, Elvis!"

"Beatles, Beatles!"

"Elvis, we love *you!*"

"Beatles, we love *you!*"

The fans fell into a rhythm so that their cheers sounded

like a mantra. Then it turned into a competition, with each side trying to outyell the other.

After Elvis had shown the Beatles the car, we went back into the house, and Elvis gave them a tour. The Colonel had recently given him a beautiful wooden sauna. It resembled a very large cabinet and sat in one of the back halls. There was a little square window in the door, so you could see inside. Some of the guys, the Beatles and Elvis were walking through the hallway and just as Elvis said, "This is my sauna," someone peeked inside it and saw a girl crouched down on the floor.

We never discovered how she had gotten into the heavily guarded house, but you had to give her credit. A couple of guys opened the door, and Elvis said gently, "Come on out." When she saw Elvis *and* the Beatles, she was paralyzed. As one of the guys picked her up to carry her out, the poor girl started screaming, "Elvis! Elvis!" He and the Beatles just laughed.

When the Beatles got ready to leave, sometime around two in the morning, they invited Elvis and the rest of us to their house in Coldwater Canyon.

"Well, I'll see," Elvis responded graciously. "I don't know whether I can make it or not."

Elvis ended up not going to see them, but several of the other guys did, and they all had a good time. After the Beatles left, Elvis said, "I like them. They're good boys. There's four of them, but there's only one of me." Then he smiled and winked. How could Elvis be threatened by the Beatles when they idolized him? Probably more than anyone else in the world, he understood their problems and their struggles to get to the top, and he truly respected them.

The only thing about the Beatles that Elvis couldn't understand was, of all things, their teeth. He and I were alone for a few minutes during their visit, and he whispered, "Man, what's with these guys, what's with their teeth? Don't they know better? They've got the money."

To Elvis, who was a dentist's dream, constantly having his teeth cleaned and cared for, having poor teeth was incomprehensible. Being able to go to the dentist, or a doctor, whenever you wanted was one of the wonderful things money could buy. He couldn't understand people who'd let their teeth go.

I was flattered and surprised when John Lennon called me during the following week.

"Hey," John said, "have you got any dope? Do you know where we can get some good grass? Or maybe some girls?"

"I'm married," I replied.

"Oh, yeah, yeah," John answered, laughing, "I forgot." John was married, too, but that didn't seem to cramp his style. A few nights later George called me, looking for grass, too. Obviously they were enjoying the fruits of success to the fullest.

I've often thought that it was too bad Elvis didn't get out more and expand his world, at least socially. There were people with him, the same people, wherever he went, but nothing made Elvis happier than meeting new people. He worried about how people would respond to him, and was surprisingly self-conscious around strangers. In private he spoke with a slight stammer, which can be heard on certain live albums and in recordings of press conferences, but he felt too embarrassed to do anything about it. Instead he avoided certain situations, like dining out in public, for example, secretly fearing that people would laugh at him if he made a mistake or be disappointed to find that the great Elvis Presley used the wrong fork. He was also self-conscious about being from the South, because he knew that some people automatically thought someone with a Southern accent was stupid. Rednecks and bigots infuriated him, and for a long time he was ashamed of the fact that the Reverend Martin Luther King's assassination occurred in Memphis.

These fears, all products of his childhood, never diminished. The real pity of it is that among the very people he was most apprehensive about meeting were probably a few who might have been friends, people like John Lennon, who respected Elvis and understood a part of him that few others could. More than anything else, though, meeting new people, rising to occasions, might have relieved his boredom, which before too long became a vicious, relentless drain, sapping his energy and his will.

When strangers happened into his world by accident, Elvis welcomed them. In December 1965 we were all back at Graceland when my high-school friend Christian Dome (who witnessed my first encounter with Elvis outside the Pan Pacific) and his wife called to tell me that they were having problems. I invited them to come to Memphis and bring their young child, and they came on the next plane. When I picked them up I was on my way to Graceland, so I brought them along.

"Elvis will let us come over?" Christian asked with disbelief.

When we got there, Elvis was downstairs. I introduced him to my friends, and he was genuinely happy to meet them. They were new and interesting to him, and he spent the next five hours showing them around the place, discussing the books he'd been reading, demonstrating some karate moves, giving them gifts and having a wonderful time. Christian and his wife also followed the spiritual teachings and were impressed by Elvis' knowledge. He was curious about them and kind in a very open, childlike way. He was starved for the type of impromptu social exchange we all take for granted.

One night after the Domes' visit Elvis and I were sitting in the upstairs office, just talking.

"Elvis, I've got something to tell you," I said. "You know, I met you in 1957."

"You're kidding," he said, laughing. "Wow!"

I ran down the whole story of my shaking hands with him outside the Pan Pacific. All that had occurred eight years before, but those eight years seemed eons away. So much had happened to us both. Of course Elvis didn't remember me; I was just one kid out of millions, and he was never the kind of showbiz phony who'd claim he remembered someone if he didn't. He got a big kick out of the story and agreed with me that there was more to our friendship than mere coincidence.

CHAPTER

5

Elvis really took to meditation, and he practiced it daily. "This is the greatest tonic in the world," he said several times. "Meditation is better than any drug I know. I can relax, I can breathe deeper, I'm calmer."

Shortly after I started working with him he decided to create a special place at Graceland where he, or anyone, could go to be alone, to meditate or to converse in private. During the fall of 1964 Elvis, Marty Lacker and I "designed" the Meditation Garden, which was completed in the spring or summer of 1965. In truth, we didn't actually come up with a detailed design or plan for it, but Elvis' ideas about the mood he wanted to create there were very definite.

The garden was located past the swimming pool, on the south side of the house. The focal points were to be a circular fountain and a statue of Jesus. Marty, who between June 1964 and early 1965 replaced Joe Esposito as the group foreman, commissioned a Memphis sculptor to create that statue, modeling it after photographs I'd taken of a similar one at the Lake Shrine in southern California. The fountain was accented by colored lights, and a few life-size figures of no particular significance were placed about. Neither was there any special meaning attached to the choice of flowers and shrubbery; I don't recall what was installed. Although initially almost everyone around Graceland found the idea of a meditation garden a little bizarre, it became the place to go to get away from people or have a quiet chat. Elvis was quite proud of the garden, and we spent much time out there when we were in Memphis.

Today the Meditation Garden is the gravesite of Elvis, Gladys, Vernon and Vernon's mother, Minnie Mae. People often ask whether Elvis designed the garden with this purpose in mind. The answer is no. Strangely, despite his deep religious convictions and his penchant for planning, he never discussed the kind of funeral service he'd like or what arrangements he'd prefer, except to remark that people shouldn't wear black. The idea of the Meditation Garden as a small private cemetery never crossed his mind. After all, why would Elvis or anyone in his family need to be buried in the backyard? Vernon was forced to move Elvis' body to Graceland when, on August 29, 1977, not even two weeks after Elvis' interment in the mausoleum at Forest Hills Cemetery, Memphis police, working with Dick Grob, head of Graceland security, uncovered and thwarted a plan to steal Elvis' body and hold it for a $10 million ransom. Vernon reached this decision under duress, but it was the correct one. On October 2, 1977, Elvis' and Gladys' bodies were moved to Graceland. Recalling how deeply Elvis loved the Meditation Garden and Graceland, and what they symbolized to him, I now find it hard to imagine Elvis being anyplace else. Elvis is at home. Had he really contemplated his own death, it's conceivable that he might have made the same choice.

Elvis expressed such profound interest in his life and the esoteric arts that I thought he would appreciate having his horoscope drawn. Astrology was on the brink of becoming the ''in'' thing, which proved to be a mixed blessing for people who seriously believed in and practiced it. It seemed that in the mid- to late sixties, the more people knew about astrology, the less they understood it. A friend of my family's and a teacher of mine was Dane Rudhyar, a world-famous astrologer, composer, musician, writer, philosopher and poet. Rudhyar was a true Renaissance man, whose major work was updating the age-old terminology of the ''art-science'' of astrology, integrating its significant aspects with Jungian psychology. Rudhyar considered himself my elder brother, and we maintained a close friendship until his death in September 1985 at the age of ninety. Among Elvis' favorite books was Rudhyar's *New Mansions for New Men.*

Rudhyar would chart Elvis' horoscope the "old-fashioned," i.e., correct, way. To do this he needed some specific information about the time, place and date of Elvis' birth, as close to the minute as possible. When I relayed Rudhyar's requirements to Elvis, he said, "Okay, let's go get Daddy."

That afternoon, Vernon, Elvis and I sat on a bench in the Meditation Garden. "All right, Daddy," Elvis said. "You've got to remember, okay?"

"All right, son," Vernon replied. He always spoke in a molasses-slow drawl, but, like his son, Vernon could be something of a showman about the simplest thing. When recounting certain events, Vernon exhibited a flair for storytelling, repeating things we, or at least Elvis, had heard a dozen times as if they were mysterious, powerful secrets.

Vernon took a deep breath and began with "A long time ago, when you were born, son . . ."

I had grown to love Vernon dearly, and surely Elvis' birth meant a lot to him, but it was difficult to sit there and not at least smile. Elvis shot me a look that said, "Yeah, that's my daddy, and here he goes." But you could see that Elvis loved hearing it almost as much as Vernon loved telling it.

"I remember, I'll tell you," Vernon continued, "that was really weird. That was mysterious, you know. We didn't have any electricity—"

"Come on, Daddy," Elvis interrupted. "This is really important."

Vernon nodded solemnly, then resumed the whole rigmarole again. He seemed incapable of, or not interested in, telling the tale any other way, so Elvis gave up. We sat for quite a while as Vernon recited his story. He spoke of Gladys' pregnancy and some of the problems she experienced because she had gained so much weight. Then Vernon got to the births.

"We were waiting around and kept thinkin', When is that baby comin'?" Vernon said. "We didn't know at the time that your mama was carryin' twins. Well, I remember walkin' outside, and all 'round that lil house there seemed to be this blue light, a strange blue light that lit up the house, and the wind was ablowin'. Then I heard all this noise coming from the house, and I ran back, and you were born, Elvis. And a few minutes later your twin brother, Jesse Garon, came, and he wasn't breathin', and there was nothing we could do. To quickly save your life, we put you in a shoebox, wrapped you warmly, opened the oven and put you in there to keep you warm. We didn't want to lose you too."

On Elvis' birth certificate (where the doctor misspelled Aaron "Aron") and the doctor's records, it seems that either he or Vernon had gotten the story wrong. These documents suggest that Jesse was stillborn first, before Elvis rather than after. Second, although Vernon and Gladys, and later Elvis, clung to the idea that the baby Jesse was Elvis' identical twin, there is no way to be sure based only on visual examination of a baby so small. Whether fraternal or identical, however, Elvis and Jesse were twins, and brothers.

Jesse was buried in a little casket in an unmarked grave in Priceville Cemetery, near some other family plots. One biographer quotes a childhood friend of Elvis' who claimed that Elvis frequently visited Jesse's grave and that after each visit Elvis was "jolly and lifted in spirits." Statements such as this, even if true, have often been used to support claims that Elvis' feelings toward his dead brother bordered on obsession. In all the years I knew Elvis, he mentioned his brother a handful of times. Like the memory of Gladys, Jesse was a precious, private part of him that he shared with very few people. Except for the occasional remark or discussion, almost everything he felt about Jesse remained Elvis' secret.

Whenever Elvis spoke of Jesse, he referred to him as "my brother." On the rare occasion that Jesse's name came up, Elvis would assume the look of a wise man. I've never met anyone in my life who spoke more eloquently without saying a word than Elvis. Of Jesse's life and death, Elvis said several times, "Larry, there's more to this than meets the eye. There's some mysteries here. And you know, don't you?"

"Yeah, Elvis, I do. I do."

That first night we spoke back in April 1964, I mentioned something to Elvis about God and the inner voice we all hear.

"What voice?" Elvis asked, excited. "What? What do you mean, man?"

I explained to him that the I Am Life principle is the living intelligence within each of us. The "still, small voice within" is the expression of divine intelligence to our outer consciousness. While Elvis was definitely interested, and this seemed to connect to something he had experienced, he did not articulate exactly what it was right away.

Several months later, after he had read *The Impersonal Life,* he remarked, "You know, I used to hear that voice my whole life, especially as a kid. I thought it was my brother Jesse talking to me. Now I know what it is. It's God. I was confused."

"Elvis, I want to tell you something," I said. "When I was a little boy, I remember distinctly being in kindergarten, and that voice would talk to me. I thought it was my father, and I used to think, Oh, wow, he's telling me things. So this is how dads do it with their kids. How else could I hear a voice that told me the truth about myself and what I should do and how to behave; what was right and what was wrong. Conscience, I guess you'd call it. All I could think when I was a kid was that it had to be my daddy."

"Wow, I know it, I know," Elvis replied. "I heard that same voice and thought it was my brother. That's what I thought. I didn't know. I heard this guidance, because I always felt that hand on me, guiding me all my life. That's why I'm here and why I'm doing this. This didn't just happen. This wasn't mere happenstance."

There were numerous events in Elvis' life that he understood, or believed he understood. Perhaps it's best to say that he believed many things as he understood them. For example, he didn't really know that Jesse was an identical twin, but he believed it; similarly with Vernon's account of the blue light around the house. Was there a blue light? I don't think Vernon would lie, but whether there was or not, he believed so, and so did Elvis. You can't dismiss the power these ideas exerted over Elvis as a child. No wonder that he always felt so special and so different.

Elvis was generally pretty straightforward, and many people around him saw him as strong and assertive, which he could be. In fact, though, Elvis harbored deep fears about saying certain things, because he didn't want to be wrong. And he had his own unique perceptions. He and I discussed very complex subjects, things neither of us ever mentioned to anyone else. Elvis believed that there was great meaning to Jesse's life and death. He was certain that Jesse had escorted him to earth and was a companion in the womb who came in with Elvis but was not supposed to live. Of course, once Elvis saw Jesse's death as an act of God, or destiny, it logically followed that Elvis' living wasn't an accident of fate, either.

Elvis admitted that contemplating this confused him before he was turned onto spiritual principles and ideas. Without the perspective of his spiritual teachings, Elvis could only see Jesse's death as unjust, inexplicable, pointless. Being alive, Elvis possessed what Jesse lost, and it was typical of Elvis' feeling about himself and others that he felt undeserving of his own life (or that Jesse must have been as deserving as his surviving brother) and so felt some guilt for having lived. Elvis experienced this in regard to his mother as well, though he never got a handle on exactly why. He could never fully reconcile this in his mind, but as he grew older he approached these great mysteries with quiet respect rather than confusion. Late in life, he accepted that there were meanings and reasons behind things that he might never fully understand, at least not in this life.

By 1966 Elvis' involvement in his studies had exceeded reading and talking about the books I gave him. In 1960 I

began studying the teachings of Paramanhansa Yogananda, an Indian yogi who came to the West in 1920 as the
emissary of Sri Yukteswar Giri. In an introduction to a collection of Yogananda's works, Giri is described as "one of a
line of exalted gurus." He had learned the secret of Kriya
Yoga, an ancient science that enables the seeker of truth to
attain a direct personal contact with God. As Sri Yukteswar
explained to his pupil Yogananda, "Kriya Yoga is an instrument through which human evolution can be quickened. . . .
This is India's unique and deathless contribution to the world's
treasury of knowledge."

Yogananda caused a sensation the first time he spoke in
the United States, at a religious conference in Boston. Reporting on his 1925 appearance in Los Angeles, the *Los
Angeles Times* described him as "a Hindu invading the
United States to bring God . . . preaching the essence of
Christian doctrine." He founded the Self-Realization Fellowship in Los Angeles around the same time.

Elvis found Yogananda fascinating. He first read the gu-
ru's international best-seller, *Autobiography of a Yogi,* in
1964 and agreed with many of the Self-Realization Fellowship's principles and teachings. Yogananda stated the
goal of his mission as "to reveal the complete harmony
and basic oneness of original Christianity as taught by
Jesus Christ and original Yoga as taught by Bhagwan
Krishna." When Elvis learned that Yogananda's body had
remained incorrupted after his death in 1952 (a fact doc-
umented by the mortuary director of Forest Lawn Memorial Park), he decided that he too would learn Kriya
Yoga.

Though by 1965 Yogananda had been dead over a decade, the Self-Realization Fellowship grew under the direction of Yogananda's disciple Sister Daya Mata. I joined
the SRF in 1960 and met Daya Mata four years later. She
had first encountered Yogananda when he spoke to an audience in Salt Lake City in 1931. She soon joined him
and, beginning in 1955, presided over both the Satsanga
Society of India (which Yogananda also founded in 1920)
and the Self-Realization Fellowship.

I took Elvis to the Self-Realization Fellowship for the

first time in 1965. Built on twelve acres, the Fellowship's Lake Shrine is one of the most beautiful places anywhere. Sitting in Pacific Palisades, the Lake Shrine includes statues of Buddha, Jesus and other religious figures, the Mahatma Gandhi World Peace Memorial, where some of Gandhi's ashes are enshrined, and breathtaking gardens.

For a time Elvis was going to the Lake Shrine quite often and bringing along other people. He liked to visit Brother Adolph, a teacher of mine who worked and lived there as a caretaker. Adolph was a disciple of Yogananda with whom the master lived while at the Lake Shrine. Elvis and Adolph took long walks around the lake. They'd sit on the benches and talk for hours at a time.

Elvis also felt a special affinity for Daya Mata. She is a beautiful woman, spiritually and physically, with graying hair and a very sweet, almost childlike voice. Elvis loved and respected her tremendously, and she loved him in return.

The first night we went to the Self-Realization ashram, I had called Sister Daya Mata and told her that Elvis wanted to be initiated into Kriya. In order to be initiated one must strictly adhere to a year-long daily program that specifies time spent in meditation, special physical exercises and a health regimen. In early 1962, after two years' preparation, I was initiated, along with another friend who had accompanied me to the Pan Pacific in 1957, Chuck Lederman, and my friend the actor Dennis Weaver. Having studied for Kriya myself, I knew what lay ahead for Elvis, and so I carefully explained to him the degree of discipline and patience required. I believe he understood me, but, as was sometimes the case when Elvis set his mind on something, his enthusiasm eclipsed all practical considerations.

That night Alan Fortas drove Elvis, Billy Smith, Marty Lacker and me to the ashram. Elvis met privately with Daya Mata. She took him upstairs, where they talked for an hour or so. When they came downstairs, Elvis was beaming with pride. In his hand he held two black leather books containing lessons, things to do in the forthcoming year to prepare for his initiation.

Once we were in the limousine and headed for home, Elvis said, "These are her personal books of the lessons. She wants me to read one lesson a week until I go through the whole thing once."

Elvis took a deep breath, sighed and happily continued. "Man, I swear to God, Larry, I haven't felt this good in I don't know how long. You were right: Daya Mata's like a saint."

Then he confessed to doing exactly what I had feared he'd do: he asked Daya Mata for a "shortcut" to attain Kriya. "I love her! You know what she said to me? I asked her for Kriya Yoga. She said, 'I don't care if you are Elvis Presley. It doesn't matter who you are, how much money you have. You've got to earn it like everyone else. You've got to be ready, otherwise it's not going to work. Not only is it not going to work, but I can't go against what is right.' "

Elvis smiled in astonishment. Daya Mata had denied his request, and he loved it. She was the first person to really stand up to Elvis that way, and it made him happy. It just showed that people who spent years kowtowing to him, thinking that was all he wanted from everyone, were wrong.

Tightly gripping the books, Elvis said, "I trust her. She doesn't have any motives, she doesn't want anything from me except that I do the right thing. She reminds me of my mom, and I don't say that lightly. There's just something about her."

Once it was clear that he'd have to work toward the Kriya himself, Elvis redoubled his efforts in the readings and meditations. We'd go up periodically to the Lake Shrine, or the ashram, where Elvis could walk among the other students and the masters unharassed. Here he was truly in a different world; his being Elvis Presley meant absolutely nothing. Occasionally someone might glance in his direction or nod, but for the most part being there was like being in the Army. Basically he was anonymous for the first time in nearly a decade.

Of course, Elvis never did get the Kriya, for several reasons. One is that while his heart truly was in it, he didn't follow the instructions the way he was supposed to. Though he enjoyed being just like everyone else at the Lake Shrine and he respected Daya Mata for not giving in to his request to compromise her principles for him, he had grown so accustomed to getting instant results that he found the program impossible to stick with. Later, sometime in the seventies, Elvis persuaded me to do something that was very wrong. After one is initiated into Kriya, one learns a special technique, which is performed each day. It is a secret revealed only to initiates, who in turn vow not to reveal it to anyone else. One day Elvis and I got into a big discussion about this, and I agreed to tell him how to do it, and I did. But I felt terribly guilty afterward, and rightfully so. It was like giving somebody a mantra without his learning his lessons in Transcendental Meditation, or the keys to a car he didn't know how to drive. It was ethically and morally wrong, and I went to see Daya Mata to confess. She was patient and loving, but she sternly warned me, "Don't you ever do it again."

Despite his failure to receive Kriya legitimately, Elvis maintained the greatest respect for Daya Mata, the Self-Realization Fellowship and the teachings of Yogananda.

Once word spread through the Hollywood grapevine that Elvis Presley was actively pursuing spiritual studies, many organizations made pitches to him. There were concepts, teachings and philosophies he liked less than others, but few he felt strongly against. In the midseventies the Scientologists had a place called the Celebrity Center, which was supposedly where people could get together and socialize. In truth, though, it functioned as a recruiting center for Scientology, where converts would proselytize and try to drum up membership. Founded in the early fifties by science-fiction novelist L. Ron Hubbard, Scientology (originally called Dianetics, the name it reverted to in the eighties) is an outgrowth of the human-potential movement. The main work of Scientology is Hubbard's book *Dianetics*, which has sold millions of copies.

Dianetics claims to be an applied religious philosophy, the study of the human spirit in its relationship to the physical universe and its living forms. Devotees of Dianetics focus their attention on clearing away accumulated physical and emotional pains and scars which supposedly alter and suppress the life force, thus preventing one from leading a more fulfilled life.

After reading up on Scientology, Elvis concluded that it wasn't a lot different from the church he had grown away from; that its leaders sought control and were overly interested in money. Elvis felt very strongly that they were perverting true spiritual teaching and doing to metaphysics what religionists did to true religion. He rejected what he regarded as their mind-control tactics, and believed Scientology to be a godless religion.

"They never mention God," Elvis said of the Scientologists. "They just want me. They want my name and my money. *That's* what they're into. I've got to be extremely careful; I just can't let my name be used for something so important except when it's right."

Elvis was convinced that the Scientologists had ulterior motives and were very dangerous, so he kept away from them. Ironically, after Elvis' death Priscilla became involved in Scientology, as did his daughter Lisa Marie.

One of the things Elvis said countless times over the years was, "I guess I'm just misunderstood." And it is as true after his death as it was in life. Just recently I saw a Christian newsletter that stated that by pursuing his study of religions outside Christianity and philosophies from other cultures, Elvis was practicing Satanism. That many otherwise well-informed writers have taken it upon themselves to explain to the world what they themselves do not understand doesn't help, either, even when they are well-intentioned. And this is not to mention people, such as Albert Goldman, whose contempt for all that Elvis was and loved is so transparent that their books tell more truth about the authors than about Elvis. I've read that Elvis studied Buddhism, practiced bending spoons, held séances through which he contacted his mother, and believed that after his death he would return in the spirit and the body of someone else. None of these statements is true.

For Elvis, his spiritual studies were part of his spiritual evolution. He believed in reincarnation as a part of that evolution, a series of steps in one's continuous development. He did not subscribe to the Buddhist theory of transmigration—that is, that if you do evil things, for example, you come back in the next life as a lizard. While he did not believe in contacting the dead, he did feel the presence of deceased loved ones, as many of us do. He held to the Christian belief that he would be reunited with his mother in death. He spoke of her waiting for him after his death, when they and everyone else dear to him would all meet again. It's interesting that he never mentioned knowing that Jesse Garon would be there with Gladys. Of course, that doesn't mean that he didn't believe that he and Jesse would be brought together again; only that, contrary to some books and movies, he didn't talk about it all the time.

Elvis liked reading books on cosmology, a branch of metaphysics that concerns the nature of the universe. The Biblical account of Genesis, depicting the creation of heaven and earth, the various kingdoms, relationships, laws and principles, was just the beginning for Elvis. He knew that answers to these questions lay beyond orthodox teachings. When he read that ancient manuscripts on the true nature of Jesus' life and teaching were locked away in Vatican archives, along with other controversial, secret materials, he said, "I'm not a prophet, but I'll tell you, someday all that information they're hiding from the masses will become known, and it will be a whole new ballgame."

Among his favorite books in this area were those by Vera Stanley Alder, such as *The Initiation of the World* and *The Fifth Dimension,* works whose focus is the application of ancient knowledge to modern life.

Elvis did believe in the supernatural. He believed in the noncorporeal aspect of living. He was interested in telepathy, healing through touch and a number of phenomena that are only now being scientifically studied. His mother had healed him through touch and prayer, and although healing was an important, accepted part of his youth, around the age of thirteen or fourteen he had stopped thinking about it. Memphis was more urbane than Tupelo, and in his eagerness to be accepted by his new school-mates and neighbors Elvis buried anything about his past that might be considered backwoods, hick. It wasn't until he and I met that Elvis realized that healing wasn't something practiced only by country people, but that it occurred in numerous cultures all over the world.

Now, among those in the group, some, such as Jerry Schilling, accepted that Elvis did have that ability. Even Red West and Sonny West, and Priscilla, have admitted as much, though they present it in a negative way. Then there were those who refused to believe that Elvis could heal. One of the bodyguards, for example, writes of allowing Elvis to heal his child, then "playing along" with Elvis by humoring him, pretending he believed it, too. Someone else wrote of "fooling" Elvis this way, but Elvis was rarely fooled. When Elvis knew that he had helped someone but sensed that he was being laughed at, it hurt his feelings very deeply. He thought he was doing something good for people; their snide comments cut him to the quick.

I once saw Elvis heal a man who was having a heart attack. Another time Elvis treated Jerry Schilling after he had taken a nasty spill on his motorcycle and was unable to move.

"The next thing I knew," Jerry said later, "I woke up the following morning healed."

Several times we healed Grandma Minnie Mae at Graceland, and she loved it. Of course, having lived with it all her life, Minnie Mae had no problem with healing. For her it was completely normal, and her grandson just happened to be one of those God had blessed with that power. Several times, after we'd given Minnie Mae a healing, Elvis would say, "I'll bet she outlives all of us."

Understandably, the healing business was kept quiet, even among our group. In the seventies, though, I witnessed hundreds of concertgoers carrying their sick or crippled children to the stage and crying out, "Elvis, please touch my baby," or "Elvis, just hold her for a minute." Few fans knew of his studies then, and yet thousands apparently sensed that he had some ability to heal.

Some around Elvis claim that he read their minds. Everyone knew that Elvis could tell what people were thinking, and in fact he could. He had an uncanny ability to know people very well; he was quite perceptive. His intuition was highly developed and finely tuned. He was an astute observer, and very little escaped his notice. But few people mention that Elvis was also with them for hours every day for years at a stretch, and that many of them were what you'd call "easy reads." Elvis wasn't a yogi or tapping into some secret power (as Parker feared that I might be). He just knew how to put two and two together.

Another misconception concerns Elvis' identification with Jesus. Elvis was fascinated by Jesus, not just the image of Jesus but who he was. He didn't think that Jesus was the only begotten son of God. He thought that all people had Christ in them and had the same potential. Knowing the Scriptures as well as he did, Elvis would pose questions like "Didn't Jesus say that you could do greater things?" Contrary to reports, Elvis' favorite book of the Bible was not the dramatic Revelations but the more mystical Book of John.

Elvis' conception of Jesus Christ differed from the Jesus depicted by modern Christianity. Elvis felt that while on earth Christ revealed very deep, profound secrets, but that what we read today of what Jesus supposedly said is a watered-down version. He thought that Jesus experienced everything that all people experienced, that he was the flower of humanity, that he suffered, and yet his suffering was ecstasy. Later in his life, whenever he felt that he was truly suffering, Elvis would say, "This is the way Jesus was. Did you ever see Jesus mentioned in the Bible laughing? Never. Not once does it say that Jesus smiled or laughed. That's because he had this compassion for other people. He knew where other people were at. He knew the sufferings of humanity. I understand that, and that's why I am who I am. That's why God put me on earth. That's part of my mission. Only today things are different. Today, everything is technical."

This is how he altered his vision of Christ. In Alder's *The Initiation of the World*, she speaks of a group of spiritual masters called the White Brotherhood, whose job it is to oversee human affairs. Elvis believed that he was working under the aegis of these masters, including Jesus. He felt somehow connected to them and thought that they had helped him, but not through messages or what some people today call channeling, because he wasn't into that. In Elvis' mind, his life was being directed divinely by the brotherhood of masters and illuminated beings, enlightened entities that have existed since time immemorial. And he truly felt that he was chosen to be here now as a modern-day savior, a Christ.

Now, many people have misconstrued this to mean that Elvis thought he *was* Jesus, which is simply not true. It's important to remember that Christ is not Jesus' second name, Christ is a word that means truth, from *christos*, Greek for "anointed one." Technically speaking, it's Jesus the Christ, not Jesus Christ.

Elvis was of the opinion that religion could be a dangerous thing in the hands of the wrong people. He despised the televangelists or anyone who used God or the promises of their faith to make money. Though televangelism wasn't nearly as popular or sophisticated then as it became in the eighties, it was hard to turn on a television down South without seeing some TV preacher exhorting his audience to send in contributions, or else.

"Look what they're doing to people," Elvis would say, pointing to the screen, "the same thing they did to me back in Tupelo. Now they've got television to do it. The same old bullshit, the same fear. Someday in the near future we'll see how the so-called ministries of God react as they see their worn-out ways and the whole 'old age' start crumbling. They'll probably be grabbing for the last penny they can get their greedy ol' hands on. They'll all get theirs. They've been building up some bad karma. I can't wait till this new age comes, so this stuff will stop."

Elvis' objections to people who controlled others through fear went beyond religion. He rarely remarked on someone manipulating someone else without mentioning his parents and his childhood. His reaction seemed to stem from seeing his mother and father "controlled" by their poverty. Elvis rejected the whole idea of external control, even though in so many ways he buckled under to it. And despite his faith in the power of fate and destiny, he believed that we're impelled by certain qualities and influences to make our own choices in life. Philosophically he opposed anything that interfered with a person's free will to choose.

In this period Elvis' public expression of his spiritual beliefs was *How Great Thou Art,* a collection of gospel hymns that, following its March 1967 release, earned Elvis one of only three Grammy Awards of his career, for best sacred performance. His other two Grammies were for best inspirational performance, 1972, for *He Touched Me,* and best inspirational performance, 1974, for the song "How Great Thou Art." In 1971 Elvis was given the Bing Crosby Award, a special-merit Grammy, "in recognition of his artistic creativity and his influence . . . upon a generation of performers and listeners whose lives and musical horizons have been enriched and expanded by his unique contributions." None of his rock-and-roll records was ever acknowledged individually.

For the movie sound-track albums someone else chose the material, which Elvis recorded, though rarely without expressing his contempt for it. For *How Great Thou Art,* however, Elvis' approach was totally different. He picked every single song; there was to be no "filler," no Tin Pan Alley junk. I spent countless hours with Elvis as he pored through his great stacks of gospel records, searching for exactly the right tunes. He took more direct control of this album than of any other in his career. As with his material in the later sixties and the seventies, each selection had a personal meaning to Elvis, especially the title song and "Farther Along."

Because the songs are Christian hymns, some people assumed that Elvis forsook his other spiritual beliefs. In fact, though, through this album Elvis sought to reach people by singing about his love of God. I'm sure that if he had ever dreamt that an audience existed for songs praising meditation and Kriya Yoga, he'd have recorded those as well. For the Colonel's part, he declined to interfere, feeling that this demonstration of religious—orthodox religious, that is—piety could work only to Elvis' advantage. It wasn't too far out for the Colonel, and it was good for Elvis' image, so why not? His first gospel album, from 1960, *His Hand in Mine,* was a hit. The 1965 success of "Crying in the Chapel," which Elvis had recorded five years earlier, was another consideration. It was Elvis' sole Top Five hit between August 1963 and June 1969.

How Great Thou Art was recorded at RCA in Nashville over several days in May 1966. This was the first time that Elvis worked with producer Felton Jarvis, whom he liked a great deal. When we were preparing to leave the Albert Pike Motel for the first sessions—it was already ten at night, and we were late—Elvis told the others to wait downstairs; we'd be down in a few minutes.

Elvis grew very serious.

"Millions of people around the world are going to hear this album," he said. "It's going to touch people in ways we can't imagine. And I know this album is ordained by God Himself. This is God's message, and I'm His channel. Only I can't be a channel if my ego is there. I have to empty myself so that the channel is totally pure and the message is heard loud and clear. Let's sit down, close our eyes and meditate. I'm not going to move out of this chair until I'm guided by that still, small voice within."

We meditated for over half an hour, sitting across from each other in facing chairs. At the same moment, we both opened our eyes.

"So be it," Elvis said softly. "I'm ready."

Elvis devoted himself to this album and spent hours on each song, getting all the parts exactly right. One thing about singing gospel music Elvis loved was that, while there are designated leads, all the singers are equally important to the sound and spirit of the performance. Elvis enjoyed the sound of voices and preferred to hear his voice combined with others. On the bus, back at Graceland, on the road, at rehearsals, he was always breaking into a gospel song, and he seemed happy when all the other singers—and even those of us who couldn't really sing—joined in. Before we left Nashville, Elvis made sure that the tracks for *How Great* were mixed and balanced to his specifications. He wanted to capture the spirit of people singing in a church, feeling that was how these songs were meant to be sung. One result was that Elvis' voice, while always distinguishable from the other singers' (the Jordanaires and the Imperials Quartet), wasn't as prominent as on his secular records.

Many months later, when Elvis heard the finished album, he was furious. Somewhere along the line the final mix he had approved was changed without his permission. Now it was too late. On the porch at Graceland, he paced back and forth, shouting angrily.

"Why are they putting my voice up in the goddamned control room in New York City? Why is someone turning that knob and amping my voice over the other voices and over the music? Because they think that's what the fans want to hear. Sure, the fans want to hear my voice, but my voice in relation to these other people's voices. I'm nothing without them. We're all together in this. But no, man, those people in New York think they know more about this than I do. Let them come down and sing the goddamn song."

Elvis went on and on about this before finally calming down. "They can't do it," he kept saying. "They're messing with my music, and when you mess with my music . . ." His voice trailed off with this unfinished threat. "If those people in New York would quit fucking around with my voice, maybe I'd get a hit."

Not long after, he spoke to the Colonel about it, but hardly in the same tone. Here Elvis finally had a record he was truly proud of, something that he had controlled, but that was ruined by RCA's commercial considerations. The sad part wasn't so much what the Colonel or RCA had done, but the fact that Elvis couldn't allow himself to be angry at the people responsible. Some of the arrogant sense of entitlement that other stars freely expressed might have done Elvis good. In situations like this, his relationship with RCA and the Colonel wasn't much different from that of any good, obedient worker and his boss.

Though Parker seemed only too happy to hand Elvis the

reins on this one, he maintained control over everything else. There's no way of knowing how much Elvis told Parker about why he wanted to release *How Great Thou Art,* but it's hard to imagine the Colonel not realizing what the album meant to Elvis. If Parker's stooges in the organization were doing their jobs, they had told him what Elvis felt about the studies, and that Elvis' interest in spiritual matters showed no sign of waning. *How Great Thou Art* was acceptable to Parker only because it was good business.

If anything, Elvis' reading was taking up more time than ever. What did the Colonel think when he learned of Elvis' desert vision, the trips to visit Daya Mata at the ashram or Adolph at the Lake Shrine and his interest in yoga? Coupled with his growing dissatisfaction with the movies, Elvis' spiritual quest must have given Parker at least a moment's pause. More than once Elvis remarked, "Hey, man, same goddamn movie. All they do is change my name, bring in a couple of new sets. It's the same flick." Elvis wasn't touring, and, while his albums sold well enough, the hits eluded him. All Parker and Elvis had were the movies.

In Elvis' twenty-third film, *Easy Come, Easy Go,* Elvis played a diver bent on discovering sunken treasure. For no logical reason the script calls for a yoga instructor named Madame Neherina, played by Elsa Lanchester, and a duet performed by Elvis and Lanchester, "Yoga Is as Yoga Does." Parker chose to express his disapproval of Elvis' esoteric interests through a little "in" joke, one that required Elvis' character (which, in the minds of some fans, was the same as Elvis himself) to ridicule something Elvis respected and loved. Everything about the yoga scene suggests that students and teachers of the art are nuts. Elvis' character makes disparaging comments about them. Only Parker—who served as technical adviser on the film— knows why. Once Elvis saw the script and heard the song, he knew what was up, and he was livid. After the scene was shot, he stormed into his trailer, shouting, "That son of a bitch! He knows, and he did it! He told those damn writers what to do, and he's making me do this."

Elvis was crushed. He faced pressure from the Colonel, who ran his career, made the deals and repeatedly told him, "Without me, you are nothing. Without me, you'll be in trouble." On the other side there were the fans, whom Elvis wanted to please however he could. By this time, there seemed to be no manager more powerful or more effective than Tom Parker. But it's hard to believe that anyone who managed Elvis Presley would not be so regarded. There's no question that Parker and Presley made a dazzling combination, and that Parker was part of the Presley phenomenon. Still, there were hundreds of Parkers, but only one Elvis.

I had been talking to Elvis about the desert's healing currents, trying to convince him to check it out. Initially, Elvis couldn't see what the big deal about the desert was. "What are you going to do in the desert?" he'd ask. After he finally went to see, he liked Palm Springs so much he bought a home there. Colonel Parker had a place there, too. Elvis and I went down together and stayed for two weeks, maybe longer, at a spa Parker recommended. Stevie and the kids came along, and we all looked forward to a relaxing vacation.

Elvis was susceptible to certain pressures, largely because he tried desperately to please almost everyone. At this time I had begun growing a beard, which was considered just a little too far out for people like Parker. One day Elvis took me aside and, somewhat embarrassed, said, "I gotta tell you something. [Producer] Hal Wallis and the Colonel saw you in the pool today and remarked about your beard. The Colonel said that when you stood up in the pool, you looked just like John the Baptist. So could you just shave off the beard until after we finish the movie?"

I agreed to; it was no big deal. What I found interesting was Parker's choice of imagery: John the Baptist?

I was out one evening when an acquaintance of Parker's approached me and said, "Larry, I want you to have dinner with me tonight."

I accepted, and later that evening I shared a table with

him and his group. He seemed nice enough, but after an hour or so I sensed something peculiar about him.

"Boy," he remarked admiringly, "you must be on some kind of diet."

"Well, I try to eat right," I said.

"Do you work out?"

"Not too much. A little bit."

He fell silent for a minute, then stared at me as though I were a piece of beef on a rack. "Boy, I bet you look good in swimming trunks."

You might think that having been a stylist in Hollywood, I would have known about homosexuals. I did, but in those days things were not as open as they are now, and I was fairly naive. I had never been approached by a man before, and didn't quite grasp what Parker's friend was driving at until I felt his hand pressing my upper thigh. I freaked out, and I think he read my expression; he had the wrong guy. He blushed, then tried to joke about it. "Boy, you're muscular too."

"Yeah, I'm in good shape," I replied brusquely.

"Well," he continued as if nothing had happened, "we're going to go swimming in my pool at the house. Perhaps you'll join us," he purred as he folded his dinner napkin.

"No." I left and went home to Stevie, stunned. I replayed the scene over and over, concluding that this guy had been sent to check me out. Could the Colonel have put him up to this? Of course. Why? I kept hearing the Colonel barking, "What the hell are Elvis and Larry doing in the bathroom all the time?" Maybe this was his way of eliminating at least one possibility.

Looking back on the events of 1966 and 1967, I can see that Parker was set on ousting me from Elvis' life one way or another. He was too smart, however, to demand outright that I leave. The incident at the spa, my inclusion in the Snowmen's League, the remarks about my alleged hypnotic powers—all were clues. I didn't read them as such right away, which was fine with the Colonel. He intended to keep Elvis with him for the long haul; he was biding his time.

While several of the guys were reporting back to Parker, and Parker had shown his contempt for Elvis' ''religious kick,'' he continued courting me all the same. Ever since we'd met, Parker had regularly invited me to bring my family to visit him and his wife, Marie, for the day in Palm Springs. Whenever he mentioned it, I'd politely decline or stall, saying, ''Maybe some other time.'' In 1966 Parker's request took on a new urgency, and something about his manner suggested that it would be best if I accepted. My impression then was that he'd think I was insulting him or avoiding him out of fear. To a certain extent, the latter was true. One day Parker announced, ''Larry, I want you at my house. This Sunday.'' This was an order.

Stevie, the kids and I drove down for the day. Parker refused to give me his address, and instead directed me to a pay phone on a main street near his home. I was to call him from there, and he'd give me the instructions then. Parker's house wasn't large, but it was well appointed. He had a fair-sized pool surrounded by Astroturf. I swam in the pool with the kids for a while, and Stevie chatted with the Colonel's wife. Marie Parker, who wasn't around much except for openings and special occasions, was very quiet and sweet. She struck me as being a little addled, though that was probably because she was so shy. The whole while, Parker watched our every move. Stevie and I both noticed that whenever I met Parker's gaze, he'd avert his eyes. He knew of Elvis' threats to join a monastery, and he seemed to be checking me for ''powers,'' perhaps out of fear that I'd turn them on him next. Today it sounds almost funny, but Parker took it all very seriously.

At about three-thirty or four in the afternoon Parker said, ''Larry, let's go in the house.''

He and I went into the den, and as I sat there Parker spoke on the phone. I can't honestly recall whether he placed the call or whether someone called him, but he spent several minutes engrossed in this conversation. He stood about fifteen feet from me and replied to whoever he was talking with by answering yes or no. There was no way anyone listening could discern what was being discussed, but before too long it was obvious that the subject was me. A couple of times he looked at me as he spoke, making eye contact and obviously trying to hold me with his gaze.

"Yeah, yeah. Yeah, right now. Yeah, well. Yeah, he's here," Parker said before hanging up.

"Let's go out," he said. "I want to buy you all some ice cream, for you and the kids."

We drove to Will Wright's ice-cream store. Wright was a character actor before he opened a small chain of shops that sold the best premium ice cream in the state. There Parker met several of his buddies, and we talked a while longer. At five Stevie and I said goodbye, thanked Parker for a pleasant day and headed home. During the drive back to Los Angeles I thought about the visit. Parker had been nice enough, and we had enjoyed ourselves, but something about that telephone call kept coming back to me. "Yeah, he's here," I heard Parker saying.

We were on daylight-saving time, so it was still light when we got to our house. As we came up the driveway I was overcome by the weirdest feeling. I didn't know why; from the outside, everything looked fine. But I sensed that something was different, out of place. Stopping the car, I saw that the back door was open. I got out, followed by Stevie and the kids. The back door swung in the wind, and as I stepped inside I heard the sickening sound of a small bird smashing its head against a windowpane, trying desperately to escape.

Two large garbage cans had been upended, and trash was strewn throughout the house, along with human urine and feces. My initial impression was that a thief had broken in. But when I looked around, I could see that most of our portable valuables were still there. Only a reel-to-reel tape deck, along with some tapes Sister Daya Mata had made for me, my files containing palm prints and numerological and astrological charts on Elvis and other friends were missing. Our bedroom had been ransacked, the closets stripped and drawers emptied onto the floor, but all that had been taken from there were Stevie's and my clothes. Whoever it was stole my suits, my shoes, everything except my underwear. This wasn't the work of a thief, or some dumb kid. This was a professional intimidation job. All I could think was, *Parker*.

I didn't voice my suspicions to Stevie or the kids, who were understandably upset and frightened. I was too angry. Today I honestly don't remember whether or not the police were called.

"Let's get over to Elvis' house now," I said. We drove to Elvis', and when we arrived he didn't appear entirely surprised to see us.

"Elvis, I've got to talk to you," I said.

He nodded. Everyone else stayed in the living room, and Elvis and I went out by the pool. I told him what had happened, beginning with Parker's insistence that I come to his house that day. Elvis listened, then looked down at the floor. Our eyes met, and he looked away. He knew that I knew that he knew exactly what had gone on.

Shaking his head, he kept repeating, "Damn! Damn!" Then he stared me straight in the eye, his way of telling me things he couldn't articulate. After a moment he said, "Lawrence, it's a dangerous fuckin' world. . . ."

He was quiet again, then softly said, "Hey, I'm sorry. I guess we've got to be smart; let's keep this to ourselves and just bear it." Elvis assumed his take-charge tone, and said, "I don't want you, Stevie and the kids in that house tonight. Just go and get a room somewhere in Beverly Hills—you know, something real nice. I want to pay for it."

He added cryptically, "The whole thing stinks, only we know there's more to this than meets the eye."

For a few months, things seemed back to normal. Then in 1966 a girl who hung out at the house in Los Angeles gave Elvis a small gift: several hits of windowpane acid— LSD. He hadn't expressed any interest in taking it, although he had heard about LSD and was mildly curious. I had dropped acid back in 1961, before the government classified it as an illegal drug. I found the experience interesting and enlightening, but could take it or leave it. The word around Hollywood was that an acid trip could open you up to new experiences and perceptions. Under the influence, some people even claimed to have seen or experienced God. In this sense, LSD was viewed by many as a "shortcut" to spiritual enlightenment. Lots of people were doing it, so I wasn't surprised when Elvis said, "Priscilla wants to take acid. She hears us talking all the time, plus she wants to understand what's in the books. She wants to experience things and understand what it's all about."

We planned to set aside a special time, and one day at Graceland things were right. Elvis, Priscilla, Jerry Schilling, Sonny West and I retired to the upstairs conference room. Elvis gave everyone else the night off and said that we were not to be disturbed by anyone. Sonny was appointed our "monitor." We all sat around a large table and dropped our hits of acid.

About an hour and a half later, we stood up to stretch and walk around. Suddenly we noticed that we had lost Jerry. No one knew where he was, and I didn't know whether Jerry was actually missing or whether I was imagining it. Nevertheless, I joined in the search, and we found him lying in a closet, under a pile of Elvis' clothes. Through all of this, Elvis obviously was really fighting the effects of the drug, trying his best to make it appear that he was not getting high.

We were having a pleasant, mellow trip, when suddenly Priscilla began sobbing. She fell to her knees in front of Elvis and cried, "You don't really love me. You just say you do." Elvis glanced at me and rolled his eyes, then tried to convince her she was wrong, but nothing he said worked. Next thing we knew, she was saying to Jerry and me, "You don't like me." When she started telling us that she was "ugly," I worried she might be having a bad trip. Fortunately, she soon snapped out of it, and the rest of our experience passed uneventfully.

Like anything else Elvis did, he tripped Elvis style. No beaded curtains, incense or Indian sitar music for us. Several hours after we had started, we turned on television and watched a science-fiction movie, *The Time Machine*, and sent out for pizza. As we were all coming down, we walked out behind Graceland and marveled at the beauty of nature, talked about how lucky we were to have such good friends and how much we cared about one another. As far as I know, it was the only time Elvis took acid.

By late 1966 the tensions were mounting again. In addition to my problems with the Colonel, there were a couple of the guys whose earlier coolness degenerated into blatant hostility. The Wandering Jew, Lawrence of Israel—these were a couple of the nicer nicknames the group bestowed on me. After hearing me talk about how each of us is on his or her own level of spiritual development, Red West specifically asked Elvis to ask me not to use the word "level" in his presence; it made him feel self-conscious and that he was being talked down to. For a while, some even criticized me for being too happy in the morning. A silly pettiness infused most of it, but for some of the guys I was a serious issue. There were a couple who didn't seem to be looking for trouble, exactly; they were more like trouble looking for a place to happen. Every now and then, without warning or reason, one would hit a flash point and violence followed.

Shortly after Elvis finished *How Great Thou Art*, we were back at MGM to film *Spinout*. It was a Monday, and I arrived at the sound stage early. There was a little set, with a couch, chairs and a table, where I saw Elvis' costar, Diane McBain, chatting with Red and Sonny, another girl and some extras. I hadn't seen Elvis yet, and so I approached Red and everyone to say hi.

"Hey, how you all doing? Red? Hi, Diane, how you doing?"

After some small talk, I excused myself and went to see if Elvis was in. I had just stepped inside Elvis' trailer and put down my briefcase when Red stormed in, right on my heels.

"All right, man," he said angrily. "Keep your hands off her!"

"What are you talking about?" I asked.

"Come on, man. Don't bullshit me. I saw the way you said hello to her," Red said, his face flushing with anger.

"You mean Diane?" I asked, incredulous. "What are you talking about?"

"Don't bullshit me!" Red shouted, moving closer. "You're after her."

Before I could blink, he raised his fist, and at about the time I spit out "Don't you—" I felt bone shatter as he punched me on the chin. I fell back on a couch, totally surprised. Red moved closer, and, knowing he was a black belt and one tough guy, I knew I'd have to fight back. The very second I raised my fist, several guys burst through the door and pulled us apart. I was dying to land a punch, but I knew Red was capable of killing with his bare hands. It was probably just as well that the fight broke up. For several years I could move a chip of my chin bone around under my skin—all in all a minor injury compared to what might have occurred. Over the years I would see several people, both inside and outside Elvis' circle, sustain far more serious injuries at the hands of the bodyguards. I got off easy.

For the most part, the guys made their distaste for what Elvis and I did known only to me. Exasperated that Elvis was so engrossed in his studies, one of them might remark, "He's still up there, scrambling his brains." Once one of them asked me, "Damn! Don't you guys ever give up?"

The only person who consistently derided Elvis' pursuits to his face and in front of others was Priscilla. At least, unlike some, she was never a hypocrite. She had no use for Elvis' spiritual or intellectual endeavors, and everyone knew it. Part of this was due to her youth. Though bright in her way, she lacked intellectual depth. Elvis' attempts to draw her into our discussions, even of such basic, straightforward works as Kahlil Gibran's *The Prophet*, were unrewarding. She glared at Elvis impatiently or assumed a pose of exasperation, as if she were being tortured. That other women, including many of his costars, such as Donna Douglas, Shelley Fabares and Mary Ann Mobley, were only too happy to discuss these things with Elvis for hours annoyed her.

At a certain point, I think, Priscilla did make an effort to understand this side of Elvis. Though her relationship with Stevie had been friendly but cool, for a couple of months right after Elvis' experience in the desert Priscilla spent a lot more time with her. Because Elvis couldn't go out in public, he sent Priscilla to a lecture by Manly P. Hall, a noted scholar, thinking she might learn something. But, as Stevie remarked to me recently, Hall wasn't an entertainer; his lectures were, well, lectures. Priscilla was bored to tears, as I'm sure many young women her age might have been.

One evening Elvis and I were upstairs at Graceland, looking at a new book called *Ten Unveiled: The Brydlovan Theory of the Origin of Numbers*. Priscilla walked in, apparently happy to see Elvis, but when she spotted the book her attitude cooled. "Oh, there you are, reading some more." Before Elvis could get out a word, she was gone. Elvis stared at the empty doorway in disbelief, shaking his head. Initially disappointed, he became angry, and said, "Damn, that girl lives with me, and she doesn't really know what makes me tick. I know you can't make someone grow, but this is my number-one interest. Good Lord, man, I pray she'll start her own search."

After a few minutes, his mood brightened and he added, "Maybe someday it'll all rub off."

Elvis often said, "You can lead a horse to water, but if you can get it to float, you got a good thing goin'." In Priscilla's case, he probably would have settled for, if not complete involvement, at least a quiet tolerance. But that wasn't going to happen. No matter where we were or who was around, whenever Elvis mentioned anything about his studies Priscilla invariably shot him an insolent look. He'd catch it out of the corner of his eye and then pretend he hadn't noticed or it didn't bother him, but you could see his heart breaking. Still, Elvis possessed an extraordinary capacity to believe in people, and once he believed in you there was little that could change his mind. And Elvis believed to the bottom of his soul that with his guidance, encouragement and example Priscilla eventually would come around. As he confessed years after their divorce, though, he realized then how slim the odds were.

On Christmas Eve, 1966, we were having dinner at Graceland with Elvis, Priscilla, Vernon, Dee, Ricky, David, Billy and Grandma Minnie Mae. Late in the evening Elvis excused himself and invited Stevie, Priscilla and me to join him upstairs. Inside the office we stood together and Elvis, smiling, said, "We have so much to be thankful for. God has truly blessed us. We are so fortunate to have the life we do."

He was unusually happy, and Stevie and I appreciated his thoughts. We *were* very lucky. Living and working in the entertainment business could distort your priorities. It was too easy to be swept up by the empty values, and that was something Stevie and I tried to be conscientious about, something that concerned Elvis too. Our lives were blessed; we had our health, our families, our kids. As I looked at Stevie, I saw that Elvis' words had touched her too. Predictably, at Elvis' suggestion that we all meditate and say a prayer of thanks, Priscilla gave a contemptuous glare, as if to say, "Here we go again."

A few seconds after we had closed our eyes, a ceiling light flashed on.

"See? See?" Elvis asked Priscilla excitedly. "This is what I've been trying to tell you about. How did that light go on?"

Priscilla stared blankly, reducing Elvis to practically pleading with her to believe him. Whether it was a real manifestation or a fluke in the power lines, I don't know. Whatever it was, though, Elvis believed it, and as I watched him beg her to listen I was embarrassed for him. How would Elvis pursue his spiritual quest, married to a girl who thought it was all a joke?

CHAPTER

6

In the two and a half years that I'd known Elvis, he had changed. He was calmer, more introspective and more content. Those who lived around and with Elvis in these years often speak of his "legendary" temper and say that they dreaded his notorious outbursts. I never did. He expressed anger toward me only once. It was around 1965, and we were at the Memphian Theater watching *Becket*, the Hal Wallis picture starring Peter O'Toole and Richard Burton as the twelfth-century King Henry II and the Archbishop of Canterbury, Thomas Becket, the king's spiritual confidant.

The movie had several meanings for Elvis. For one thing, he couldn't help but note the film's high quality, and it made him furious—partly because he knew he'd never get to work on such a project, and also because he believed that Wallis, the producer, used money he earned from Elvis' artistically less ambitious films to underwrite better, serious movies, such as *Becket*. I suppose Elvis felt that if it was his work that was funding such quality productions, he deserved at least a chance to perform in them himself.

On a deeper level, the movie's symbolism was quite obvious, so much so that I'm a little embarrassed to mention it today. Here were the King of England and his spiritual adviser, who got along until Becket opposed the King's policies toward other members of the clergy. In the end, Becket is abandoned by the King and murdered by the King's men.

Stevie and I were seated a couple of rows behind Elvis, enjoying the film, when suddenly over the sound track I heard Elvis yell out, "All right, Larry! I know what you're thinking!" I didn't answer, and a few seconds later he resumed watching the screen. It was never mentioned again.

One morning when we were working on *Paradise, Hawaiian Style* I was waiting in Elvis' dressing room for him, sitting in one of the big soft black leather chairs. Elvis entered, with the guys trailing behind, and he was in an ugly mood. Once inside the door, Elvis sank into a barber-style chair and glared at his reflection in a mirror. During this phase of shooting, Milton Berle, who was also working at Paramount, would come by each morning and visit. He really liked Elvis, and he'd have us all laughing at his jokes.

When Uncle Miltie came in, Elvis cheered up and was soon cracking up. Once Berle left, though, Elvis instantly fell back into his funk. This time he didn't just sulk. He sprang from his chair and began berating the group. Apparently, the girlfriend of one of the guys had told Priscilla something to the effect that Elvis had said he didn't want her with him in California and kept her in Memphis so he could be "free," i.e., chase women. When Priscilla relayed back to Elvis what she had heard, he hit the roof.

"That's it, that's it! I'm fed up with you guys and all the small talk, gossiping and bullshit. Now fuck off, all of you. Just call Daddy and get your checks, then get the hell out. You and your stupid women, always running off at the mouth.

"I'm tired of you anyway," he said, pacing the room. "You're all a pain in my ass. I don't want to see your faces anymore. Call Daddy, tell him every word I said. This will make him real happy."

Charlie Hodge, who had joined recently, and I sat there with Elvis, knowing he didn't mean us. Then Elvis turned and stomped out, with me and Charlie following. By four that afternoon he had rehired everyone, as they knew he would. They knew him too well not to expect a change of heart. If he felt deeply guilty, there might even be a new car in it for everyone.

The spiritual teachings didn't necessarily change Elvis so much as they gave him a freedom to express his true self. His newfound, or more likely rediscovered, personality was quieter; energetic but not manic; disciplined and more sensitive. Some people found these refinements unacceptable. In their eyes he had become a bookworm and a bore. Even Priscilla longed for the "mischievous games" he used to indulge in on the movie sets—the very antics that prompted the derision of coworkers and superiors in Hollywood.

In embracing the spiritual teachings as Elvis did, he redefined the parameters of his life. While I know that this might sound like an overstatement, it is true. Not only were the changes that occurred in the wake of his spiritual awakening evident to his friends, but after a while people outside his inner circle noticed them as well. Norman Taurog, who directed a number of classic films as well as nine Presley movies (including Elvis' favorite, *Blue Hawaii*), was especially impressed with how Elvis had matured in the few years he had known him. Now, rather than run around and toss water balloons on the set, Elvis sat reading in his trailer or holding his own intelligent conversations with other people working on the film. When Taurog remarked to him, "Whatever change you're going through, keep going. You finally came of age," Elvis entered the trailer smiling, looking as if he would burst with pride.

"Mr. Taurog just gave me one of the best compliments of my life," he said. "He told me that I was tapping into my potential. He said he always knew hat I'd wake up someday."

As much as Elvis kept to himself socially, he was sensitive to how other people saw him. He rarely spoke about it, but he understood how he was initially perceived by the entertainment industry outside the record business: as a rube, an unsophisticated, uneducated teen idol. Elvis would never cease believing that if only he had gotten a chance, or some acting help, he could have realized his dream of being a credible actor. Still, he was enough of a realist to understand that by late 1966 the die had been cast. If there was no chance of his being taken seriously as an actor, then at least he could be respected as a person. Norman Taurog's compliment represented that kind of acceptance. After that, Elvis knew that other people—*intelligent* people—recognized the value of his studies and liked the changes they saw in him. Elvis was rarely happier than when he was in a position to enlighten someone else. I don't think he was that way because he liked to show off, but because he wanted very desperately to be seen as an intelligent, thinking person.

But all of these positive changes and reinforcements occurred in the outside world, and in Elvis' life the outside world was a distant place he ventured out into but never really lived in. To outsiders, Elvis' observations on philosophy and religion were interesting; to most insiders, they were annoying. Elvis' home and his life existed on the inside, and the inside had, by late 1966, solidified into the hard form it retained until the end. The routines, which so rarely deviated to begin with, grew immutable. The occasional employee might leave, or come back again; Elvis might move from one house in Los Angeles to the other; his recreational interest might shift from miniature slot cars to go-carts, but these were only imperceptible ripples in an otherwise static existence. Things happened, of course, but even the most dramatic event assumed the texture of an episode on a television series. Everyone was Taking Care of Business. Whatever the problem, it would be solved, business would be taken care of, ruffled feathers would be smoothed, and before long things would be back to normal.

Normal. It's a funny word to use in reference to Elvis, because precious little about him or his life ever really was. Every now and then I flash back on a specific moment we shared, and I'm still amazed at how bizarre an existence it was. I use the word "existence" deliberately, because psychologically, socially, artistically Elvis' life offered all the stimulation and challenge of the average factory worker's. Years of buffers separated Elvis from the outside until the real world paled and before long was no more real to him than the scenery on a movie lot. Never having asserted himself as an adult in that world, he lost the ability and the desire to do so. Several of Elvis' more unusual personality quirks stemmed from this.

After 1960 his life proceeded without much variation. Except for his experience in the desert and the recording of *How Great Thou Art,* there were no events of significance by which he could mark time. The movies and the sound tracks melted together into one big ugly gob; during these years Elvis never even took a trip to someplace special where he wasn't required for work. I don't think he knew what a vacation was. Those occurrences by which Elvis marked his own life—his first success, his mother's death, the Army—were years gone. I think that his inability to enjoy and measure his accomplishments the way most normal people did inspired his later hobby of collecting police badges. Elvis couldn't talk about when he traveled to this country or that city, went to see a show or shopped in an interesting store or spent time with a fascinating stranger, because he never did those things. Each badge, however, represented a particular time and a place, and Elvis had a story to tell about every single one of them—who gave it to him, how he went about getting it, who said what to whom, and so on. It was typical of Elvis that he so treasured the things most of us take for granted, such as his high-school diploma.

Take, for example, his attitude toward money and giving gifts. He loved to give, because he knew it made others happy. Among the numerous beautiful presents I received from him were a black sapphire ring (sapphire is the stone associated with 8, the number Elvis and I shared), a Cadillac, a motorcycle, a mobile home, a five-gaited quarterhorse, a pickup truck and countless articles of his clothing. Since I am a couple of inches taller than Elvis, his clothes were always a little small on me, so I gave them to friends and to fans. Elvis would say, "You've got to have this!" as he handed over one of his studded belts or a piece of jewelry. Once when we were sitting in the room adjacent to his bedroom at Graceland he opened

a box and handed me a watch without a wristband on it.
"Here, you take this," he said. "I want you to have it."

I turned it, and on the back was inscribed, "To Elvis
from Nick." Nick Adams, who would die from a drug
overdose under mysterious circumstances in February
1968, was a young actor who had appeared with James
Dean and Natalie Wood in *Rebel Without a Cause* and in
the sixties starred in his own television series, *The Rebel.*
Shortly upon his arrival in Hollywood Elvis was befriended by Wood and Adams, both part of the era's brat
pack. Adams had accompanied Elvis back to Tupelo for
the historic "homecoming concert" in fall 1956. It was
hard to tell what, if anything, the watch meant to Elvis.
One day many years later a friend of mind admired the
watch, so I gave it to her.

Another watch he gave me—which also ended up with
a fan—was one of several Elvis designed and ordered
custom-made by a Memphis jeweler. The face was black
and designed so that every thirty seconds it showed a cross
and a Star of David together before fading to reveal the
watch's numerals and hands; ten seconds later, the cross
and star reappeared. He gave out these watches to people
on one of the movie sets and in doing so made a very
profound statement about who he was and what he believed.

Of course, there's no question that Elvis could afford to
give everything he gave away, but, knowing him as I did,
I can safely say that even if he had lived out his life as an
obscure truck driver he'd still have given things away. Not
cars, of course, but whatever he had. Elvis' generosity
often drove Vernon to distraction. As far as Vernon was
concerned, Elvis threw away money and didn't know the
value of a dollar. In a sense, that is literally true. Except
for the cost of cars and jewelry, two things he seemed to
be buying all the time, Elvis had no idea what things cost
and couldn't care less. Even though he was a millionaire
himself, whenever he heard of someone earning $50,000,
or learned that something cost several thousand, he was
amazed; those were tremendous sums. I eventually realized that Elvis' whole conception of a dollar's value and

the cost of living had been frozen back when he made his first million—in 1956. He hadn't really kept up, and how could he? After all, Elvis didn't go grocery shopping.

It wasn't that he was ambivalent about money; he understood that it had changed his life. Many poor children who become wealthy erase the pain of lack by treating money as if it doesn't matter once they get it. That's what happened to Elvis. He often said, "The only good thing about having money is that you don't have to worry about it."

Vernon would probably have said, "The only bad thing abut having money is that you do have to worry about it," and worry he did. Vernon lived in constant fear that something, God knows what, would befall them, and that one day he and Elvis would find themselves back in Tupelo or living in a seedy apartment building. No matter how much money Elvis made, it was never real to him or to his father. Many times when Vernon confronted Elvis about the amounts he spent—on cars, guns, anything—Elvis said, "Daddy, even if we lost it all today, we'd start all over again from square one. I'd get it all back tomorrow. It doesn't matter, Daddy. We have each other; that's what's really important. Nothing could stop us."

While Elvis took comfort in such thinking, it struck terror in Vernon's heart. He knew that his son was incapable of preparing himself a bowl of canned soup, paying an electric bill or reading a checking-account statement. Elvis's attitude toward money was one of freedom; Vernon, however, saw it as just plain recklessness.

Elvis was ripe for change. Sometime in late 1966 when he was out riding his motorcycle in Mississippi, he spotted a fifty-foot-tall concrete cross. When he inquired about it, he learned that the ranch on which the cross stood was for sale. A few months earlier Priscilla, who loved horses and riding, had encouraged Elvis to keep horses at Graceland. Priscilla enjoyed outdoor activities, and it's to her credit that she persuaded Elvis to take up riding. She also convinced him to get outside during daylight hours, which was quite an accomplishment. Before too long he had purchased several horses. Finding the ranch, which was located near Walls, Mississippi, less than ten miles from Graceland, could have been one of the best things to happen to him.

Elvis wanted everyone to move to the ranch, which he named the Circle G after Graceland. All the guys, their wives and their kids came, each family with its own mobile home and pickup or jeep and, of course, horses. The cost was enormous (the mobile home Elvis gave me cost in excess of $20,000, for example), but Elvis didn't care. He was very happy on the 163-acre ranch. It symbolized a chance to make a new start, to live close to nature and to get away from the old routine.

Any time Elvis made a gesture toward change, whether small or large and regardless of what it concerned, something inside him instinctively resisted. This behavior took its toll, eventually squelching even Elvis' inclination and enthusiasms, until he didn't dare consider change. For a moment, though, this seemed different.

"This ranch is my dream," Elvis said. "I've been looking for something like this for a long time. This ranch represents how I really want to live my life. Lord God, I can't stand staying out in Hollyweird too long. But this place is back to the basics, and that's what I need, like my life's blood, for some balance, 'cause without it you can really lose yourself 'out there.' I'm talking about hanging on to your very soul.

"I'll always keep Graceland, only the ranch keeps us in touch with Mother Nature, this is for my damn health and peace of mind. And you know as well as I do, I don't care how much money you got, you can't buy something like that. And this is God's country. You can see it, feel it, man, you can just breathe it in here. And this is for us, to be together and to teach us all how to live with the old fundamentals. This is going to be like a commune."

The ranch presented countless opportunities for giving gifts. There seemed to be no end to how many things—trailers, cars, pickups, ranch equipment, livestock, tools—he could buy. Vernon was understandably alarmed, but this was Elvis: everything to the max.

One day after we had received a number of brand-new pickups, Alan Fortas said, "Elvis, everyone here already has a pickup, and there's one extra. What should I do with it?"

Without hesitating, Elvis replied, pointing to the crowd of fans who had gathered across the road, "Alan, damn, man, just give one away to one of them. Don't bother me with details like that!"

The Circle G Ranch might have become Elvis' sanctuary, his true home away from home, so to speak, but that never happened. For one thing, within days of his arrival, word got out. Within weeks the place became a tourist attraction, and carloads of people blocked the two-lane country roads. It's hard to say whether buying the ranch was the result of a crisis or whether a crisis came of his owning the ranch. Whatever it was, Elvis' behavior started to change. He ate more than ever and before long had put on a good amount of weight.

Elvis had something on his mind, and in early 1967 he and I fell into a discussion about marriage. Not mine or the possibility of his, just the idea of marriage and what it meant. More than once Elvis remarked, "Look at Jesus. He never married." Again, I don't think that this necessarily pointed to a "Christ complex," although certainly Elvis suffered from that to a degree. Regardless of what Elvis did or the books he read, at his core he was always a profoundly religious and moral man. His allusions to Jesus' never having wed were more an expression of his own ambivalence, of rationalizing a way out of a commitment he was having second thoughts about.

Interestingly, the second thoughts were not about marrying Priscilla; he loved her very much. She was a lot of fun, and she adored him. But at age thirty-two Elvis sensed that a real marriage involved commitments he wasn't sure he could meet. His concerns were well founded. His and Priscilla's "courtship" was a perpetual junior-high-school date. After so many years of their living together, Elvis and Priscilla's relationship should have matured, but instead it hit a pitch very early on and never progressed. Elvis was still trying to impress her, trying to convince her that the teachings were important. But, as strange as their affair may have seemed to me or anyone else, his relationship with Priscilla could not possibly have been any more or less normal than the rest of his life. This wasn't what most people would regard as the typical situation with a man and his wife-to-be, but then Elvis and Priscilla were not typical in any way.

We were upstairs at Graceland in mid-December 1966 when Elvis said, "I haven't spoken to anyone else. The Colonel doesn't know and neither does Priscilla. Don't say a word to anyone. I told Daddy only last night, and he's the only one."

Elvis paused. "I'm thinking of marrying Priscilla. How do you feel about it?"

"Elvis, I think it's a good thing. You're thirty-two; it's about time. And you're always saying how much you want children."

"What do you think the fans will think?" he asked, his voice betraying a hint of doubt. Elvis' fans were everything to him.

"They'll love you even more and be very happy for you. Besides, everyone knows about Priscilla by now. In a certain way, it will only make you even more real to them."

"I'll tell you what I'm gonna do," he said softly. "I'm not sure just when, but we're going to get married soon. And I'm going to have two best men, you and Marty Lacker—but I'm telling Marty at the last minute."

"I'd be honored, Elvis," I said, smiling.

Elvis grinned. He loved making plans and sharing secrets.

It was a strange time, because, on the one hand, Elvis was looking ahead, making new plans, trying to change his life, while, on the other, everything seemed strangely the same despite his efforts.

Around then Elvis stopped traveling by bus between Los Angeles and Memphis. He suffered from a profound fear of flying, but as time passed his procrastinating about leaving Graceland grew more elaborate. Finally he had messed around for so long that we had no choice but to fly to L.A.; not even driving all night would get us there on time. There wasn't even time to arrange for a private plane, so I found myself with Elvis at the Memphis airport, preparing to board a commercial flight.

One thing about being with Elvis was that the intensity of people's reactions to him never diminished. Seeing Elvis Presley suddenly appear in the flesh was more than a lot of them could handle. Over the years I've seen people scream, cry, stare slack-jawed, and faint. To me, he was just Elvis. I guess he was "just" Elvis to them too, and that's why they reacted as they did.

All of the other passengers were seated on the plane, preparing for takeoff, when Elvis walked on board. We weren't booked for first class, and our seats were near the rear. As Elvis made his way down the aisle people's heads turned. They looked at Elvis, they looked at each other, they looked back at Elvis, all the while their faces saying, "Do you see what I see?"

Unfortunately for Elvis, it turned out not to be the kind of flight to cure anyone's fear. We hit stretches of turbulence, the plane bucking like a bronco. Elvis tried to control his reaction, but several times he turned white and had to dash back to the restroom and vomit. Still, he'd return to his seat, determined to sit it out.

He probably never would have flown again, but not long after that we were late for a recording session in Nashville and had the chance to rent a private six-seater. Again there was no choice, so Elvis clenched his jaw, and away we went. Everything went beautifully this time, and suddenly Elvis didn't much mind flying. On the trip back, we started talking to the pilot, and the subject of Elvis' phobia came up. "I was a pilot in World War II," the man said. "Let me show you the maneuverability of this plane."

Elvis was game, and before I knew it we were flying straight up, then straight down, then upside down, with an occasional hair-raising nose dive thrown in. Wherever the plane was, my stomach lagged several feet behind. I glanced across at Elvis, who was simultaneously scared out of his wits and having the time of his life. The roller coaster at the Fairgrounds was nothing compared to this,

and after a couple of daredevil maneuvers Elvis' fear of
flying vanished. Priscilla and Vernon met us at the airport,
and Elvis was so excited about flying that he asked the
pilot to take them up for a demonstration.

The next film was his twenty-fifth, *Clambake,* easily
one of the worst. Now that he had the ranch, Elvis was
particularly reluctant to go back to Hollywood. He had
spent an incredible sum of money on the ranch—probably
close to a million dollars—and during that time had put
on an excess thirty pounds. No wonder he was miserable.
Every call to preproduction was a fresh slap in the face.
Now, with marriage on his mind, Priscilla and the ranch
beckoning him home, and a generally more serious out-
look, he was bothered by the movies in a different way.
Making them was more than a drag, more than an insult
to his talent; it was a humiliation. Perhaps if Elvis had
had a means of earning comparable amounts doing something else, he might have left Hollywood for good in 1966.
Ever since the desert incident, that was clearly on his mind.
But he just couldn't do it.

Back in Los Angeles, Elvis was visiting Daya Mata and
Brother Adolph occasionally and over time met a number
of other people deeply involved with various aspects of
metaphysics. He took Priscilla with him for a spiritual
session with the woman who ordained me, the Reverend
Jean Allen.

Among the other people he met was a woman named
Paula André, who was the last disciple of Cheiro, one of
the greatest seers of the twentieth century. Cheiro (born
Count Louis Harmon) was an astrologer, numerologist and
palmist. Among those who sought Cheiro's advice were
Mark Twain, Sarah Bernhardt, Rasputin, Mata Hari, King
Edward VII of Great Britain, King Leopold I of the Bel-
gians, King Umberto I of Italy, the Czar and Czarina of
Russia, Pope Leo the XII and Oscar Wilde. At the time
of his death in 1936, at the age of seventy, he was acknowledged as the best-selling author of books on numerology, astrology and palmistry. Elvis loved Cheiro's books,
and in the seventies he spoke of producing a film biography of Cheiro in which he would portray the seer.

I met Paula when I wandered into her bookstore, Greengables, which was across the street from the Paramount lot. We started talking, and it was she who first introduced me to Dane Rudhyar. I brought her to meet Elvis, once at his house on Perugia Way, where she gave him a highly accurate palm reading, and again at the movie studio.

After the first reading Elvis told me, "She said the first line and my strongest line is my fate line. Paula said that is the heaviest fate line she ever saw. That no matter what I would have done when I started singing, I couldn't help but be a success."

I also introduced him to a woman who had perfected a massage technique similar to Rolfing. When she did body work on Elvis she warned him that his diet was unhealthy and that she could feel certain things which indicated he would develop intestinal and digestive problems if he didn't change his ways. Elvis found all of this fascinating, but not enough to make him change his diet.

Knowing how people around Elvis, including Parker and Priscilla, felt about the studies, I was never convinced of being on solid ground with anyone but him. Out of the whole bunch, the only person who defended me and wanted me there was Elvis. I trusted him implicitly; I knew that his loyalty to me was challenged repeatedly and that he always stood firm. Still none of that blinded me to the fact that Parker would never surrender in his fight to banish me. In my heart I knew that when it came right down to it, it was Parker, not his boy, who ruled the roost.

It was the first day of either shooting or preproduction for *Clambake*. It was my custom to meet everyone at the studio around seven or else go to Elvis' first and then we'd go to the studio together. Because it was our first day working at a new studio, I drove to Elvis' house. I sat down in the living room with a couple of the guys waiting for Elvis to come out. Ten, fifteen, twenty minutes passed, and still no Elvis, which was unusual, since generally by the time anyone arrived he was at least up and having breakfast.

Finally Elvis emerged from his room, walking slowly, as if dazed. He wobbled a bit as he made his way across the room, then collapsed into a nearby chair with a sigh. Shaking his head in disbelief he said, "Oh, man, I got hit. I really got hit last night, man. I hit my head. You won't believe it. Come over here and feel this."

One by one we each gingerly touched the golf-ball-sized lump on the back of his head.

"What happened?"

"I don't know," he replied uncertainly. "That's the strange thing about it. The only thing I remember is that I walked into the bathroom and felt like I was being hit or pushed or something. So I grabbed onto the TV, and the next thing I knew I was falling and holding on to this tripod for support, because I'd hit my head."

Now, in Elvis's bathroom there was a small television on a tripod, which stood in a sunken tub. For years I, like most people, assumed that Elvis must have walked into the bathroom and, perhaps half asleep, tripped over the television cord and fallen against the tub head first. But that's not really what Elvis said. His first words were "I got hit." And if he had fallen forward, which he would have done if he had tripped over a cord, the bump would have been on the front of his head, not the back. At the time, all of us who worked with Elvis prided ourselves on our smarts, yet today I can't understand how we missed this simple, glaring discrepancy. Elvis was obviously quite confused, so it's possible that his account lacked something. Still, I keep coming back to the difference between his description of the accident and the resulting injury. The story just doesn't hold.

Elvis complained of not feeling well and of having blurred vision, so someone called the Colonel. Shortly thereafter Parker arrived. He wasn't in the house more than two minutes when he walked directly up to me, brandishing his cane in the air, and said, "You get rid of those books right now! And he's not to read any more books whatsoever."

"All right," I replied, stunned.

Apparently satisfied, Parker went into Elvis' bedroom

with him and closed the door, and we didn't see Elvis again for a long time. Soon medical people came in, wheeling various apparatuses, and some studio executives arrived, looking quite concerned. This would cost the studio money, so it was a crisis. For all the alleged concern over Elvis' purportedly serious physical condition, he did not enter a hospital for observation. About an hour later the Colonel emerged from the bedroom and said, "No one's to talk to him. No one. You leave him alone. He's very sick. We have a problem here. And there's a movie supposed to be made here," and so on. Parker took this very seriously, and later I would see why.

For the next week or so no one was allowed to see Elvis except Priscilla, the doctors and the Colonel. In fact, I believe Parker spent more time with Elvis during these days than he had spent with him in the entire preceding decade. What went on during that week we'll never know. Elvis certainly didn't know or couldn't remember. When he was finally permitted visitors, I came into his room and sat on the bed. The minute I saw him, I knew this wasn't Elvis. I mean, obviously it was Elvis, but he looked very strange, as if he were under the influence of something, and there's no doubt in my mind that he was drugged. For the first time in our relationship, he wasn't looking me in the eye. When I spoke to him he looked at me as if he'd never seen me. His eyes were glazed, haunted-looking. And I don't think it's any coincidence that Elvis' descent into experimenting with the next level of psychoactive medication, very heavy downers and synthetic narcotics, followed his "recovery."

I have no idea what happened during this time, and again neither did Elvis. Two weeks after the incident a meeting was called. Parker sat beside Elvis, who was still propped up in bed, still out to lunch. While Elvis might agree with Parker when he didn't want to, I always knew how he really felt. You could see the resentment and anger in his face, because Elvis was a tiger. He didn't kowtow to anyone without making his true feelings known. But the Elvis I saw this day resembled a zombie. He sat there quietly, gazing down at the bedcovers, never meeting my eyes.

"Things are going to change around here," Parker began. "We're going to have to cut back a little. Elvis is spending too much money. Too much money has been going out. Everybody's going to have to take a pay cut. Everybody brings their problems to Elvis. And some of you"—Parker turned his cold gaze on me—"think maybe he's Jesus Christ who should wear robes and walk down the street helping people. But that's not who he is."

The tension in the room was palpable. The other guys kept shifting their glances from me to Parker to Elvis to me to Parker again. And Parker hadn't said the last of his piece; there were other things. We were instructed to no longer discuss our personal problems with Elvis but to take them to Joe Esposito, who, though already the group foreman, was now officially anointed by Parker.

"I don't want him reading any more books! They clutter up his mind!" the Colonel said forcefully. Although he never addressed me personally, I—and everyone else—knew whom he was talking about. Throughout Parker's tirade Elvis never looked at me once. But, although I didn't know it until nearly two decades later, Elvis didn't give up on me just like that. In Priscilla's autobiography she writes, "Later the Colonel told Elvis that he should get Larry out of his life, that Larry used some sort of technique to manipulate his thinking. Elvis argued that this wasn't the case. He was truly interested in his readings." Somehow, though, the Colonel won out, as Elvis must have known that he would.

Later that evening Elvis called for me and Stevie to come to his room. He was leaning against some pillows; Stevie and I sat on the edge of the bed.

"I just want you to know that I love you guys. No matter what happens," Elvis said, again saying more with his eyes than his words ever could. "I love you. Don't ever forget that."

The following weekend we began working on the movie. In our usual routine I arrived before or with Elvis, and we always started the day with a friendly conversation, or we'd discuss some new book while I did his hair. Once Elvis returned to the set after his convalescence, though, everything changed. Usually pleasant and easygoing, he was now surly and uptight, as if angry at everything and nothing. He ranted and raved about insignificant matters. The Colonel's edict had come down: I was forbidden to be alone with Elvis for even a second. Whatever time I spent with Elvis had to be chaperoned by one of the guys, lest we talk about anything really important to Elvis.

One day shortly after work resumed Elvis stormed into the trailer, and as he sat having his hair styled he railed about what was wrong with the spiritual teachings.

"Those damn masters, they're trying to control people's minds, that's what they're trying to do," he said darkly. "They're trying to hypnotize people. They want to control you for their own purposes. They have motives."

Elvis sounded paranoid. I said nothing; there was no point to arguing. When I heard him utter the words "control" and "motives," the pieces fell into place. Who had the motive? Who had the control?

At one point during a tirade, he stopped, then softly said, "Forgive me. Don't take it personally. It's me."

Later that day, during a break in shooting, I stood on the sound stage and witnessed a spectacle I hadn't seen in a couple of years: Elvis and the Memphis Mafia chasing one another around the sets, chucking water balloons and screaming like unruly children. One of the sound men glanced at them and, shaking his head, said, "Oh shit. We've heard about this, and here they are." You didn't need any special powers to read the crew's thoughts; they were written all over their faces: Despite the compliant attitude and the Southern manners, Elvis really was a dumb jerk after all. It broke my heart.

I stayed on for a couple of months more, but Elvis and I never spent another moment in private. For the Colonel, Priscilla and most of the guys, my defeat was a sweet victory. Suddenly it was open season on the Swami, and the guys made no effort to be discreet or cute about the name-calling. Elvis just stood by silently, watching. I felt not only that I had lost a friend, but that my friend had

The Colonel, Elvis and Larry on the set of Spinout, 1966.

Larry's father with various of his harmonica groups.

Elvis with his Texas army buddy, Eddie Fadal, en route from a concert at the Cotton Bowl in Dallas to one in Waco, Texas.

5

Gladys and Vernon visiting Elvis on the set of Love Me Tender. *This was the only time they visited him on a movie set.*

6

7

Elvis with his helicopter pilot and the Colonel at Graceland in 1958.

Vernon, a Paramount executive, Norman Taurog who directed many of Elvis' movies, and Elvis signing a new contract.

8

Gladys, Elvis and Nick Adams' mother in the backyard of Graceland.

A rare picture of Grandma Dodger in her room at Graceland.

CONTENTS

11

CONTENTS

SNOWMEN'S LEAGUE Of America

Chief Potentate COLONEL TOM PARKER

• • • •

Confidential Report Dealing with Advanced Techniques of Member Snowers

The Colonel's infamous Snowmen's League of America book given by the Colonel to Larry.

12

Drawings from Through the
Eyes of the Masters:
Meditations and Portraits,
*by David Anrias, showing
where Elvis got the ideas for
some of his costumes.*

13

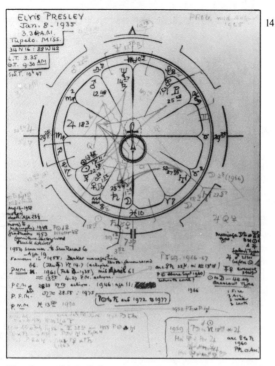

Natal astrological charts for Elvis and Priscilla Beaulieu.

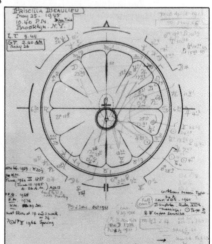

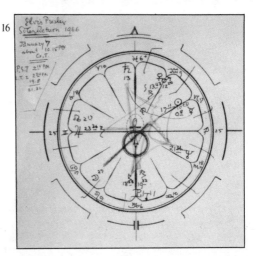

special chart
r Elvis called
olar Return 1966."

Solar chart of
Gladys Love Presley.

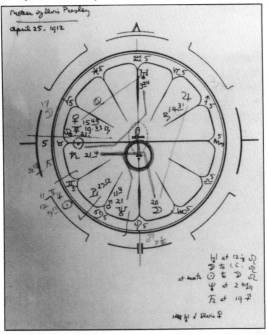

New Age Voice, *the magazine Larry published, which gave its name to Elvis' backup group.*

18

20

EDITOR   Larry Geller
TYPE   L. Van Ranst
TITLES   Celest Werner
LAYOUT   Larry Geller
ART   Pineal Playhouse
SYMBOLS   Karen Uris
PRINTER   Trade Printers of
                California

The New Age Voice is Published by
the New Age Foundation,
P. O. Box 69970,
Los Angeles, California 90069
©1972

Though I speak with the tongues of men of angels, and have not love, I am become sounding brass, or a tinkling cymbal.

And though I have the gift of prophecy, understand all mysteries, and all knowledge, though I have all faith, so that I could remove mountains, and have not love, I am nothing.

And though I bestow all my goods to feed the poor, and though I give my body to be burned, and have not love, it profiteth me nothing.

Love suffereth long, and is kind; love envieth not; love vaunteth not itself, is not puffed up.

Doth not behave itself unseemly, seeketh not her own, is not easily provoked, thinketh no evil;

Rejoiceth not in iniquity, but rejoiceth in the truth;

Beareth all things, believeth all things, hopeth all things, endureth all things.

Love never faileth; but whether there be prophecies, they shall fail; whether there be tongues, they shall cease; whether there be knowledge, it shall vanish away.

For we know in part, and we prophesy in part.

But when that which is perfect is come, that which is in part shall be done away.

When I was a child, I spake as a child, I understood as a child, I thought as a child; but when I became a man, I put away childish things.

For now we see through a glass, darkly; but then face to face: now I know in part; but then I shall know even as also I am known.

And now abideth faith, hope, love, these three; but the greatest of these is love.

I CORINTHIANS 13

19   *The picture of Jesus opposite the masthead is the one Larry was sent in the mail and opened in the presence of the narcotics detectives.*

Elvis on tour in 1976, Larry in background. 21

Steve Smith, Elvis, David Stanley and Larry boarding the Lisa Marie.

22

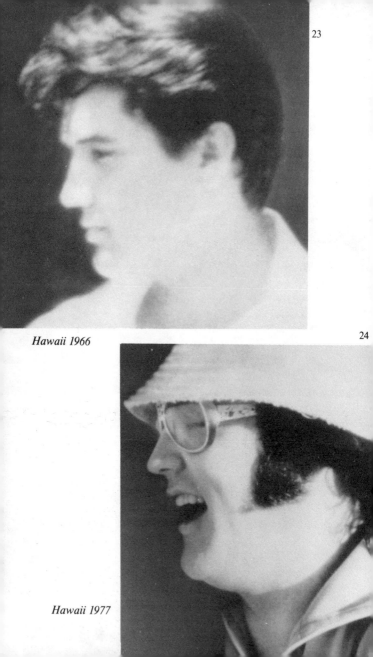

23

Hawaii 1966

24

Hawaii 1977

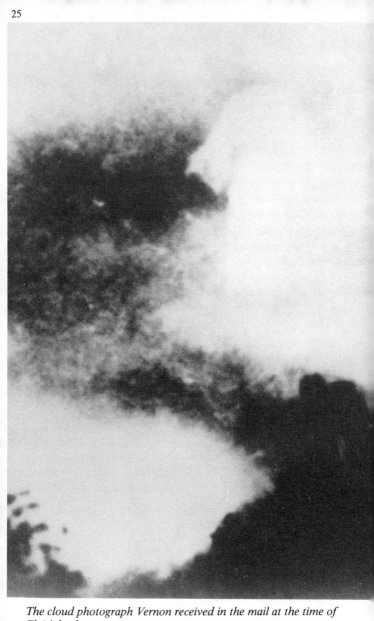

The cloud photograph Vernon received in the mail at the time of Elvis' death.

*Elvis with Ginger
and Elvis with Larry.*

26

*In the backyard of the rented
Hawaiian beach house, March 1977.*

27

28

Larry in England doing a benefit on what would have been Elvis' fiftieth birthday, 1985.

lost himself. Despite all that, I don't think that Elvis had
it in him to fire me. The Colonel probably suspected—and
correctly—that there was no reason for me to hang around
just to do Elvis' hair. It was my profession, one I could
practice anywhere in the world with just about anyone I
wanted. There was no financial reason for me to endure
the insults and the coldness. Probably deep inside I was
hoping that Elvis would snap out of it, whatever "it" was,
but after several weeks that hope diminished. Sooner or
later I'd have Parker on my case, and the thought of being
fired by him was intolerable. When I reached a dead end,
I quit.

One day in late April 1967 I called Elvis' house to tell
him that I wasn't coming back. Jerry got on the line and
said, "Larry, you'd better come to the house right now.
We're all going to Vegas."

I didn't respond. So they were all going to Vegas. What
else was new?

"We're all going to Vegas," he repeated, as if I would
pick up on his meaning.

"No, Jerry," I answered. "I can't go."

"Well, you've got to be here, man," he said. "Otherwise we're going. We're leaving town."

"Jerry, I just can't go," I insisted. "I'll let you all go."

Jerry didn't tell me what was happening, because he
didn't know. But from his tone of voice I knew that something unusual was going on. I was so wrapped up in how
I was going to tell Elvis, and what this meant, that I didn't
care what went on there. I had made plans to drive to
Yosemite National Park, about eight hours from Los Angeles, to be alone with my thoughts. I was leaving the
next day or so. I told Jerry goodbye and hung up.

The next day when I went to the market to pick up some
groceries and the paper, I saw the front-page headline,
ELVIS PRESLEY IS MARRIED, running above a large photograph of Elvis and Priscilla smiling happily in their wedding attire. I couldn't believe my eyes, not because they'd
gotten married but because it had happened so suddenly.
The timing of it was bizarre, to say the least. Now I really

CHAPTER

7

On the drive to Yosemite I composed in my mind the letter to Elvis. It was more than just a goodbye; it was, as far as I knew, the last communication between us. It would have been much easier if Elvis had been a faddist, someone whose interest wasn't sincere, whose need for a spiritual life wasn't profound. Then I could say, Well, this is really what Elvis is about. He's really content reading football magazines and behaving like a fourteen-year-old. Maybe our meeting was a total fluke; maybe Elvis' self-knowledge wasn't meant to be. Maybe he really wasn't that bright, that deep, that emotional.

But none of it was true. Brother Adolph once said to me, "I've met a lot of people in my life, but Elvis is closer to God realization than most people. He has that power and energy about him." Clearly, Elvis' spiritual drive was part of him. Elvis needed the teachings desperately. He was more than what most people—even those who loved him—thought. He had depths they could not see, much less appreciate. I'd have accepted my banishment if I could have believed that something or someone else would enter Elvis' life. Perhaps he would continue visiting Daya Mata, or begin attending church somewhere, or keep reading his books. It didn't have to be with me, although after only a few days away from him I missed him very much. The tragedy lay in the realization that as long as they could stop it, no one and nothing would ever penetrate the human fortress to "disturb" Elvis again. It came as no surprise when, just a couple of months before he died, Elvis confessed to me that he had succumbed to Priscilla's pressure and burned some of his books.

I didn't have the presence of mind to copy the letter I sent, nor was Elvis the type to keep things like that, so there's no way to recreate my exact words. The feelings, though, I could never forget. Loosely paraphrasing from memory, this is what I said:

Elvis, I'm communicating to you this way because this is one of the most difficult decisions I ever had to make in my life. . . . Our time together was precious and special for both of us, and for years to come we'll both derive a lot from it. But I feel that it is time to part from you. I don't want to, but I have to. There are too many heavy things going on. It hurts me, but I know you understand. It's better if I leave. . . .

And so on. I folded up the two pages, sealed them in an envelope and drove back home. I gave the letter to Jerry Schilling, who promised me Elvis would get it. I recall thinking at the time that Elvis might never see it, not because I distrusted Jerry, but because the barriers between Elvis and the outside world were now higher and wider than ever. Staff at Graceland, under orders from Parker and/or Vernon, were already screening his mail and discarding any correspondence they deemed inappropriate, such as newsletters from the Self-Realization Fellowship and similar materials.

For the next five years I knew no more about Elvis than any other fan. These years were, professionally and privately, arguably Elvis' best. There were still the movies, sound tracks and halfhearted record releases, but between 1969 and 1973 Elvis reclaimed much of the light and power of the fifties. From everything I read and heard, marriage was a good thing for him, and in February 1968 his only child, Lisa Marie, was born in Memphis. Elvis had spoken so often of having a child and a family. I knew he must be happy.

I decided to devote my life to helping others. My bookstore, HELP (Health through Education promotes Love and Peace) was a typically sixties attempt to enlighten people and promote positive values. In the meantime I launched several other projects with similar goals. With the help of singer Johnny Rivers, I attempted to establish an alternative school at Big Sur. Our proposal was accepted by the federal government, and things seemed about to fall into place, but for one reason or another it didn't work out. Another venture was an alternative, spiritually oriented magazine, *The New Age Voice,* which I founded, edited and published one issue of. Through all of this, I continued to pursue my spiritual studies.

There was no contact with Elvis during these years. Neither of us ever picked up the phone or sent a card or a letter. I missed him very much, as you would miss any good friend, but after a couple of years passed there seemed little chance that we would ever speak again. Deep down, I felt differently, but it was a feeling that couldn't be supported by anything but my faith. Several times I glanced into my rearview mirror and saw one of his cars following me for several blocks, but that was Elvis' way. I didn't really think about it that much. If he ever needed to see me or talk to me, he knew where I was.

And, of course, I always knew where he was. Every time I turned on the radio, he was there, singing some song. The local movie theaters seemed to be perpetually screening the latest Elvis movie. In December 1968, though, something changed. Elvis as the King of Rock and Roll was resurrected through an hour-long television special. Its real title is "Elvis," but within minutes of its airing it became know as the "comeback special." I distinctly remember sitting in front of my television that Tuesday night, curious to see if Elvis would be as great as I knew he could be, and he didn't let me or anyone else down.

From the moment his face filled the screen, Elvis took total control. He was stunning—slim, dynamic, as handsome as ever. And although I detected some nervousness in his gestures and expressions, it was beautiful to see, part of his genius and his charm. But the best thing about the special was that for the first time in years Elvis was doing all that he ever really wanted to do: sing before his fans. "Magical," "charismatic," "virile," "humorous" were just a few adjectives reviewers used. People look back on that special and say, "Of course," as if it couldn't possibly have turned out any other way. In truth, though, no one really knew how Elvis would handle it, or how his audience would receive him. Critics and hipper, latter-day rock fans expected a banal Christmas special, full of mediocre songs. As it turned out, that was precisely what Parker wanted from Elvis, and it was largely through the efforts of a tenacious producer, Steve Binder, that "Elvis" developed into the perfect vehicle. Odds were, it would be awful, an Elvis movie tailored to the small screen. Even the truly faithful had to wonder.

Years later, when Elvis told me how nervous he was before they began taping in June 1968, I understood that he wondered, too. It had been almost eight years since he stood before a live audience anywhere, yet, standing there in studded black leather, it was as though he had never gone away. It wouldn't be fair to Elvis to compare watching him on television that December evening with seeing him on Ed Sullivan's show back in the fifties, but something about the experience felt the same. There was the flash of revelation, of truth, a purity of expression and perfection of form that was the essence of Elvis. His presence was so commanding that even those who knew him personally and intimately, who could separate the show-business image from the man, were not immune to it. A song especially written for the special, "If I Can Dream," went to number twelve on the charts, the best showing of any Elvis record since 1965.

"I'm planning a lot of changes," Elvis told a reporter around this time. "You can't go on doing the same thing year after year."

Shortly after he had completed taping the "live" segment of the show the previous summer, Elvis made up his mind that he wanted—needed—to be onstage again. How and why he ended up returning to the stage in Las Vegas,

or "Sin City," as Elvis always called it, has never been
clear. Elvis always hated Vegas, and he longed to travel,
not just across America but around the world. The response from the television special indicated that he was
welcome anywhere. But Parker devised another scheme
and arranged for Elvis to make his Las Vegas debut at the
International Hotel—the largest in the city—on July 26,
1969.

Elvis' Vegas shows inspired the same high praise and
enthusiasm as the special. He stood at another pivotal
point, from which he could have stepped in a dozen different directions. For what proved to be the last time in
his life, he possessed the power to do anything with his
career that he wanted. Somehow, though, Elvis wound up
snared in another trap. His whole career fell into three
phases. The first, of course, was the fifties. The sixties
were the movie years, followed by the seventies. Looking
back, you see that the seventies were essentially a reprise
of the sixties. The difference was that Elvis was perform-
ing before live audiences, and not making goofy films.
And while the "product" was unquestionably superior,
the routine that evolved in each phase wore on Elvis. Per-
forming live began to assume a sameness, and no sooner
had he proved himself onstage again than even that, as
exciting as it was, crystallized into another predictable
pattern. For Elvis, who was nothing if not a creature of
habit, someone willingly seduced by familiarity, this was
possibly the worst thing that could have happened. He
needed to be revitalized, stimulated and challenged, but
not just once in a decade, or even once a year—all the
time. He had too much energy, too much intelligence.
Even achieving things no one else in the world could
achieve lost its appeal. It had nothing to do with the fans—
he loved them. He lived for them. That was just the way
Elvis was.

Elvis' reemergence during this time took place not only
on the stage and the record charts, but in the American
consciousness. In 1970 a documentary on his Vegas show,
Elvis—That's the Way It Is, was released, followed exactly
two years later by another documentary, *Elvis on Tour.*

Elvis' name began appearing regularly in the press. In 1971 he was named one of American's Ten Outstanding Young Men by the U.S. Jaycees. The highway that ran in front of Graceland was rechristened Elvis Presley Boulevard. In late 1969 "Suspicious Minds" became his first number-one hit since April 1962.

Elvis spoke to the press more frequently, though always in tightly controlled press conferences. Personal one-on-one interviews were extremely rare, but even in his brief, guarded answers I saw evidence that he hadn't entirely forgotten the teachings. In his speech to the Jaycees he answered a question about religious commitment by saying, "God is a living presence in all of us," and then said of the other nine honorees, "They are building the kingdom of heaven." During his famous press conference before a series of sold-out shows at New York's Madison Square Garden, he expressed in only a couple sentences the feelings that tormented him for so many years. When asked if he was satisfied with his image, Elvis replied, "Well, the image is one thing, and the human being is another. It's very hard to live up to an image. I'll put it that way." From just those words I knew that despite whatever happiness he had, some things in his life remained unresolved and unanswered.

In 1970 or 1971 I went to Las Vegas to check out Elvis' show. I didn't tell him or anyone else I was coming. As I sat back in the crowd watching him it seemed it would be only a matter of time before we were reunited. As I headed back to Los Angeles, I just let the idea go. Whatever was going to happen would happen.

Rumors had been circulating for quite some time that things between Elvis and Priscilla were strained. Finally in February 1972 Priscilla left Elvis for Mike Stone, a karate instructor whom Elvis had introduced her to several years earlier. Her leaving him was, after Gladys' death, probably the toughest single blow in his life. It's true that Elvis was rarely home in those days and that he didn't like wives, including his own, to come on the road. He and Priscilla led essentially separate lives. It was an unorthodox marriage, to say the least, but in Elvis' romantic way he believed it would never end. The worst part for him, though, was the humiliation. If Priscilla had simply left because she couldn't live with him, or taken off with another man discreetly, it might have been different. But Priscilla committed adultery and, once she was out of Elvis' house, flaunted if for all the world to see. Not that Elvis had been entirely faithful, either, but at least pictures of Elvis and his lovers weren't splashed across tabloid covers. If Priscilla wanted to go she could go, but he couldn't understand or accept that it had to happen this way.

In June 1972 Stevie and I broke up; we divorced two years later. That August Johnny Rivers called me and said, "Larry, let's go to Vegas and see Elvis. He really needs you. Now's the time. I'll have my secretary call and make arrangements for us."

Johnny phoned Joe Esposito and told him we'd be coming. Our seats were in Elvis' private booth, so of course he knew we'd be there. I had only to see Elvis onstage for five minutes for it to be clear to me how deeply in trouble he was. Everyone else in the audience was so overwhelmed by him that they couldn't possibly have guessed the truth. But I could see by the way he walked, the look on his face, his whole demeanor, that he had taken a lot of drugs. When he spoke he drawled far more that he had ever done in conversation, and his words ran together. To say I was shocked by Elvis' appearance would be an understatement.

"Johnny," I said, leaning across the table, "he won't live for another five years like this."

Still, Elvis gave a masterful performance. At one point during the show he asked to have the house lights turned up. He thanked the audience for being so kind, then he introduced Johnny Rivers. As Johnny stood up at our table, acknowledging the applause, Elvis stared at me. After the show, a maître d' came to the table and said, "Elvis would like to see you in his dressing room. Please follow me."

When Elvis saw me, he smiled widely, and we hugged each other. In a certain sense it was as though I had never left. Our meeting had none of the awkwardness people

sometimes experience after long separations. There was
no "How are you doing?" or irrelevant chit-chat. Elvis
and I hugged and patted each other on the back and shoulders.

My happiness at seeing Elvis again couldn't surmount
my horror at the drugs' effects on him. Yes, this was the
early seventies, but, outside of certain rock groups, blatant
drug use onstage wasn't done. That's not to say that there
weren't plenty of people in the business using drugs, heavy
drugs, but it was still in the closet. At that point the cultural mores were such that using drugs entailed a great
professional risk, especially for someone like Elvis, Mr.
America himself, who only a couple of years before had
received an honorary agent's badge from the Bureau of
Narcotics and Dangerous Drugs through the help of President Richard Nixon. Clearly, Elvis had lost his center,
and the drugs numbed his emotional pain.

In late 1972, I was back in Las Vegas, and Elvis and I
spent our first time together in years. When we got to his
bedroom, I felt I was back home again. The first thing I
noticed were the books, maybe twenty or thirty of them,
strewn all over the floor—*The Rosicrucian Cosmo-
Conception, Urantia,* the works of Madame Blavatsky, and
several others. Elvis felt particularly drawn to a biography
of Madame Blavatsky. Every time he held the book, he'd
say of Blavatsky, "She looks so much like my mom I can't
believe it. Look at the eyes, Larry, the shape of the face,
the cheekbones. I've never seen anything like it!"

Picking up the books one by one, I could see that these
were the books I had given him. They were dog-eared,
peeling, crumbling. As I held a ratty-looking copy of *The
Initiation of the World,* I said, "Elvis, I'll get you a new
copy. It's out in paperback now."

"No, no," he said. "I want *this* book; my markings
are in it. It doesn't matter how old it is or what, it's mine."

At one point I said, "By the way, I have a present for
you."

"What?"

"Let me go up to my room."

When I returned, I handed him a copy of *The New Age Voice,* my little journal. Though it was the first and last issue, I was very proud of it. Several leading writers in the field, including Manly P. Hall and Dane Rudhyar, had contributed pieces, and I had handled all the design and the layout. Elvis was very impressed, and read it with interest. He especially liked my editorial, which consisted solely of Corinthians I:13. Sitting down to write the "big statement" a new publication called for, I had found that no matter what idea I came up with, it had all been said before. My solution was to run this verse, which for obvious reasons was a favorite of Elvis':

> If I speak with the tongues of men and of angels, but have not love, I am become sounding brass, or a clanging cymbal.
>
> And if I have the gift of prophecy, and I know all mysteries and all knowledge; and if I have all faith, so as to remove mountains, but have not love, I am nothing.
>
> And if I bestow all my goods to feed the poor, and if I give my body to be burned, but have not love, it profiteth me nothing.
>
> Love suffereth long, and is kind; love envieth not; love vaunteth not itself, is not puffed up.
>
> Doth not behave itself unseemly, seeketh not its own, is not provoked, taketh not account of evil;
>
> Rejoiceth not in unrighteousness, but rejoiceth with the truth;
>
> Beareth all things, believeth all things, hopeth all things, endureth all things.
>
> Love never faileth; but whether there be prophecies, they shall be done away; whether there be tongues, they shall cease; whether there be knowledge, it shall be done away.
>
> For we know in part, and we prophesy in part;
>
> But when that which is perfect is come, that which is in part shall be done away.
>
> When I was a child, I spake as a child, I felt as a child,

*I thought as a child; now that I am become a man, I
have put away childish things.*

*For now we see in a mirror, darkly; but then face to
face; now I know in part; but then shall I know even
as also I have been known.*

*But now abideth faith, hope, love, these three; and the
greatest of these is love.*

Elvis invited me to a party in his suite. It was really
nice to see them all, including many of the guys. Through
everything, there was a camaraderie among us. Elvis introduced me to some of the newer people, the singers and
musicians who toured with him, and each person would
say, "Oh, so you're Larry Geller," or "I've heard so much
about you from Elvis." It was nice to know that he'd
thought about me while I was gone. Among the new people was a singer named Kathy Westmoreland, a very sweet
young woman with a beautiful voice. When Elvis introduced us, he fell to one knee and said to Kathy, in his
hyperbolic style, "Kathy, this is the heaviest motherfucker
I've ever met in my life. You'll never meet anyone heavier
than this. Just talk to him."

She said to me, "Elvis told me so much about you."

Kathy had joined Elvis in 1970 as a background singer.
Elvis often said of her, "She has the voice of an angel."
Whenever he felt that the audience was getting too wild,
he would interrupt the show and ask Kathy to do a solo
number, because he knew there was something about her
singing that calmed people down. Before I returned to
Elvis, he and Kathy had a brief romance that ended in a
deep friendship. Kathy and I got to talking, and I learned
that she was a deeply spiritual woman who had been reading many of the books Elvis and I were into for years. In
my absence Elvis had spent many hours discussing those
very things with her.

As the evening wore on, my idea of what had occurred
in Elvis' life over the past few years changed. It hadn't
become the spiritual desert I had feared. The one thought
that overrode all the others was that perhaps Parker really
hadn't gotten to him after all.

During this visit Elvis asked me to rejoin him on a full-time basis. "I'm going to Hawaii to do the special," he said, referring to his upcoming show that was to be broadcast live around the world via satellite. "Will you go?"

"I'd love to," I said, "but I'm committed to Johnny for a tour of Europe. I'll be gone for a couple of months, but let's talk again when I get back."

We were in his suite at the Hilton (as the International had been renamed), and Elvis was wearing a bathrobe. He motioned for me to follow him into our old "study," and there he nonchalantly sat in the bathroom sink. He was obviously pretty heavily medicated.

"Larry, Daddy gave me physical life, but you gave me spiritual life. You helped give me my internal life. What you went through—the guys hated you, and I know it. I know what happened."

For a minute I couldn't grasp what he meant by "what happened." So many things had happened. Then he said, "I know things now that you had to go through that I don't think you know that I know. You left for the right reasons. I didn't want to accept it, but I knew it had to be, and there were a lot of funny feelings at that time. I hit my head, went through that bullshit trip, got all those drugs in me. Then the Colonel had all those people come in. The Colonel just sat with me and talked to me and brain-washed me again."

Again? My mind was racing a mile a minute, but I couldn't stop Elvis for explanations. I'd find out one day.

"The Colonel was so suspicious of you. He told me things about you. But let me tell you something," Elvis said firmly, "everything is different now. *Everything is different now.* It will never happen again. None of that stuff that happened to you will ever happen again, and you know what I'm talking about. You'll never be violated.

"Larry, you don't know the shit I went through after you left, man. You don't know. Some heavy stuff. I came back here to Vegas. I was scared. I had to start all over again in my own mind. And you know what got me through it? My knowing that God is with me. Everything that you taught me, everything that I learned, is what got me through. I've had dark nights, and I heard your voice. I heard you talking to me. All the words that you used to tell me would be right there, and that's what kept me going.

"Things have really changed. Everyone has grown a lot, and they can accept things now that they couldn't accept before. They're ready for things."

He mentioned some things I'd done recently, and when I asked him how he knew he smiled and replied, "Hey, Lawrence, do you think I was going to let you out of my life? Just like you, I knew we'd be back together. And I always knew where you were. I knew about your bookstore. I kept tabs on you."

With Elvis' comeback complete, RCA's foreign affiliates and promoters everywhere were vying to lure him to their countries. Elvis longed to see the rest of the world, and knowing how well loved he was in such places as Great Britain, Japan, Europe and Australia, he naturally wanted to perform for those fans. Offers promising millions flooded in, and yet Colonel Parker turned them all down. The Colonel's "solution" to the worldwide demand for Elvis live was a compromise at best, a history-making media event, and Elvis' last peak before the long free fall.

"Elvis: Aloha from Hawaii," telecast live via satellite on January 14, 1973, to over one billion viewers in forty countries, gave millions their first glimpse of Elvis live and all their last look at Elvis in his prime. Lean, beautiful, dynamic in his white jeweled jumpsuit and gold-lined eagle cape, Elvis proved again that his comeback was no fluke; he was the King. To the opening bars of his theme song, he paced across the proscenium, opening his arms wide as if to embrace the whole world. When "Aloha" finally aired in the United States on April 4, audience reception was no less enthusiastic.

When I returned from touring Europe with Johnny Rivers a few months afterward, I drove to Las Vegas to see Elvis. As the Hilton marquee came into view, the words "the Voice" jumped out. Elvis had formed a male backup vocal trio and named them the New Age Voice, after my

little homemade magazine. Since the marquee couldn't ac-
commodate the full name, they became known as the
Voice. When Elvis introduced me to the singers, Donnie
Sumner, Tim Batey and Sherril Nielson, he said to them,
"This is who you're named after." Then he turned to me
and added, "I'm sorry that the marquee doesn't have their
full name, but just the Voice. Looks pretty damn good
under my name, though."

Being back with Elvis was great. That's not to say that
certain members of the entourage welcomed me any more
warmly than they had the first time out, but everyone had
matured and grown to a certain extent. And we were all
getting older. Elvis started wearing reading glasses, which
it took me some time to get used to seeing. Somehow it
just didn't fit. The guys had changed, too. Now everyone
hugged when greeting, something that had been considered too "faggoty" in the sixties.

Parker couldn't have been thrilled to have me back in
the fold, either, but he was courteous and kept his distance. Besides, he knew that even without me around,
Elvis had resumed his studies. Not all the books were
burned. With his family blown apart and his drug usage
up, Elvis needed the teachings. They did no harm, and,
with Elvis occasionally threatening to dump Parker, the
old man had bigger fires to fight.

Despite the negative influences in his life, Elvis had
somehow managed to bring into his world several very
good people, among them Linda Thompson, a former Miss
Tennessee. They had met in the summer of 1972, and not
long afterward she became his constant companion. I liked
Linda a lot. She was everything Elvis usually looked for
in a woman—beautiful, demure, accommodating—and
more. She had intelligence and spirit. While Linda would
do almost anything to make Elvis happy, she drew a line
and was never afraid to speak up to him. She kept at him
about exercising, eating properly and taking his vitamins;
she was quite vocal about the drugs too. Everyone around
Elvis was quite fond of Linda, including Lisa, who developed a special relationship with her.

With his career back in high gear, a new woman in his

life and the world at his feet, he should have been, if not happy, at least content. But Elvis experienced true fulfillment only when he rose to a challenge. For him it wasn't the having but the getting that brought him joy. As time wore on, potential conquests dwindled. There was only a finite number of things Elvis could do, only so many mountains left to scale. In his mind the next—and probably the last—frontier lay outside U.S. borders. Financially, no matter what it cost, a world tour was a no-lose proposition. When "Aloha" was broadcast, for example, over 90 percent of all Japanese homes were tuned in. Parker's plan had backfired; "Aloha" didn't just fail to satisfy the world appetite for Elvis, it whetted it for more. Other offers followed, only to be rejected out of hand by Parker, possibly because, lacking a passport, he couldn't risk crossing the border.

The whole time, though, Elvis made it clear that he was going abroad. Parker's answers to Elvis—whatever they may have been—didn't quiet him. One day when Elvis returned from a trip to Hawaii, there were some businessmen waiting for him. He met with them privately for a while, and later he nervously told me about it. He didn't tell me what they had said, but he let me know what their visit meant.

"Larry, this is a dangerous universe," he said ominously. "It's dangerous. No matter who you are, the higher you are, the more dangerous it is. In the twenties and the thirties the gangs would mow you down in the streets, or they'd dump your body in the river. Now those people are in legitimate business. They're businessmen, they run corporations. They own the great things of America, so they go about things in a different way now. They're very nice, and they negotiate, and they'll talk to you."

The sadness and resignation in his voice made me want to scream. What those men had said to him I could only guess. It's amazing that Elvis was so easily run around by people like Parker and RCA, but again it comes down to not what was or was not true, only what Elvis believed.

In 1964, shortly before I went to work for Elvis, I met Sam Cooke. The singer was at the height of his career and power. Just thirty-three, Cooke was a renowned gospel, then pop, singer, as well as an industry pioneer, one of the era's few black artists to control his own career, even establishing his own record label. Cooke's string of hits for RCA included "You Send Me," "Wonderful World," "Chain Gang," "Shake" and "Bring It On Home to Me."

Sam was a regular customer of Jay Sebring's, but one day when Jay ran behind schedule I took over. Sam was a very kind person, and we got to talking about all sorts of things. As it turned out, he was also into the teachings, so I lent him several books, including *The Impersonal Life*, *Autobiography of a Yogi*, and *Fourteen Lessons in Yoga Philosophy*. In early December of that year we were stunned to learn that Cooke had been shot to death in a Los Angeles motel. The official story portrayed Sam as a man who, after luring a woman to his motel room, attacked her. When she ran to the motel office for help, the manager, a middle-aged black woman, shot Sam three times and clubbed him with a stick. The police found him dead.

For people who knew Sam, no matter how casually, the story didn't hang together. It didn't sound like Sam, and even today, nearly twenty-five years after the fact, there are some who suspect a cover-up. Elvis was a big gospel fan, of course, and a fellow RCA artist, so the rumors didn't escape his attention. But the effect Cooke's death had on Elvis was unusual. Now and again he would allude to it, and after he was refused "permission" to tour outside the country the subject arose again.

"Why do you think Sam Cooke is dead?" he asked me. "Everyone thinks he was murdered in a motel. Oh, he was murdered, all right. He was murdered because he got out of line. I got it from the horse's mouth. Cooke was told that he had a big mouth, to stay in line, and he didn't do it.

"You can go so far, Larry. You can only go so far."

Since there's not enough evidence available for anyone to say with absolute certainty exactly what happened to Cooke, let's accept the official story as true. But whether

it is or isn't, who was the "horse"? And why did the horse
say these things to Elvis? It's no secret that Parker knew
how to scare the hell out of Elvis. And from Parker's point
of view, the only good Elvis was a frightened Elvis. After
I rejoined Elvis, he told me about the rap Parker had given
him after the bathtub incident. As ever, it was a speech
aimed right at Elvis' Achilles heel—his honor, his trust,
his sense of obligation, his guilt, his overwhelming sense
of responsibility to everyone around him. As Elvis lay in
bed, his head full of drugs, Parker let loose.

"Do you know how much money the studio has lost?
Do you know how much a day it costs?" Parker asked.
"What about your daddy? What about Priscilla? What
about your aunt and your grandmother and your fans?
They're going to find out that you're blacklisted from Hol-
lywood. . . ." and so on.

Whatever else was said, Elvis got the message: don't
make noise. Someone said something to scare Elvis. And
it worked.

Elvis's susceptibility to these suggestions is easier to
understand when you consider how sheltered his life was
and how dangerous the outside world could be for him.
He felt safe because he was surrounded by armed security
people and was heavily armed himself at all times. No
matter how many guns he added to his arsenal or how
many bodies he put around him, he was powerless to elim-
inate the hazards. All he could control was his vulnera-
bility. Crowds in the fifties were wild and an ever-present
threat. But the seventies were a different time. Contrary
to popular belief, Elvis was not obsessed with conspiracy
plots and assassinations. Like many people, he was very
intrigued by the riddle of John F. Kennedy's death, and
living in the wake of the Manson murders he reexamined
and beefed up his own security arrangements like any ra-
tional celebrity.

The sad fact is that there are crazy people out there,
and even minor stars attract them. As Elvis often said,
"Every night is a full moon." His main concern was Lisa
Marie, obviously an attractive target for kidnappers. After
heiress Patty Hearst's abduction by a radical terrorist group

in early 1974, Elvis became more cautious than ever. We were all extra vigilant whenever Lisa was around, taking turns accompanying her between Graceland or wherever Elvis was and her home with Priscilla in Los Angeles.

I arrived in Las Vegas just as Elvis was beginning a run at the Hilton. When I got to his suite I noticed a tension in the air.

"Come here," Elvis said. When I was within an arm's reach, he grabbed me by the shoulder with one hand while thrusting a loaded handgun into my belt with the other.

"I know you don't like to wear this," he said seriously, "but I think there's going to be trouble tonight." He explained that they had gotten word that someone was going to try to kill him that night during the show. There'd been a threatening note, and the FBI and other law-enforcement agencies were taking it seriously. Preparations were made for intensive security. We were all given guns, and two ambulances were stationed outside the stage door, just in case. This wasn't the first or the last time such threats were made.

Barron Hilton, the son of the chain's founder, Conrad Hilton, and its chief executive, spoke with Elvis before the show. He told Elvis that he could cancel, that he didn't have to go on. Elvis declined, saying, "Mr. Hilton, if someone is going to kill me, they're going to kill me. If it's not tonight, it's going to be tomorrow night. I'm going to go out there and face it. This is what I live for."

When someone suggested that he wear a bulletproof vest under his jumpsuit, he replied, "No way am I going to wear one of those things. My damn jumpsuit weighs a ton already. I won't be able to move."

One thing that Elvis did not say, but that has been widely reported, is that if anyone in the entourage caught the guy who shot him, we should kill him. This is a popular story, especially with the bodyguards, since it presents Elvis as a ruthless, macho kind of guy. The truth is, it was the bodyguards who had the killer instinct, not Elvis. The "murder-my-assassin" story was simply their projecting onto Elvis what they believed he should have said. Fortutunately, nothing happened that night, but after that we were always ready in case something did.

Late one night in 1974 Elvis and I were sitting outside his house in Palm Springs, relaxing and watching the stars in the clear desert sky. I was shaken out of my thoughts by Elvis' voice. He tried to say something but was stuttering so badly I couldn't follow him.

"I, ah, ah . . . I wanna tell you something." He stopped, then began saying nervously, " 'Cause, ah, you're the only person who could possibly understand. Back when you left, and for about a year or so . . ."

Whatever it was, Elvis couldn't get it out. He seemed embarrassed, and his face was flushed with anger and frustration. Finally he said defensively, "Look, ah . . . you just gotta try and put yourself in my shoes. I mean, just be Elvis for a minute. Think back when I had that experience in the desert. I didn't only see Jesus' picture in the clouds—Jesus Christ literally exploded in me. Larry, it *was* me. I *was* Christ. You know what I mean. In fact, it will always be part of me. Something like that never leaves you. But, at any rate, reading about the masters and God's master plan, and, being *Elvis,* I, ah, I swear to God, Larry, I thought I might be him. I really thought I was singled out, not only to be Elvis, but, ah . . ."

"Elvis," I said, calmly, "are you trying to say you thought you were Jesus Christ?"

Elvis, with visible relief, grinned. Then he quipped self-consciously, "Elvis Christ, Jesus Christ. I went through the whole gamut. You wouldn't believe what flashed through my mind. You were gone. Daddy, the Colonel, Priscilla, the guys—everyone was on my case. And I didn't open a damn book. And you know me, I really had to back down. You know how forceful my ego can get. Just putting the books away.

"Plus Priscilla was fixing to have Lisa. Believe me, she didn't want to hear nothing about anything spiritual. I couldn't really be myself and be totally open to her. She didn't want to hear me. I stood alone, Larry. I had a secret. I'll tell you, she would have called the boys in the white suits and locked up my ass if I told her what was really goin' on in me.

"So, here I was, hanging on my own cross. It tore me up. I didn't have a living soul I could really talk to, you know, like we do. All I had was my prayers. I said many times, 'Lord, I'm not reading, meditating, healing—nothing. So if You want me, if I am the one, You gotta show me. 'Cause by myself, I'm lost. And if I'm wrong, if I'm not what I suspect, then show me, give me the strength.'

"I struggled like you can't believe. I swear, I heard many things you told me. I played them over in my head. Nothing helped. This was something I had to go through by myself. I had to really grapple, and it took a long time to figure it all out: you know, how Elvis fit into the big picture.

"Now I know what my mission is, and that's to uplift people, bring happiness into their lives. People are suffering everywhere, and it's only goin' to get worse. I'm not a preacher; I'm an entertainer, a singer. That's how God and the Brotherhood are helping and usin' me, that's my role, and I love it. I thank God for the position I've been put in. And who knows? Maybe there's something else in store for me. Maybe God wants to use me in bigger ways. I feel it's so. I hope so."

Interestingly, one of Elvis's favorite expressions around this time was "Everything in moderation." And he truly believed and never regarded his own extreme behavior as hypocritical. Not only from the teachings, but from his own understanding, he knew that too much of anything was bad, and he would periodically declare his intention to break his bad habits.

One day in 1973 he asked, "What do you eat?" As if he didn't know. My "bizarre" eating habits—I was a vegetarian then—were the subject of countless Memphis Mafia wisecracks. "Well," I said, "I eat as much raw food as I can, raw fruits and vegetables, and I don't eat meat." After I had explained my approach to nutrition, he nodded.

Later that night, as we were all sitting down to dinner

at the Holmby Hills house in Los Angeles, he said, "So that you all know what's happening around here, I'm changing my diet. Because the spiritual teachings say that you have to eat right, I'll be eating a lot of vegetables now, a lot of salads, and raw fruits. I'm telling the maids, and that's what they're going to make for me."

Out went the brownies, the ice cream, the chicken-fried steak, the burgers. Elvis ate only fresh, nutritious, healthy foods—for two days. Then it was back to the same old nonsense. Elvis was nothing if not a creature of habit. No matter how bad the habit, he was faithful to it.

In fact, by 1973 the only good thing he did for himself was continue practicing karate. Within several months, however, that also ceased. He had always loved karate and derived much pleasure and pride from it. Intellectually, he knew what a positive force it was, but before long he couldn't think about karate without recalling what his enthusiasm for the art had led to: Priscilla's meeting Mike Stone. His involvement tapered off until he lost the drive completely in 1975. He never really exercised again until right before his death. In his prime, Elvis could do some amazing things. The second day I was with him in 1964, he said, "Watch this." We were sitting in the bathroom, and he walked over to the basin and chopped it, making a noise that sounded as though the marble was going to split into pieces. Later Elvis' fingers, which were unusually fine and lithe for a man, gradually became slightly gnarled and knotted from calcium deposits caused by minor fractures in the bones.

Elvis was a legitimate black belt, but in his later years he continued receiving belts of even higher degrees, up to the eighth, indicating a rare mastery of the art. In fact, though, some of the more advanced designations were bogus. He wouldn't say so, but deep in his heart Elvis knew the truth. Most people, including several physicians, law officers, even President Nixon, found it hard to say no to a man who could probably talk the Pope into donning a yarmulke. He was that charming. Through all the short-lived enthusiasms he had embraced and discarded, only karate and the teachings endured. After late 1974, there was only the teachings.

Even as Elvis' existence was getting further removed from everyday reality as most of us know it, during the midseventies he would venture out into the world every now and then. One day in the early seventies when Linda was out of town, Elvis felt lonely and decided to meet a woman. We were standing in front of the house, and Elvis said to me, "Come on, let's go for a ride. Let's take the Stutz."

I got into the car with him and one of his three stepbrothers, Ricky Stanley, who came along as security. (We never left the house without one armed person with us.) As we were driving Elvis said, "Where do you meet someone? Where do you meet girls?" He was totally perplexed.

We drove to Hollywood Boulevard, then down Sunset, and all the while he was looking out the car window, checking out women—not hookers, mind you, just normal, everyday, nice-looking girls—and didn't have a clue what to do next. Elvis could easily have stopped the car, stood on the sidewalk for two minutes and taken home a dozen women, but that didn't occur to him. In his mind, he wasn't a sex symbol, and he couldn't imagine how to approach a woman on the street. We drove around for a while, but Elvis seemed incapable of doing or saying anything to any woman. The whole time, he kept imploring, "Larry, you've got to set me up with someone. I know you know girls. You've got to fix me up."

Finally I relented and, through a friend, found a nice girl, who came over to the house. She was very sweet but not Elvis' type, and after entertaining her for several hours he had someone drive her home. For some time after, Elvis teased me about the girl, directing his comments not toward her but at my inability to come up with someone more appropriate. Not long after, he briefly pursued a woman very close to me, which presented an awkward situation.

Ironically, while he was in the living room being the perfect gentleman and gracious host to the inappropriate young lady, a bunch of the guys were in the den, watching *Deep Throat* on a Betamax. At one point, Elvis and I walked back to see what they were up to. When Elvis saw that they were watching pornography, he turned and walked out. In his day, he had looked at dirty magazines, like everybody else. In the sixties he owned one of the first home videocassette recorder players, and a couple of times he taped girls taking off their clothes, but that was as far as it went. Women who had normal sexual desires intimidated him, partly because of the drugs and partly because of his puritanical upbringing. As the drugs curtailed his libido, he avoided situations that might get out of hand and started viewing women in ever more romantic terms.

Even though Elvis had Linda in his life, it took a very long time for him to come to terms with Priscilla's leaving, if he ever did. Not only did he lose a wife, but his little girl was spending most of her time away from Graceland, coming only to visit whenever she could. The shock, the humiliation, the surprise of it all were more than he could absorb. For one thing, almost no one ever quit on Elvis; it was always the other way around. And even if someone did leave, Elvis never failed to lure them back. Except Priscilla.

"She was a child, and I taught her everything she knows. She just became a different person; she finally grew up," Elvis said during one of our long conversations. "Priscilla was like a little sister to me. It just took me too long to figure that one out. If I'd known better, I would have pushed her out of the nest to fly on her own a long time ago. She grew up, and the person that grew up and I are just apart. We're not in love with each other.

"Man, when you go through that pain, you're never the same again. Never the same. It teaches you about life and about women, and how you've got to be so sure when you make a move like that. You've got to really know if you're loving someone or if you're *in love* with someone." Besides ending his marriage, the divorce from Priscilla symbolized many other things for Elvis. Out of the 365 days

of the year, Elvis chose his thirty-eighth birthday to sue
for divorce.

The seventies found Elvis working harder than he had
worked since the fifties. He spent at least a third of the
year on the road, alternating between one-nighters across
the nation and weeks-long stints in Las Vegas or Lake
Tahoe.

During the early seventies Colonel Parker's gambling
became compulsive and he played to play. Winning ceased
to be the object of the game for Parker. He simply could
not walk away from a game, which made him the kind of
customer no casino would turn away, provided, of course,
he could make good on his debts. And Parker could, because not only was he wealthy, but his "collateral" was
Elvis, and Elvis generated money for Vegas just by being
there. Aside from the business Elvis drew to Las Vegas
during his appearances, there were other perks for the hotel, such as the considerable bills Elvis and his entourage,
including singers, musicians and staff, ran up. Rooms,
meals and drinks for ninety to a hundred people came to
a substantial sum. It's no coincidence that throughout the
seventies we stayed exclusively in Hilton hotels.

Elvis knew all this, and yet he took it upon himself to
save Parker by working the extra dates. His relationship
with his manager, at least in this area, was a revolting and
sad example of Elvis' supermasochism. He loved perform-
ing, but touring is a draining, nerve-racking business for
even the healthiest person.

Elvis' attitude toward his medications had become more
sophisticated as well. In addition to his own health problems—hypertension, high blood sugar, glaucoma, and a
twisted colon that caused him to retain pounds of water
weight—Parker's problems created stresses for Elvis, add-
ing yet another good "reason" for him to up his dosages
of sedatives, hypnotics and uppers. Elvis had lived this
secret life for so long that it never occurred to him that
his medications might be getting out of hand.

Once Elvis looked me in the eye as he gulped down a
handful of pills. "Lawrence, do you think there's a tie-in
between medication and meditation?" He grinned, obvi-

ously amused by his observation. "It must mean something. It's too similar there."

Sad to say, without medication Elvis wasn't as good, onstage or off, as he was when he had it. There were times when he was more lucid with the drugs than without them. He was an addict. The medication ritual—a number of various prescription drugs doled out to him by his doctor in a small manila envelope like the type numismatists use for coins—bothered me, and Elvis knew it. For a period, he stopped taking his pills in front of me.

"The mind is stronger than these medications," he often said, trying to reassure me, and most likely himself, that he was still in control. "The mind is stronger than any drug in the world. I can overcome anything." So the drugs had him believe. And he wasn't about to listen to anyone who wasn't an expert in the field. The only experts he recognized were his doctors—such as Dr. George Nichopoulos, whom he had met in 1966—and what they said to him only they and Elvis knew.

Elvis' only involvement with a heavy "street" drug came in 1973, when he briefly used liquid cocaine that he obtained from one of his physicians. At that time cocaine was not yet recognized as an addictive drug, and few experts in the drug field considered it dangerous. I had stopped over at Elvis' house and was waiting for him to come down. When he finally did at around four, I said, "Hi, how are you?"

"What's wrong with your nose?" he asked, concerned.

"What are you talking about?"

"You're congested," he replied.

"No I'm not."

"What do you mean? I can tell," he said with authority. "Go like this," he ordered, then made a sniffling sound. After I complied with his weird request, he said, "See, you're all congested."

"Elvis, I am not congested," I answered impatiently.

"Come with me," he said. Then I realized he was up to something. Up in his bedroom he produced a large bottle, which he opened and then, holding a wad of cotton over the mouth, tipped it to saturate the cotton. As he pushed the cotton into my nose, he remarked nonchalantly, "There's a little cocaine in here. Eight percent cocaine."

Within seconds I felt as though I'd been hit by a bolt of lightning. Every bone in my head throbbed, even my teeth hurt after a while, but I felt like Superman. Elvis just grinned; I was in on his little secret.

In 1974 Elvis woke up one day and told Charlie and me that he wanted to get drunk. "I just want to know what happens when you get drunk," he explained. It sounded reasonable enough; he never drank and to the best of my knowledge had never been intoxicated in his life. For the next four days Charlie and I hung around with Elvis as he downed fifteen to twenty drinks a day—mixed drinks of all sorts, hard liquor—and got blitzed out of his mind. Elvis had an unhumanly high tolerance for any psychoactive chemical, and it took a lot for him to get drunk, but he did it, like everything, to excess. He was a funny guy to begin with, and the alcohol turned him into a one-man comedy show. I don't think Charlie or I ever laughed so hard in our lives, and Elvis seemed to be having a fine old time. Each night we'd carry him up to bed, and the next morning he'd start all over again, as if he were embarking on a new adventure. After several days he stopped, and he never drank again.

Around the same time, Elvis went on a marijuana binge for a few days. Again his tolerance was high, and he had to smoke so much pot to get off that it hurt his throat. Fearful of losing or damaging his voice, he gave up on marijuana.

Although Elvis' denial was very strong, he occasionally acknowledged that his medications were a problem, and several times during the seventies he checked into the hospital in attempts to clean up. Withdrawal from any of a number of the medications he took could conceivably have caused death, so medical supervision was necessary. It was impossible to tell how "detoxed" Elvis got during these trips to the hospital, because he had used drugs for so long that he was rarely high and only rarely appeared to be under the influence. Like anyone who is physically

addicted to any substance, Elvis had had years to learn to
cope and maintain. He was, after all, a master showman.
In everything. Even on those occasions when he forgot
lyrics or rambled on inanely, the audiences still applauded. Elvis didn't read reviews, and in his mind he had
overcome his medications. After all, he was maintaining
a tour schedule that would put many lesser men under in
a week; he was a sellout everywhere he went. Stepping on
the stage, he fell into the unquestioning collective embrace
of thousands. From Elvis' point of view—the only point
of view he understood—he *was* stronger than those medications. He was out there, wasn't he? They loved him,
didn't they? He was fulfilling his purpose, wasn't he?

In early 1974 I married my second wife, Celest. She
had worked with me in my bookstore, and we had a great
deal in common. She was very fond of Elvis, as he was
of her. She was very supportive of me, and because she
cared so much for Elvis she never complained about the
amount of time I spent away from home to be with him.

In the fall of 1974 Barbra Streisand came backstage in
Vegas to offer Elvis a costarring role in a remake of *A Star
Is Born*, which she was producing with Jon Peters, her
boyfriend. Elvis would have played Norman Maine, a successful actor, updated to rock star, who turns to drugs
when he is eclipsed by his wife's (Streisand) fame. Elvis
was very excited by the chance to return to films with such
a good property, and he knew he could do it. Parker, however, couldn't seem to countenance the fact that Streisand,
a superstar in her own right, insisted on (and clearly deserved) equal billing with Elvis. Elvis was his boy, all
right, but in movieland, of the two of them, Streisand was
the serious actress, the bankable name. This wasn't another stupid teenybopper movie; and Parker, who so rarely
misread a situation, was in over his head. He underesti-
mated Streisand's strength. When she and Peters wouldn't
go along with his demands, the deal was off.

Elvis had been thinking about returning to the movies
in some way, and at one point during this period he spoke
on the telephone with Paul Newman about the possibility

of acting in a film Newman and his people wanted to produce. "Man, I made some good movies in the fifties," Elvis said, referring to *Love Me Tender, Loving You, Jailhouse Rock* and *King Creole.* "I know I can be a great actor; it's in me. All they have to do is give me the chance. Just give me the chance."

One day he said, "Come with me right away." He was very excited about something, and when I got up to his room in Holmby Hills he said, "All right, here's the deal. We're going to make our first movie. I want you to write it; I know you can do it. You know all about the significance of colors and about the secrets of breath and about spirituality. All the martial arts were founded upon spiritual principles, and this film will be based on that. You're the one to put it together. Do a little research. I'm going to give you a check. Charlie! Charlie, get me a check!"

"I don't need any money, Elvis."

"No, no, no," he replied. "You got to have money right now. This is it. We're in business. I'm going to produce my first movie. We're going to do it with Ed Parker [Elvis' karate instructor, bodyguard and friend], and all the guys are going to have a piece. And I'm going to be the executive producer, and I'm going to narrate, and you're going to write my narration." He stopped to catch his breath, then winked. "All right? What do you think of that?"

"Great! What is it about?"

"It's on the origins and development of karate, how it started, where it came from, how it got to where it is now. We're going to send film crews to different tournaments," he continued happily, talking about all the various aspects of the film and how it would work. He was so caught up in telling me about it when someone in the group reminded him that Linda Thompson's parents were waiting downstairs to see him, he forget his manners and said, "They'll wait!" Elvis loved plans and projects, and it was a joy to see him like this, so full of life. He reminded me of how he'd been after he bought the ranch, and at the time I felt that if there was anything that would wrest him from his depression and his medication, this was it.

Twelve weeks later I had my first treatment outlining the film's contents, which Elvis thought was great. For the first time in his career he also got involved with some outside people, producers and businessmen of some sort. I also recall a master from Belgium, who came to the house to meet with Elvis. Elvis made it very clear that this was his baby; the Colonel would get a little piece of the action, but nothing like what he was used to. In return, Elvis expected the Colonel to put together a distribution deal for the finished film. Needless to say, Colonel Parker got wind of the project and wasn't happy. All it took to set Vernon against it was that *it cost money*. Pretty soon, Elvis was hearing from those two how outsiders weren't to be trusted, and how did he know what he was doing—and the whole nine yards. Exacerbating the situation was the fact that several of the regulars weren't friendly with Ed Parker, whom they distrusted. I liked Ed very much; he was a sincere, intelligent man—the type Elvis needed more of around him—which was all the more reason for everyone else to want him out.

That fall Dee and Vernon had separated after ten years of marriage. Two of Dee's three sons, David and Rick Stanley, remained on Elvis' payroll. Dee demanded a substantial divorce settlement from Vernon—which really meant from Elvis—and Vernon was miserable. It was not a happy time. The full force of these pressures ground everyone down. There was a general feeling of dissolution, as if everyone and everything was breaking down and no one could stop it. Looking back, I see this period as Elvis' last attempt to break free. In the next few years other things he would do and say would suggest that he might make some substantial move toward changing his life, but the movie business was truly the last time Elvis stood any real chance of pulling his neck out of the guillotine.

Just twenty days after Elvis's fortieth birthday, he checked into the hospital again. There doctors diagnosed an enlarged colon, extensive liver damage, and glaucoma. A few days later, Vernon suffered the first of several heart attacks. By some stroke of luck, Vernon was felled while at the hospital visiting his son. Otherwise it's likely he would have died.

In one fell swoop, the production company was gone, and Elvis was back on the road until August, when he canceled most of his Las Vegas dates and returned to Memphis and the hospital. He checked out in September 1975, went home and didn't do much until December; then it was back to Vegas, so that Elvis could make up the dates he'd canceled in the fall.

Financially, Elvis should have been doing quite well, but Parker had been busy concocting deals, the goal of which was to position himself to take the maximum amount of Elvis' earnings as quickly as possible. A classic example of Parker's shortsighted greed was a deal to sell the masters to all of the songs Elvis had recorded before March 1973 to RCA Records for a flat fee, waiving all rights to future royalties and other income. For $5.4 million (of which Elvis got only $2.8 million and Parker took $2.6 million), RCA owned these masters. In addition RCA agreed to pay Elvis and Parker for other services. In the end, Elvis came away with a total of $4.65 million, substantially less than Parker's $6.2 million. As large as the sum Elvis received might seem, it represents only a small fraction of the amount he and his estate would have earned if the masters had not been sold and he had continued to receive royalties on the sale of those titles.

Next Parker created Boxcar Enterprises, Inc., a corporation to handle all merchandising of Elvis products. In this business, Parker held a 40 percent controlling interest, with remainder of the shares doled out so that Tom Diskin, RCA executive George Parkhill and music publisher Freddie Bienstock each got the same percentage of total shares as Elvis, 15 percent. These were typical of the deals that were finally brought to light (and to court) in 1980, when Lisa Marie Presley's court-appointed guardian ad litem, Blanchard Tual, was charged with investigating and reporting on Elvis' business affairs and his dealings with Colonel Parker. Tual's report stated the obvious: the Colonel had "handled affairs not in Elvis' but in his own best interest."

What with these deals and Parker's renegotiating his contract with Elvis—bringing his take up to 50 percent (three to five·times the industry standard)—and with Elvis' and Vernon's business naiveté, there would have been very little left for Elvis if he had ever stopped working. Elvis didn't know about tax shelters, and he didn't want to. ''I want the government to have whatever I owe them,'' he said. ''I'm an American, and that's the way I want it.''

Even if someone could have talked some sense into Elvis, Vernon couldn't comprehend anything about money unless he could hold it in his hand. Making even the most conservative investments, Elvis would have been a billionaire. Instead he left an estate worth only a small fraction of his lifetime earnings. One day in 1973 I was talking to Vernon about how the price of gold had reached unprecedented heights, and why it was such a good investment. Vernon listened, nodding his head, and promised he'd think about it. Six months later he said, ''Larry, I took your advice. Come here, I want to show you something.'' With a flourish he produced a single gold piece, worth not more than one hundred dollars. Vernon was so proud of himself; he'd made an ''investment.''

Vernon was getting even more nervous about the money, and about his son. Deep down, he sensed the severity of Elvis' problem, but on another level he knew just enough to know that he didn't want to know any more than what was in front of his face. He loved his son, but he too was ill. Vernon never was a take-charge person, and he was so weakened, emotionally and physically, that he couldn't have changed if he'd wanted to.

Elvis and Vernon could read each other like books. The love they shared was beautiful, but at times Elvis would lose his patience and snap at Vernon. Once he said angrily, ''I'm the boss, Daddy, and don't you forget that!''

Vernon was stunned, and hurt, because despite his limitations, he was loyal to his son. Vernon knew the score with a lot of people around Elvis, and, while he would have loved to disband the whole entourage, he was particularly against Red West, Red's cousin Sonny West and Dave Hebler, a relatively new addition to the security force. In recent years Elvis had been named a defendant in several lawsuits brought against him by people who—innocently or not—ran afoul of this trio. He never laid a finger on anyone, but the bodyguards were employed by him, so it was Elvis who got sued, often for millions of dollars. The bodyguards not only cost money in legal fees and possible future settlements but caused Elvis constant worry about when the next lawsuit was coming. Only his loyalty to the guys, especially to Red, kept him many times from firing them himself. Vernon wasn't the only person who considered the bodyguards a liability, but he was the most vocal. On July 13, 1976, Vernon gave Red, Sonny and Dave notice that they were fired.

Red, who have befriended and defended Elvis back at Humes High School, took it especially hard, even though he and Elvis hadn't been close in years. Unlike many of the other guys, Red made a life for himself outside the entourage. While in Elvis' employ he had also worked as a stuntman and an actor and had written a couple of hit songs. Over the years, most of the guys came and went, leaving to start new ventures, then returning when things didn't work out. Red didn't fall into that category, and his anger wasn't about money, or even the job, I think. He was hurt.

That fall several people close to Elvis got phone calls from Ed, Sonny or Dave, asking them about dates and other details. They were, they said, writing a book about Elvis. No one who really cared about Elvis cooperated with them. We knew the bodyguards well enough to know that revenge was their motive. I imagined what would be in the book if it were ever published, but that was a big if, and few took the threat seriously. Elvis knew of the bodyguards' plans but believed they were acting out of anger and that once they calmed down reason and their loyalty to him would triumph; there would be no book. In fact, those three hadn't been off the payroll more than a few weeks before we were all speculating about when Elvis would offer them their jobs back. That was Elvis' way, and it was just a matter of time.

Elvis appreciated the loyalty of those still around him

and kept trying to involve them in his spiritual studies. As they all grew older they had also grown more tolerant. They had seen more of the world and, in many ways, matured. Elvis' studies didn't attract the derisive comments and snickers they had inspired years before. After so much time everyone—including Vernon and, to a certain extent, Parker—accepted Elvis' studies because they were important to him. Elvis, however, wasn't so content to leave things at that. One summer day in 1976 he said to Lamar Fike, "Lamar, I want you to read."

In front of Elvis, several guys and me, Lamar opened *The Sacred Science of Numbers* and began reading aloud. Elvis then handed him a copy of *The Prophet,* and asked him to read some more. After a few pages, Lamar looked up at Elvis and said, "I don't know a word I read."

Elvis stood and, looking at each person, said, "Lamar, when you and everyone else here starts searching for truth, and you want to know who you are and what the truth of life is, that's what's going to make me happy. You all want to make me happy? You start searching for God and truth, and you'll make me happy. That's all I want from you guys."

They all nodded as if they understood, and in fact several people close to Elvis did become more spiritually involved. Elvis' cousin Billy Smith, Charlie Hodge, and eventually his stepbrothers Ricky and David, followed Elvis' lead. Elvis tried to draw the others into his personal life not because he was crazy about converting everyone, but because he wanted to share with them the happiness he'd found. Also he sensed a loss of real contact with them in the last years, and he thought the studies might provide some common ground, as had the slot cars and the water-balloon fights. Many times we would come off tour and the minute all the business was taken care of, everybody scattered. Several times someone said to me teasingly, "Uh-oh, Geller, he's gonna want you here, and you're going to have to stay with him," as if this were punishment.

By the fall of 1976 Elvis was seriously ill. Over the last year I had noticed how labored his breathing had become even when he was sitting down. He rarely spoke more than a couple of sentences without stopping to draw a long, deep, noisy breath. Besides being overweight due to his ridiculous eating habits, he carried a lot of water, so much that there were times after 1973 when he couldn't zip up his boots. His hands and feet were bloated, and he complained constantly of general pain and weakness. He wouldn't say, "I hurt here or there," but "God, I hurt all over." When I gave him his nightly massage after shows I noticed large, dark bruises everywhere. They weren't concentrated in one place or a couple of spots, but all over. He'd awaken some days to find his face covered by strange blotches and discolorations. Elvis knew that something was terribly wrong with his body, something more than the colon, the liver or the medications.

Most people faced with these developments would run to a doctor. Elvis had Dr. Nichopoulos on twenty-four-hour-a-day call and could have been tested and treated at any time. But he did nothing about it. Elvis couldn't face the truth about his physical health. During this period he had other distractions. His relationship with Linda had begun to wind down by then. Their romance was cooling and mellowing into a deep friendship, a relationship more typical of siblings than of lovers. We were on tour in August or September of 1976 when he realized that Linda was interested in someone else. Elvis had suspected as much for some time.

Elvis and I were up late, talking, when he suddenly asked, "Where's Linda?" After I replied that I thought she was downstairs playing Scrabble with some of the other guys, he said, "Larry, do me a favor and get Linda. I need her now."

After searching in a few obvious places, I found Linda in the hotel restaurant, sitting at a back corner table with Elvis' keyboard player, David Briggs. Though she had a healthy attitude toward sex and liked to flirt, I don't believe her relationship with Briggs was sexual. She was too moral a person to do such a thing.

There seemed nowhere for Elvis to turn. Vernon was growing weaker by the day; tensions between Elvis and

Parker occasionally flared. Everything was fading away,
even himself. He spoke excitedly of grand, sweeping
changes he wanted to make in his life; about a new start.
Then an hour later he would be lost in a fond memory of
his mother or his childhood.

All that the present offered Elvis were problems and
pressures—variations on the same problems and pressures
that had been plaguing him for the last two decades. Regardless of how much of his past he had disowned and
rejected, he found comfort in and embraced all things familiar. He knew who he'd been in the past. The future was
a blank canvas on which Elvis could create the rest of his
life. Of course, one of the future's drawbacks is that it
doesn't yet exist, but for Elvis that was its charm. If the
good things it promised weren't yet real, then neither were
the bad.

Beginning in 1976 I worked on two projects: writing my
book about hair care and launching my own line of hair
products. Between tours I'd huddle for hours in libraries,
researching and preparing the manuscript. Though free
moments on tour were rare, the manuscript came with me
wherever I went.

I've never been able to explain fully what made me start
writing about my life with Elvis, but sometime in late
November of 1976 I began jotting down notes about him
in my papers. In my diary I wrote of having a strange
feeling about Elvis' health and his state of mind, but looking back I recognize that there was more to it than that.

During those last months Elvis was besieged by crip-
pling physical illness, substance addiction, the threat of
exposure, the fear that he would be forced to face a questioning public, an overwhelming sense of having failed to
protect his father, and especially his daughter, from the
glare of negative, damaging publicity he had so deftly
eluded until then. The mistakes of his past, the pressure
of his present, and the uncertainty of the future crushed
him. And at the end he spoke of himself often: who he
was, what he meant, what he believed in, what he hoped
for.

At some point Elvis decided that he wanted to write his own book, and because his tour schedule was booked so many months in advance, he wouldn't be able to begin really working on it until early 1978 at the earliest. He charged me with taking notes for it from our conversations. As I did that I was, to a certain extent, examining my own thoughts about what I was witnessing. It was a frightening time and I found writing about it comforting and therapeutic. Many of the specific conversations, incidents and thoughts I recorded all reflect a sense of foreboding, a sense that something ominous and unthinkable was lurking nearby.

Sometimes I recorded whole conversations in my own shorthand, knowing I'd never forget expressions, scenes, feelings. These follow, interspersed with a narrative based on diary entries that I've since filled out with memory. The balance is as I wrote it over a decade ago during what turned out to be Elvis Presley's last nine months on earth.

CHAPTER

8

In mid-November 1976 Elvis met the last love of his life, Ginger Alden. Ginger was a local girl, a first runner-up in the Miss Tennessee contest. George Klein had actually tried to arrange something between Elvis and Ginger's older sister Terry, Miss Tennessee 1976, but when Ginger came along with Terry to Graceland, Elvis fell for the younger sister.

It was the afternoon of November 29, and I had just gotten up to Elvis' suite at the Hilton in San Francisco. That evening he'd be doing the second of two shows there before flying down to Anaheim. In addition to our whole entourage, several people, including my sister Judy, were along. Elvis, dressed in his royal-blue pajamas, with shaving cream slathered over his face, was just stepping out of the bathroom.

"Lawrence, good timing. Come on in here a minute. I gotta lay something on you."

I followed him into the bathroom, and as he stood at the sink a sly sheepish grin spread over his face. After shaving his chin, he suddenly whirled around and exclaimed, "I feel a big change is about to happen! Remember that girl I told you about last night? Ginger? Well, I can't get her out of my mind. Man, I just can't forget that night. Nothing happened—I mean, all we did was talk, you know. All I can say is that when our eyes locked, the sparks flew. I was floored, and I know she felt the same way."

Smiling, Elvis turned back to the mirror and continued shaving.

"Larry, I can't get my mind off her. This might sound strange . . ." He stared silently at his reflection before continuing solemnly. "She reminds me of my mom. When I first saw her eyes, it hit me. I haven't felt like this in years. Let's just keep our voices down in case Linda should walk in."

Wiping away the last traces of lather, Elvis stole a quick glance out the door. "I'm just being extra cautious," he explained. He then outlined his elaborate plans to have Ginger flown in to meet him, by which time he hoped to have Linda out of town. I asked him how he intended to tell Linda what was happening.

"Here's the game plan," he said. "I already told her that I need a few days alone before we go into Las Vegas, and this way she can shop for clothes in L.A. and I'll fly her in next week."

His plan of action set, Elvis carried on about how much he respected Linda, how much she'd done for him over the years, how she'd been there for him after Priscilla left, and so on. But he admitted what we all knew: he and Linda were finished.

"Since I met Ginger," he continued, "I feel that ol' lovin' feeling again. I can feel it in my bones. There's something about Ginger. I'm sending the ladies home on the *Jet Star* [the smaller of his two jets], so explain to your sister, Judy, that I'm preparing for the Vegas show. That's why the ladies have to go."

"I can't wait to meet Ginger," I said.

When I did meet Ginger that evening, she was exactly as Elvis had described her to me: pretty, with dark eyes and long deep-brown hair. She was understandably shy, having never been out of Memphis or far from her family, and self-conscious about her age. We of the entourage took being with Elvis for granted, but any newcomer was obviously overwhelmed by the hustle and bustle of the tour. Ginger seemed in awe of the surroundings, which, though normal to us, were unusual to her. She didn't say very much.

The next afternoon I was surprised to find Elvis just as happy as the day before, which was unusual, especially since he woke up each morning groggy from his medications. His boyish smile seemed to light up the room.

"We talked for hours last night," he exclaimed, speaking of Ginger. "I asked her if she would like to go into Vegas with us and finish the tour, and she said she would. Man, I really like her. And all we did was talk, we didn't even kiss! I feel right with her. Larry, what do you think of her?"

"Obviously she is beautiful," I began slowly. I tried choosing my words carefully, but I blurted out, "By the way, how old is she?"

Elvis paused, looked away, then replied with forced casualness, "Twenty. Actually she turned twenty just two weeks ago, on November thirteenth. Hey," he said, trying to change the subject, "that makes her a four, the best number for an eight like us. Four means balance, and, Lord God, I sure need a little balance."

NOVEMBER 30, 1976

San Francisco

Tonight we flew from San Francisco to Anaheim, California, for the last concert before playing two weeks in Vegas.

Elvis' happiness shone through every song he performed. He was truly on the wings of song: free, for the moment, of all that was tearing him down. Elvis had found love again. The quality of his performance and the texture of his voice were a reincarnation of Elvis Presley age twenty-three.

Elvis' feelings swept over the audience. Even John Wayne, who was in the audience, and my parents were elated. I wanted to stay with my parents after the show; impossible, however. The first order of business was to get Elvis back to our plane safely and on to Vegas before the tens of thousands in the audience broke through and overwhelmed the hundreds of security police.

DECEMBER 1, 1976

1 A.M., Las Vegas Hilton

We finally arrived at the Las Vegas Hilton. It looked like a ghost town. Even the Hilton's gambling casino—Vegas' finest—seemed dead. Most of the blackjack tables were empty.

12 Noon

I went downstairs for breakfast. Everywhere I looked, the Hilton was showing signs of renewed life. Elvis is in town. *The giant Elvis booth at the hotel's entrance was buzzing with people. As always, the Elvis hats, buttons, banners, posters were drawing tourists like magnets. I walked over to the blackjack tables to say hello to Tony, one of the dealers.*

"Larry, thank God you're all here," is how Tony greeted me, sighing. "This place has been a morgue all month. We all couldn't wait till Elvis arrived. Hey, man, say hello to Elvis; tell him we all thank him."

7:30 P.M.

I went downstairs for dinner. The Hilton was alive, teeming with people. Elvis' pictures were on all the walls, and there was the old electricity in the air. The groupies had arrived and were milling around by the elevator—Elvis' elevator. Everything seemed back to normal; at least, on the surface.

9:30 P.M.

I went upstairs to Elvis' suite. Elvis and Ginger were sitting by themselves on the couch, wearing matching blue bathrobes. Elvis was reading to Ginger from Cheiro's Book of Numbers. *I reminded him that I had to do his hair. We'd waited long enough, and he was opening tomorrow. Elvis looked up from his book, then at Ginger, then at me. I could see him trying to figure out some excuse.*

"Lawrence," he finally answered with mock solemnity,

"there's a time for everything. However, son, this is definitely not the time. I'm tryin' to paint a white picture for Ginger, and you want to dye my hair black." Then he smiled. "No, I'm only kidding. I'll tell you what: we'll definitely do it tomorrow before the show. In the meantime, enjoy yourself, and I'll check with you later."

DECEMBER 2, 1976

Around one this morning Elvis had me paged. When I entered his suite, Dean [Nichopoulos, Dr. Nick's son] said, "Larry, Elvis needs you. He said to just go in the bedroom." As I entered the bedroom they were both perched up on the bed in the blue hooded robes with a dozen books strewn on the bed.

"Well, I see you've been studying," I said with a chuckle.

Elvis replied, "Lawrence, I'm about my Father's business." He turned to Ginger. "Honey, I need to talk with Larry for a minute. I'm just going in the other room; I'll be right back."

I followed Elvis into the bathroom adjoining his bedroom. After he'd closed the door behind us, he said, "Lawrence, I swear to God, I looked into Ginger's eyes, and I saw my mother's eyes." Although Elvis was coherent, he was a bit woozy. What was he on? "I think I'm fallin' in love," he continued. At that his body swayed, and he grabbed onto the ledge of the sink. With his typical Elvis humor, he exclaimed, "Well, I'm definitely fallin'!

"Listen, will you go to your room and bring me that book you have on the sacred numbers? Ginger doesn't say much, but she sure is a good listener. I really think she's open; she told me she wants to learn."

6 P.M.

"Man," Elvis exclaimed, "I can't believe Ginger! She's so open to the things I believe in. Larry, maybe I found my soul mate." I haven't seen him so happy in years, but

*it's all too unreal. How long can the drugs and his feelings
about Ginger keep him on this high?*

*"Larry, find me some material on soul mates, will ya?"
Then, with the hair dye still on his head and dripping
down over his face and neck, Elvis excitedly called out to
Ginger, "Honey, tomorrow you're getting a brand-new
wardrobe."*

It was after five the next evening when Elvis finally woke
up. I was sitting with a few of the guys watching the news
on television when Elvis emerged and groggily made his
way to the sofa. No sooner had he sat down than Ricky
Stanley came in and said, "Boss, Linda's been calling."

Elvis looked annoyed, then brushed Ricky off, saying,
"Right, Ricky, I know, I know. Get Sam [Thompson, Linda's brother] up here; I want to talk with him."

Ten minutes later, when Sam arrived, Elvis asked everyone else to leave, then added, "Lawrence, stick
around."

He and Sam walked over to the suite's dining room, and
Elvis said, "Sam, I know you must feel strange about
Linda not being here and seeing me with Ginger. I have
to bring this situation out into the open and talk about it.
I love your sister; she means a lot to me, you know that.
She was there when Priscilla and I split up, and she helped
me through some rough times. I mean, when I was in the
pits . . . But Sam, I'm sorry: it's Ginger. I'm in love with
her. You know how I feel about your whole family, so
don't think this will interfere with our relationship or your
job here. It won't. I respect you and your work, so I don't
want you to feel insecure or anything like that, all right?"

Sam seemed relieved. "Elvis, I'm really glad you said
what you did. I respect you for it. I understand. I did feel
awkward and didn't know what to say to you. I'm grateful
you broke the ice, because no matter how it turns out, I
want to work for you."

Elvis stepped forward and gave Sam a warm hug. "I
need to talk to Larry. I'll see you later."

After Sam had left the room, Elvis slowly made his way

back to the sofa. He looked as if he'd just finished fifteen rounds in the ring with Muhammad Ali. He started to sit down, then just fell back.

"It never stops, son," he said wearily. "There's always something to deal with. But I feel good about talking to Sam. It takes the edge off." With that he exhaled loudly and fell silent.

DECEMBER 5, 1976

After the show that night Elvis seemed unstable physically. His performance has been way off, although, ironically, his voice sounded better, with deeper resonance and more strength. But his movements and overall quality were strained, lackluster.

He complained of weakness. We were in his dressing room downstairs, and Ed [Parker], Dick [Grob], Ricky and I quickly got Elvis into the private elevator that goes right up to his penthouse suite. It was apparent to us that he was really out of it. Two fans managed to get by our security and rushed up to us as we entered the elevator. Obviously unaware of Elvis' condition, the two fans, a man and a woman, cried out, "Elvis, you're the King!" as the doors were closing.

Elvis, weak, leaning back against the elevator wall for support, mustered up his strength and responded: "I might be in the saddle, but I'm not on the throne." The doors shut on "throne." Elvis looked at me and winked— desperate for confirmation that I would find the way to relieve his pain.

As soon as we entered Elvis' suite, I called Dr. Elias Ghanem. After Dr. Ghanem left Elvis' bedroom, Ginger asked me to come in. How strange: hearing Ginger speak. In his bedroom, Elvis was lying on his back with a wet towel over his eyes. He asked Ginger to excuse us for a few minutes.

"Lawrence, I know the medication gives me some temporary relief, but I also know that spiritual healing is the most effective. The doctors don't really understand that, so please, go to work; I really hurt." For the next thirty

minutes I gave Elvis a soothing rub, massaging him with prayers until, peacefully, he fell asleep. Exhausted, I too crashed.

DECEMBER 6, 1976

Elvis came out of his bedroom sometime after four this afternoon and sank into the sofa. "I feel rejuvenated," he mumbled as he peered over at me, looking listless and groggy. Ginger emerged from the bedroom and sat down next to Elvis; both of them in the blue robes. As Elvis ordered breakfast, Joe, Charlie and Ricky came in from the dining room.

"Joe," Elvis said impatiently, "when is the Colonel gonna set up that tour for Europe? Man, the English fans, the German ones and all the rest of them expect me to come over, and I wanna go. What the hell is going on?"

Joe, trying his best to appease the Boss, replied, "Well, the Colonel says Concerts West is working on it—"

"They better be working on it! That's all I've been hearing every time I bring up the subject. What the hell are they doing?"

Joe went into a long song and dance about security precautions and the stir Elvis would cause, none of it all that convincing. But when Joe said, "If you went over there, Elvis, it would be like the Second Coming or something," Elvis looked over at Ginger and grinned. Chuckling, he added, "Hey, Joe, I also want to go to Japan. You tell the Colonel I said that."

The show that evening seemed a bit livelier than last night's. The crowds were as wild as ever—girls throwing panties at Elvis, trying to get onstage. But Elvis was really struggling. Throwing out his scarves to the audience seemed to take a real effort.

DECEMBER 8, 1976

This afternoon Joe told Elvis that Ginger's mother and father and her two sisters had just arrived, along with Vernon and his lady, Sandy Miller, on the Lisa Marie *[the larger plane]. Vernon entered while Joe was talking. Daddy*

Vernon looked tired and pale. Since his heart attack he rarely travels. Elvis asked everyone to leave so that he could talk with his daddy.

1:30 A.M., Elvis' Dressing-Room Suite

After the show Elvis came out of his inner dressing room to the larger living-room area, where the rest of us, along with well-wishers, were mingling. I still can't believe what I saw and heard. He must have taken extra medications, because he seemed really out of it. Everything he said and did was irrational: talking a mile a minute; keeping Ginger's family waiting; procrastinating. It was obvious that he was too nervous to go upstairs; he even went next door to the Sweet Inspirations' dressing room and talked and talked with Myrna, Sylvia and Estelle.

Then [comedian] Jackie Kahane brought in a few of his friends to meet Elvis, and they talked and talked. We had to pry him out of there, and we all finally went upstairs to his suite, where another crowd was waiting. Ginger introduced him to her family. How ironic life is: Here was Elvis, nervous as a little boy, tranquilized to cover up his shyness. And there they were, Ginger's family, nervous and self-conscious themselves, all caught up in their own fantasy.

DECEMBER 9, 1976

As the orchestra played his theme, "Also Sprach Zarathu-stra" [the 2001 theme], Elvis put his hands together and brought them to his forehead in a prayer position while bowing his head and saying his little prayer as he always did before performances: "Send me some light—I need it bad."

He was tired—drained from the tour, Ginger, his worsening health, those damned drugs—but his whole countenance changed as soon as he appeared onstage. As each song was sung he seemed to draw upon a reservoir of energy that radiated from him to the audience, who in turn sent him their energy and love.

As hard as he tried, though, Elvis missed a few lines tonight; slurred his lyrics. When he started singing "Funny How Time Slips Away," he forgot where he was, stopped, and after a few measures had the orchestra start from the top again and began the song from the beginning. Blanking out, Elvis had to read the lyrics from the sheet music of "My Way," despite having performed it hundreds of times. The crowd—sympathetically, lovingly—went berserk anyway. Their Elvis was immortal and could do no wrong.

DECEMBER 10, 1976

There was a typical commotion after tonight's show. The dressing room was alive, teeming with people, and, to compound Elvis' personal health problems, his daddy collapsed. Elvis quickly grabbed Vernon's limp body, set him gently in a soft armchair, and yelled out to Dr. Ghanem, who was in the adjoining room.

Vernon appeared as if he were having a heart attack, looking white as a ghost; one could hear him struggling for breath. Dr. Ghanem and Elvis immediately took him to the hospital, the security force following. When Elvis returned to his suite around 2:30 A.M., he took me by the arm and ushered me into his bedroom.

"Lawrence, Daddy had a mild heart attack. Dr. Ghanem wants to keep him in the hospital tonight; y'know, check him out. But we know how effective spiritual healing is, so let's do a special service for Daddy. I want you to lead the ceremony, and we'll all join in: Ginger, Charlie and us. All right?"

I said, "Absolutely, E. Your daddy is going to be fine."

Elvis said good night to all the others.

Charlie, Ginger, Elvis and I all sat cross-legged, joining hands in a circle, on Elvis' bed. I began a prayer that led into the healing service. Elvis took up where I left off, reciting the Lord's Prayer. I said softly, "Just visualize light pervading and penetrating Mr. Presley's body, bathing and soothing his entire being." We meditated, holding

*hands, keeping our eyes closed, with Elvis every once in
a while quietly saying, "Amen. Amen. Amen."*

DECEMBER 11, 1976

*I was having an afternoon snack and saw Vernon and
Sandy walk into the coffee shop. Vernon looked well, even
rejuvenated. He saw me and came over with Sandy to my
table.*

"Well, you're looking fit, Mr. Presley."

*Vernon, in his usual fashion, chirped, "I'll tell ya,
Larry, I feel great. You know, I had a mild heart attack
last night, but I'm feeling much better today. The doctor
said I'll do all right." I didn't mention the service we had
for him early in the morning. I'll leave that for Elvis.*

The next afternoon a few of the Memphis Mafia were
lounging around the living room, waiting for Elvis to come
out of his bedroom and begin his day. Suddenly Elvis
emerged, looking quite shaken and in pain as he walked
across the room and sank into the sofa. He sat motionless
for a few minutes and then asked everyone but me to leave.

As the guys left, I noticed beads of perspiration running
from Elvis' upper lip down his chin. His eyes had a
strange, haunted look. He stared at me, taking in deep
gulps of air and breathing erratically. Trying to stand, he
lost his balance, and as he fell he grabbed at the drapes
with both hands to keep from hitting the floor. His head
jerked around and he cried out, "Lawrence, Lawrence!
Quick! Help me to my bedroom!"

I ran to him and picked him up, supporting his body as
we staggered into his bedroom and made our way to his
bed, where he collapsed. He moaned, "This is it—I'm
going out. I . . . ah . . . I took too much . . . or someone
gave me the wrong thing. I'm going . . ."

I quickly raised his head, supporting it with my right
arm, and placed my left palm on his chest, over his heart.
I could feel it pounding furiously.

"I'm calling for help, Elvis."

"No, no," he pleaded. "I'm leaving my body—I'm dying. Don't leave me."

"You're not dying, Elvis," I said, trying to sound calm. "I won't leave you. You're going to live. Just relax. Feel the warmth of my hand."

His heart was still pumping madly, he was gasping for breath, and his eyes were rolled back and crossed.

"Relax, Elvis. Breathe deep from your diaphragm. Don't panic . . . relax . . . breathe deep. Know you're going to be all right. Be still and know, Elvis, relax . . ."

I could feel his sweat soaking through his bathrobe and my shirt. All the color had drained from his face. Silently I pleaded to God not to let him die. I kept repeating, "Elvis, just relax. Feel yourself coming back into your body—breathe slowly." He was convulsing in my arms. I kept praying and talking to him while massaging his chest. "Elvis, you know you are going to be all right, you know God won't let you go. Feel the heat of my hand and relax."

His eyes began to focus, and I could feel his heart slowing back down to normal. Finally he spoke. "Yeah, yeah. I feel the heat . . . I'm comin' back . . . I'll be all right."

After a few minutes the crisis passed. "Man," Elvis said as he came to himself, "your hand felt like a red-hot iron—whoa." He started to raise himself and then sat up with pillows supporting him.

"Ol' Lawrence, I thought that was it. Thank God you were here; you brought me back. I can still feel the heat from your hand." Then he added, "We can't let Daddy know about this—it'd kill him."

After a few more moments, he was smiling. He looked at my drenched shirt and said, "Is that your sweat or mine?"

Once the worst was over, I called a doctor.

Elvis and I left his bedroom and went into the outer suite, where a few of the guys were sitting around. Elvis looked a bit disheveled, and I got some strange glances. If they only knew.

Dr. Ghanem was in another room talking with Vernon and a few of the guys. I got his attention and then privately told him that Elvis had been hyperventilating earlier and that his heart was beating rapidly. He told me not to worry—that he'd check Elvis later.

Later that night, backstage

A few moments before showtime, Elvis and I stood behind the curtain. A few of the guys were standing around as well as some police officers and stagehands. Elvis felt extremely weak and he mumbled, "Larry, my throat is killing me. Give me a healing. Lay your hands on me."

"Elvis, there are a lot of guys looking at you. Are you sure you don't mind everyone watching?"

Elvis answered with a serious tone, "I need to be healed. It doesn't matter what they think; maybe it'll do 'em some good." The two of us stood motionless as I said a short prayer. Elvis ended with three amens. I placed my hands on his throat, then on his heart, and finally on his head. We must have been quite a sight.

DECEMBER 12, 1976

Closing Night. Finally.

Elvis probably had no idea how bad this tour would be when he told me a few weeks ago about big changes that had to be made. These have been two weeks I'll never forget. This run has been a long and dreary one. Elvis is a wreck. He won't—and can't—stop. And now Ginger. He's killing himself striving for her love and attention. I don't think she understands what is going on; what all the dynamics involved are. She never talks to anyone, but as Elvis says, she listens. But what is she listening to?

The closing-night party ended at around four-thirty in the morning. After everyone left, Elvis, Ginger and I sat around talking about the tour. Elvis turned to Ginger and said, "Well, honey, now that you've had your first taste of showbiz, what do you think of it?" It was obvious that he took great pleasure in exposing his new love to the bigger world; a world that, ironically, was so quickly closing in on him.

"It's very interesting," she replied flatly. "I'm really enjoying myself."

Elvis was pleased and continued cheerfully, "And it was so great to see so many of my friends who came to see my show. I mean, Merv Griffin, Liza Minnelli, Wayne Newton, Engelbert, Roy Orbison, Glen Campbell. I had a good talk with Glen. Honey, you really would be surprised. We had a deep talk in the dressing room about life, God, religion. He's really a very sensitive guy, and he's been through many changes. He's not like his image, I'll tell you that." Elvis had been on a roll, but at this last thought he paused. "Well, that's usually the case. Do you think the public knows about me? No way! They know about Elvis, the image, but not me. They have no idea about the inner me, or all the changes I go through."

This single thought had obsessed Elvis before he and I even met, and here, over thirteen years later, it continued to haunt him. I could see that he'd come no closer to closing the gap between the two Elvises. Just as his thoughts threatened to turn even darker, he suddenly grinned, turned to me and winked.

"Lord knows, I've been through a few changes just in the last few days." He glanced at Ginger to check her reaction to his little compliment; she was asleep.

Elvis and I walked out to the balcony. Silently we each surveyed the awesome view. All of Las Vegas, with its gaudy neon, sparkled like a cheap gemstone against the subtle hues of early morning. There was a cool, soft breeze. The world felt fresh and new.

"When I look into Ginger's eyes, I see my mom's eyes," Elvis said quietly. "She makes me think of a youthful version of my mom. When I look into her eyes, I fall in. Ginger is what I've been looking for. This is it—this relationship is totally different from the others.

"Like my mom, she's moral. We've only kissed and fooled around a little bit, and I mean a little. We haven't gone all the way. I've held back, and that's what I'm going to keep doing. Man, that girl in there is pure. She would never hurt me. I'm finally falling *in* love with a woman."

From the way Elvis spoke, it sounded as though he wasn't trying to convince just me, but himself. He sensed my reservations about Ginger. He may have shared them.

"What do you think?" he asked.

"I know how you feel and where you're coming from," I began gently. "I'm aware of the anguish and pain you keep within yourself. But, Elvis, I have to tell you how I truly see it. That's what you really want to know, isn't it?"

He nodded.

"First off, I like Ginger. She seems like a good person, but you've only been together a short two weeks, and in that time it's been a roller-coaster ride. The truth always comes out. Slow down, give it some time, and you'll know one way or another. I could be wrong, but remember, Ginger's just turned twenty."

Elvis looked solemn, then said, "Yeah, I met Priscilla when she was just fourteen."

"That's right," I replied. "And look how that turned out. Look how you're still suffering. I really think Ginger is a symbol for you. She represents a composite of many factors that are affecting you: her youth, her beauty, her innocence, her morals, the connection you feel between her and your mother. Elvis, if this is the one—and I have my doubts—time will tell."

"Lawrence, you're right. But I still want Ginger."

DECEMBER 13, 1976

We should have left for home after the show closed last night, but Elvis was too fatigued to move. Hopefully we will leave tonight. Christmas is only nine days away, and the next tour kicks off two days after that.

9 P.M.

I walked down to the gambling casino. It was beginning to look like the night we arrived. The casino was almost empty. The crowds had gone. As I scanned the large gambling room, there was one group circled around one of the tables. I approached and saw Colonel Parker sitting at the table where the game "The Wheel of Fortune" was being played. The curious who gathered to see the famed Colonel were blocked off for the Colonel's safety and convenience.

I stood watching Colonel Parker steadily lose huge piles of chips. The Colonel—smoking his perennial large cigar, and with enormous bravado, blowing out large smoke rings as if he were winning millions—called out, "Larry, come over here and sit with me and bring me some luck; I need it." For the next two hours he steadily lost. He was losing so badly that not even the Midas touch would help him out of the hole he was in. I politely excused myself and left.

2 A.M.

I took another stroll into the gambling casino. I looked over at the Colonel's table, where he still sat, still with a cigar in his mouth that was being chewed upon furiously. As I walked behind the outskirts of the crowd, I overheard rumors of losses ranging from one to one and a half million dollars.

Around 5 A.M.

Elvis came out of his suite shouting angrily, "Let's get out of this town before it bankrupts us!"

The following day we left Las Vegas, each of us going our separate way, home to see families and get ready for the next tour, a five-city, five-date run beginning in Wichita on the twenty-seventh and culminating with a New Year's Eve show in Pittsburgh. On Christmas Eve I was at home in Los Angeles when Elvis called from Graceland, sounding very happy and full of life.

"Merry Christmas, Lawrence," he said cheerfully. "I wish you were here."

"Merry Christmas, Elvis. You sound good. How are you feeling?"

"Great. The ol' battery is recharged, and I'm ready to get back on the road again. This will be a short one, so I think Lisa, Daddy and Ginger's mother and sisters will come along. Ginger says she'll feel better if they're with us. Well, whatever makes her happy."

"How is everything with you and Ginger?"

"Hey, man, I think this one is gonna work out according to the master plan. I think she feels the same. By the way, pick out a good book for Ginger; you know, something basic."

I promised I would and then told him I would fly to Wichita and meet him at the hotel.

"No, no, Lawrence," he said adamantly. "You can't do that. Just fly here the day after tomorrow, and bring me some books and Ginger's book. This way we can spend some time before the tour begins, and we can fly to Wichita together."

"Come on, E, I want to spend some time with my family."

"I know, I know," he answered in mock exasperation, knowing he'd get his way, no matter what. "But you gotta fix my hair, and this is the perfect time. Plus, we'll have some time to talk, and I really need to talk with you, so just be here? I'll make it up to you—you won't be sorry."

"Okay, Elvis. I'll see you tomorrow." Though over the years I'd been able to say no to Elvis many times, now I just couldn't. There were so few positive things happening in his life, and it was hard to shake the feeling that time was running out.

I arrived at Graceland after six on the evening of the twenty-sixth. Compared to the crowds Elvis used to invite there during Christmas week in the sixties, Graceland was practically deserted. Only Grandma, Aunt Delta, Mary, the maid, David Stanley and Charlie Hodge were there, and Lisa Marie was visiting from California. I called Elvis' room from the kitchen, and he asked me to come up.

As I ascended the staircase to the second floor, I saw Lisa Marie sitting listlessly on the floor outside her father's bedroom door, just staring at nothing.

"Hi, Lisa, honey," I said, trying to cheer her up. "Merry Christmas! What did you get from your daddy for Christmas?"

"A golf cart," she replied nonchalantly, "so I can drive *myself* around Graceland."

"Oh, that sounds like great fun. Will you take me for a ride later?"

She nodded yes, then looked up at me and said, "Larry, is my daddy up yet?"

This scene was becoming too familiar. Lisa often waited for long periods of time for Elvis to get up and get himself together. Often he awoke too groggy to deal with her or anyone. Her time with him was so precious that she naturally wanted to be with him constantly. I tried explaining the situation so that she wouldn't feel hurt.

"Yes, Lisa, he's up, but he needs to see me right away. I have to give him a haircut for the tour tomorrow."

It wasn't enough, and as I entered the room I turned to see Lisa peering inside the door, a look of longing and sadness on her face.

Once I was inside, Elvis rose and greeted me with the customary bear hug. Then he gave me that familiar sly grin, indicating that he knew he'd gotten his way, because I was there. Quickly, however, his mood changed to one of annoyance.

"Ginger's not here. Had to go home and spend some time with her mother—again. Man, is she attached to her family, running over there every time her mother or sister calls."

"Well, good," I replied. "That'll give us some time to do your hair." When he saw that I didn't share in his annoyance over Ginger's absence, he shrugged and changed the subject.

"Right. Well, we'll do it later. What about my books? Did you bring them?"

"Are you kidding? Have you ever seen me come without books?"

He smiled as I handed him a stack of new titles.

"Which one is for Ginger?"

I removed another book from my briefcase. "Here, E, a deluxe edition of *The Prophet*. This way she can have her own copy, and a special one, so Merry Christmas."

"That's a beautiful copy," he said, examining the slipcase. "It's better than mine, but I'll give it to Ginger. She'll love it." He paused, then joked, "*The Prophet*, eh? I think we should change the spelling to p-r-o-f-i-t. I've spent over a hundred thousand dollars on her already, and it's not even been a month. A car for her, one for her mother, clothes, rings, bracelets. I'm only kidding, you know. I love her. Daddy's really happy I found someone I really care for, but he thinks I'm spending too much money too fast on her. I told him, 'Daddy, don't worry. I know what I'm doing. We're not going broke.'"

Billy Smith came in to make some adjustments on the videocassette player, and when the door opened I remembered Lisa sitting out in the hall. As I told Elvis of my encounter with her on the way in, he lowered his head. When he looked up and tried to speak, words failed him. Anguished, he said, "Good Lord, Larry, every day, whenever I wake up, she's outside my door. Sittin', playin', waitin'—waitin' for me. I tried to explain to her that I don't get up early like everyone else. She's my whole life—what the hell am I doing to my baby? Damn, I'm going to spend time with Lisa."

Later that evening he and Lisa played together.

DECEMBER 27, 1976

5:30 P.M., aboard the Lisa Marie

We flew from Memphis to Wichita, Kansas. I cut and styled Elvis' hair on the plane before the show. He seemed relieved and back in stride again. While I was blow-drying his hair he said to Charlie and me, gratefully, "Thank God we're back on the road. I mean, singing, being on-stage, making people happy—that's my life's blood. That's my moment of glory."

DECEMBER 30, 1976

Backstage at the Omni, Atlanta

Joe came in and said that Billy Carter was outside and would like to come in to say hello. Elvis was pleased, and said, "Sure, I'd love to meet the new President's brother."

Joe returned a few minutes later with an entourage of about ten Secret Service agents protecting President-elect Jimmy Carter's younger brother. In the shape Billy was in, he needed protection. He staggered in, swaying back and forth and barely staying on his feet, drunk as a sailor. Elvis looked over at us, surprised at this sight—and at all those Secret Service men in their clean business suits monitoring Billy's every move as he careened off the walls. When the group left the dressing room, Elvis humorously gave an exaggerated look of awe and exclaimed, "Man, they should use his breath as a national-defense weapon; it nearly knocked me out!"

DECEMBER 31, 1976

Pittsburgh

The drive to the auditorium tonight was bleak and depressing. The old buildings, the abandoned factories. It seems time itself has stood still. Pittsburgh reminded me of newsreel footage of the Great Depression. Here it is, 1976 going on 1977, and it appears nothing has changed in decades.

As the clock countdown approached midnight, the crowd, still wild, would not let Elvis go. Now every night's performance seems wired with the energy of a full moon. Pandemonium has become commonplace. Elvis proudly introduces Ginger to the audience at every show. He also introduces his daddy, who always receives a loud ovation.

By two in the morning we were back at the Hilton, in Elvis' room. Elvis, worried about Vernon traveling in sub-zero weather, said, "Larry, I think we should fly back to Memphis and get Daddy home. It's too damn cold here. What do you think?"

"I agree," I replied just as the phone rang. When I answered, a voice said, "Is Mr. Presley available to speak with President Carter?"

Covering the receiver, I relayed the request to Elvis, who nodded. "Happy New Year to you, Mr. President," Elvis said. All I heard for the next ten minutes was Elvis saying, "Yes," "I'd love to," "It sounds good," and "It would be an honor." Elvis was positively beaming when he hung up.

"Lawrence," he said excitedly, "I've been invited to Washington. President Carter just asked me to be a special adviser to him on the youth of America, the music scene and other projects. Man, I can't believe it! He said he would like to have a special meeting with me after the Inauguration, for me to come over to the White House."

Elvis got most of his information from television news programs and documentaries. He preferred watching television to reading because it was quick and immediate and told him all he felt he needed to know. He had no interest in politics, which is interesting considering how pro-America he was. His attitude toward voting was typical of Elvis. He believed that everyone should exercise their right to vote, yet he never did so himself. He worried that he'd create too great a commotion at the polling place, and deep inside he didn't think his one vote really counted anyway.

While Elvis had no use for the more mundane aspects of the political process, grand plans such as this one inspired him. He always had a vague idea of things that he could do to help the country, like helping fight the war against drugs. Elvis saw this as an important contribution he could make. "I'd love to serve my country and use whatever influence I have. And you can help and be *my* adviser. Yeah! Mr. Carter said he would create a special post for me." As distant as the possibility seemed, Elvis was totally absorbed. I realized for the millionth time how few challenges Elvis' life presented him, how few opportunities to do something outside his little universe.

5:55 A.M.
Aboard the Lisa Marie

To top all of our miseries, after an icy wind blew us across the airstrip we entered a subzero airplane. Elvis' Convair 880's heaters took over twenty minutes before they began emitting any heat. Everyone was frozen, teeth chattering, and unable to move. We all quickly huddled together, with blankets covering us, until we finally felt some semblance of heat. Then we took our seats and awaited departure. The control tower radioed Captain Elwood and told him there would be a delay, as there were two separate phone warnings of bombs hidden on the plane, timed to explode after takeoff. Captain Elwood told Joe we couldn't get clearance to leave unless we signed a waiver assuming full responsibility.

Finally we prepared for takeoff. There was an eerie silence for the first two or three minutes, although we all sensed it was a hoax. Or was it? What a way to start the new year. I pray 1977 will be a better one than 1976.

CHAPTER

9

JANUARY 3, 1977

Graceland

I was blow-drying Elvis' hair when he looked up at me and said, "Lawrence, I just realized why my first attraction to Priscilla happened: It's reincarnation. How else would a grown-up man be so drawn to a fourteen-year-old girl? Man . . . I used to think she was my soul mate."

Elvis laughed to himself, as if to say, What a fool I was, and continued. "Now I know she wasn't the one; at least, not my real *soul mate. She was only a dress rehearsal, Larry, not the real thing. It must be some sort of karma we obviously had together, only I'm sure it's all from another life."*

7:40 P.M.

We flew back to the West Coast. Lisa and I were dropped off in Los Angeles, where I escorted her home in the limo awaiting us at the VIP airport next to LAX. Elvis flew on to Palm Springs, where I'm to join him in a few days.

JANUARY 8, 1977

Palm Springs, California

When I arrived at Elvis' house this afternoon, a few of the guys asked to talk to me privately. They wanted to go to the bookstore and buy Elvis some spiritual books for his

*birthday today. They had no idea what to select and asked
me for a list.*

*How ironic: They bitch and complain because they have
to carry his trunks filled with his portable library; they
have no philosophical, psychological, metaphysical or
spiritual bent; they scoff at anything we study; they laugh
behind Elvis' back and at me openly. Now they are anxious to bring him material they don't believe in or want
anything to do with themselves!*

6:15 P.M.

*Elvis came out of his bedroom after I styled his hair. He
looked especially good tonight. Today is his forty-second
birthday, and he had on a black suit with a blue silk shirt.
In his hand was a stack of crisp new one-hundred-dollar
bills. After everyone gave him their birthday gifts (mine
was a complete assortment of vitamins and minerals), Elvis said, "Would you guys excuse us? I wanna talk with
the ladies privately."*

*For the next one and a half hours Elvis gave the wives
and girlfriends of his group a spiritual dissertation and
read passage after passage from some of his favorite spiritual books. He then gave them each a hundred-dollar bill
and said, "This is my birthday, and what makes me happy
is not just receiving gifts, but giving. This is my gift to
you."*

JANUARY 9, 1977

Palm Springs

*The whole group was gathered in the living room, waiting
for Elvis to come out of his bedroom. Finally, after eight,
he and Ginger appeared, and he announced, "I'm gonna
have the manager of Robinson's open the store tonight so
that Ginger can go shopping, and I want all the ladies to
go with her and pick out whatever they want for themselves. I'll send Dick and a few guys from security so that
no one will bother you. Y'all should have a great time; the*

store is all for you. So pick out whatever you need. And keep an eye on Ginger. Make sure she doesn't go hog-wild," he said jokingly.

The next tour wouldn't start until mid-February, so I returned home and resumed work on my book. Of course I thought of Elvis often, especially after the last eight weeks. Elvis always had his highs and lows, but this was something else. His happiness over Ginger was all-consuming, and yet he expressed the doubts many of us had about her. No sooner would he indicate that he realized there was something amiss in their relationship than he'd be off again, rhapsodizing about her and their future together. Generally, just about everyone in the entourage was cool toward Ginger. Only Rick and David defended her. They were the closest to her in age and attributed her quietness to the fact that she was young and probably uncomfortable in Elvis' environment.

I was sound asleep when my phone rang in the wee hours of January 13. It was Elvis. He was in Palm Springs, and he wanted me to rush down and perform a marriage ceremony for his friends Dr. Max Shapiro, his dentist, and his fiancée, Susanne, that evening. He sounded happier than I'd heard him in a long time. Thirty minutes later I was on a flight to Palm Springs, and before dawn I had pronounced Max and Susanne man and wife.

After Max, Susanne and I had hugged and everyone had congratulated the new married couple, Elvis said softly, "Lawrence, would you come in my bedroom and talk to me and Ginger?"

Once I was in the bedroom he embraced me. The three of us sat on his bed, and Elvis exclaimed, "Larry, that was the best wedding ceremony I ever witnessed. I mean, did you feel the presence, the spirit in that room?" Choked with emotion, he then turned to Ginger. "Honey, what did I tell you?"

She broke her silence and said, "Yes, Larry, that really was special."

Elvis then continued dramatically, "I knew this was really going to be something, but that service went beyond my expectations. What really got me was that most ceremonies just go through the motions. They always use the right words, but the words are dead, like there's no life, no spirit, behind them. That room was filled with light and the holy spirit. That's the way weddings should be—not just religious, but spiritual."

Elvis paused, looked around the room, then at Ginger, then me. Almost blushing now, he softened his dramatic tone of voice and stammered, "Larry, I haven't even told this to Ginger, but now is as good a time as ever." He paused. "A few nights ago I had a vivid dream. Ginger appeared before me dressed all in white. She looked like the perfect bride." Clasping Ginger's hands, he said to her, "Honey, I knew we sort of touched on the subject of marriage a few times recently, but I want Larry to marry us—just like the ceremony tonight. Do you agree?"

Ginger's face lit up at the mention of marriage. She was speechless for a moment, then she smiled and answered, "Yes, of course."

Elvis stroked her face and kissed her.

"Lawrence," he began as a smile of victory stole over his face, "Lawrence, will you marry us?"

"Yes, of course. It will be an honor."

In my heart of hearts, I strongly doubted that their marriage would ever take place. Elvis was caught up in the moment's emotion and promise, and Ginger went along.

Elvis assumed a serious tone. "Now, don't tell anyone; this is our secret. I don't know yet when we'll do it. Probably toward the end of summer—August or September. We'll have to wait and see. I'm sure everything will happen the way it's supposed to."

At around six in the morning I left Elvis' bedroom and walked into the living room, where a few of the guys were sitting around. Every now and then throughout the marriage ceremony I'd caught several of them yawning or rolling their eyes as I read from the Bible or the Self-Realization Creed. One of them remarked now, "Well, here comes the wandering rabbi."

"Tell me something," I said. "Who is your Lord and Savior?"

With great pride and assurance he replied, "Jesus."

"That's right," I said. "Jesus, a nice Jewish rabbi.
Welcome to the fold. In fact, everyone who wrote the Old
and New Testaments was Jewish, except for Luke, and he
was half Jewish. You know that chai Elvis always wears
around his neck? He wears it because he feels connected
to the Jewish faith. Why don't you tell *him* how you feel?"

No one answered. I turned into the hallway, and there
stood Elvis. He put his arm around my shoulder and took
me aside, out of earshot of the guys.

"Larry, you know I know what's goin' on around me.
I've been aware of what you've been called for years. Actually, you're lucky: it only proves one thing." Then Elvis
assumed a melodramatic tone and proclaimed, "The darkness hates the light."

I left Palm Springs, anxious to get back home. Late on
the evening of the twenty-third, Elvis called from Graceland.

"Larry, tell me one thing: Why am I sitting here at
Graceland?" he demanded, clearly frustrated. "What the
hell is going on? I need to be out there. Why aren't I
working? I feel myself wasting away here. I mean, I
haven't done a show all month. What the hell is happening, huh?"

Calmly I replied, "Elvis, you should be happy to have
a short break—"

"Hey, easy for you to say," he shot back. "At least
you're writing a book between tours, while they have me
here in some kind of holding pattern."

"E, take advantage of these few weeks off. You've been
working yourself into an early grave. You need a rest, you
know that. Plus, there's no shows touring right now anyway. Most of the country is snowed in. They say this is
the coldest winter of this century; it even snowed in Florida. So relax. You really need to. Maybe it's a blessing in
disguise."

"Yeah, but what about the fans?" Elvis asked impatiently. "They expect to see me. They don't care about
the bad weather. I can't let them down. If it weren't for

my fans I wouldn't be where I am now. They put me here.
I owe everything to them.''

I again listed all the reasons why he wasn't out on tour,
but he wasn't listening.

"We all need you, Elvis, but we need you healthy and
well. So," I added cheerily, "here's the ideal situation:
record-breaking bad weather. Your fans will understand if
you're home for a couple more weeks. You have to get
well.''

Elvis broke in sharply to avoid the subject of his health,
and it became clear what was actually bothering him.
"And the fans are gonna read those lies in that goddamn
filthy book that's comin' out. Those guys are trying to kill
me. I can't fathom it. My oldest friends—lifelong friends—
and now they're trying to distort my image to the public
and my fans.''

"Elvis," I pleaded, "let it go for now. You've got to
calm yourself and think of more important, more positive
things. You're loved, man. Your fans would go to the ends
of the earth—''

"I know! I know!" he shouted. Then, as if to reassure
himself, he said, "Hey, the fans are not dumb. They won't
believe this. They'll see through it. My fans are very special. They know the truth.''

"Right on, Elvis. All you have to do is live your life
and do the best you can. The fans will never leave you.
You couldn't get rid of them if you tried.''

"Hey, I told Daddy about the wedding you did in Palm
Springs and what our plans are. He's a little overly cautious, you know. He said, 'Go slow, son.' " Then, resum-
ing his confidence, Elvis signed off with "Well, just get
your butt down here as soon as possible, you hear?''

As his friend, I tried to walk the line between sharing
his happiness about Ginger and letting him know that it
was okay to express his doubts. I certainly had my own.
In early February he asked me to come to Graceland earlier than planned. It was typical of Elvis to call and ask
people to rearrange their plans on a moment's notice, but
suddenly he seemed particularly in need of companionship, and he wasn't taking no for an answer.

On the evening of February 2, I was working at my desk when the phone rang. It was Elvis.

"Lawrence," he said enthusiastically, "I need to talk to you. I need you *here*. Phones serve their purpose, but there's nothing like personal contact; you know, eyeball to eyeball. Look, I want to buy you a new condominium here in Whitehaven. That way I'll save all these long-distance phone bills, and you should be here anyway. I mean, I'll buy you one free and clear, the most expensive condo in Memphis—"

"Elvis, that's a beautiful offer. I really appreciate it, and I'd love that, only I can't accept, not right now anyway. I have to be here in L.A. between tours to complete the book and be with my family. At least for the next six months. You know what this book means to me. Can I take a rain check?"

Knowing that I was determined, Elvis gracefully gave in. "Well, I understand," he replied. "I want you to finish your book. I believe in it. I know it will help people, and I'm proud of you, so you got your rain check.

"But, Larry, listen carefully, son. I'm not exactly sure, but in the past few months I've been having prophetic-type dreams, and last night I had one that was somethin' else. I mean, it was a dream, only it was more than just a mere dream. It was real—it was like a direct message."

Elvis' voice took on a more solemn tone, and I could hear him sigh. "I dreamt that Ginger and I were outside, in the back of Graceland, by the fence. Ginger was dressed all in white." After a moment's silence, he began again, as if just struck by a revelation. "Whoa, Ginger was wearing white in that other dream I told you about. White, huh?" Then to himself he mumbled, "White is definitely symbolic. Larry, what do you think white represents?"

"Well, basically white represents purity, and the Divine—"

Elvis broke in. "Hey, wait a minute. Let me find that book you gave me, *Color and Music in the New Age*. It's here somewhere. Hold on."

I could hear Elvis asking the book where it was hiding, then he returned to the phone. He thumbed through the pages and then read, " 'As all creation is inherent in God Himself, so does the Great White Light contain within itself all the colors of the spectrum. And it plays directly upon the divinity within—within man. As his latent divinity is awakened, he comes into attunement with the White Light as a power.' " Elvis muttered softly to himself as he skimmed over some irrelevant passages before continuing. " 'The Glorious One who manifests through the White Ray is beyond all planets, all stars, all constellations. Him we identify only as The Supreme Being.' "

Then he took another book by the same author and read, " 'White Light is weighted with the power to bless. It is God, speaking through the manifold activities of creation.' "

Elvis was on a roll, searching for the meaning of his dream. He seemed happiest when he was looking for answers.

"All right, listen to the rest of my dream. The best is yet to come." He paused for dramatic effect, then said, "Okay. Ginger's dressed all in white—like the other dream—and she also has on a white shawl over her shoulders. We're holding hands and gazing into each other's eyes when—you won't believe this—Ginger turns into my mother, even her voice.

"I mean, it *was* my mother! The eyes never changed— Ginger *became* my mother. They were wearing white, the same clothes, but those eyes! Ginger's eyes and my mother's eyes were exactly the same, piercing right through me, looking into my very core. I can still see them, right now. It was that vivid.

"Then suddenly Sun [one of Elvis' horses] walks over to us when Ginger becomes my mother. Not a word is spoken. We are communicating with our eyes. Our eyes are locked. Then my mother mounts Sun—bareback."

Elvis stopped for a second, amused by this last detail. "That's right—she was bareback. I'm sure that means something, too. Then my mother, with our eyes fixed, says, 'Son, our love is eternal, I'll never do anything to hurt you, you know that, never. No matter what, our love for each other is unconditional.' Then as she starts to ride off, she stops, turns back, and from a distance she says, 'I'll never hurt you like Priscilla did. Elvis, I know how you suffered, I know the deep burden you carry within yourself, but face it—she was immoral.'

"Good God, Larry," he said, choked with emotion, "as she begins to turn and ride off, she becomes Ginger again, and she and Sun start to gallop and fly into the sky and clouds, and all I hear is, 'I'll never leave you, I'll never leave you.' And they fade out, just like a movie in living color. That was not just a mere dream. That was a divine message, don't you think?"

"Elvis, I agree with you: it was not a mere dream. The symbolism has so many ramifications and connections to your life. The dream is loaded with meaning and possible interpretations."

Elvis then replied, "Seriously, Larry, I really think there's something profound here. Help me."

When I arrived at Graceland on February 10, I called Elvis' bedroom from the kitchen, and he asked me to come upstairs immediately. He and Vernon were sitting on the edge of the bed. Vernon hung his head and gazed at the floor, puffing on a cigarette, while Elvis shook his head from side to side in disgust. He was still in his blue bathrobe; his hair was disheveled and matted. Spiritual books covered the bed and were stacked upon the nightstand, next to vials and bottles of laxatives, eyedrops, nose spray, atomizers and various medications. Both television sets were on, with the sound turned off.

"Remember our last tour in Vegas?" Elvis asked rhetorically. "Well, I heard the Colonel lost one point four million dollars." His rage seemed to build with each word. Vernon sat silently, his head engulfed in a cloud of smoke.

"Larry," Elvis continued, "*one point four million*—in one night. Man, that's outrageous. Most people don't make that kind of money working hard for their entire lives. And he lost it in one damn night gamblin' in Sin City!" He turned to Vernon. "Daddy, you were probably right. We should've gotten rid of him back in seventy-four."

Mr. Presley glanced up and weakly shrugged his shoulders, as if to indicate it was all beyond his control and always had been. "Well, son, you always knew how I felt about him, and you remember how your mama felt about him. She thought we were all bein' taken in, but you're the boss."

After a long silence, Elvis muttered under his breath. "Yeah, Mama was always right." Then his voice grew louder. "Look, don't get me wrong. I'm grateful to the Colonel for all he's done. I've always been loyal to him—and everyone else. That's my nature. Only, like the song says, 'The times they are a-changin',' and I think his time is about up. Gentlemen, let me put it this way: I think we need some new blood."

He stopped, then repeated, practically snarling, "Man, one point four million dollars, blown in one night!

"I like Mr. Barron Hilton—he's a good man—but damn, I don't ever want to go back to Vegas again and perform. Ever. And I won't. One point four million, that's downright immoral. Something's gotta change. I don't know what it is yet, but things are definitely gonna be different around here."

As Vernon slowly rose to go, he said wearily, "Elvis, I think I'd better get home now. It's gettin' past my bedtime, son." The weight of this problem was too much for Vernon.

Elvis got up to embrace his father and said lovingly, "Well, Daddy, don't you worry yourself. As long as I'm around, everything will be all right."

Vernon, looking pale and weak, replied, "Well, son, I know it will, too. Don't worry about me. Good night, Elvis. Good night, Larry." When he reached the door, he turned and said, "Try not to stay up all night worrying yourself to death over the ol' Colonel. It ain't worth it. You gotta get ready and go on tour, you know."

"Daddy, this too shall pass. You know me, I just had to get it off my chest. Larry is here. He'll fix my hair and you know us, we'll ponder the universe and figure it all out. It'll be all right. I love you, Daddy."

Vernon nodded. "I love you, too, Evis."

With Vernon gone, Elvis said, "Daddy has always resented the Colonel. He thinks he's taken advantage of his position. He'd love me to get rid of the Colonel's ol' ass. That's firstly what I'm gonna do.''

Elvis' face hid nothing, and when he spoke those words he looked as though he was going to—finally—avenge himself.

A couple of days later we left for a tour of the South and the Southwest. In West Palm Beach I met a fan who told me that hearing Elvis' recording of ''How Great Thou Art'' had saved her from committing suicide. Her name was Darlene, and after a long talk in the Hilton coffee shop I told her of the circumstances surrounding the recording and promised I would let Elvis know about her. Who knows how many other stories there were like Darlene's that Elvis would never know?

FEBRUARY 12, 1977

Hilton Hotel, West Palm Beach, Florida

Elvis, Ginger and a few of the guys were sitting around the suite. Elvis was still in his robe and hadn't begun preparing for tonight's show. I asked to speak with him privately in the bedroom. Elvis sat on the edge of the bed as I told Darlene's story and my account of what happened over ten years ago in Nashville.

Elvis was moved. He stood up and walked to the window, contemplating the story. After a long silence he said, ''God works in mysterious ways, Lawrence, that's for sure.'' He turned and looked out the window. What a sight: here's Elvis Presley, wearing his blue bathrobe with its hood up, gazing out his guarded room with a look on his face like he's trying to figure out the riddle of the ages.

He shifted his weight from one leg to the other, turned his head to me and calmly and lovingly said, ''All I ever wanted was to help people; love them, lift them up, spread some joy.'' Elvis was reaching for the significance of Darlene's story. ''That girl downstairs, man, she's the living proof, Lawrence. You know, I've told you many times that my moment of glory is being on that stage and singing and

*feeling all the love the audience sends to me. It's a com-
pleted circle of love we send each other. If you could experience that for one moment, you would know what I was
talking about. It's beyond any mortal high, I'll tell you
that.*

"What did you say her name was?" he asked.

"Darlene."

*"Right. Darlene. Well, if that happened to Darlene,
what about others? This means more to me than experiencing 'my moment of glory.' I mean, a person's life was
saved! That's a fulfillment that transcends everything.*

*"Remember when you flashed me about my only true
love affair? You hit the nail on the head. I've never had a
lasting love affair like everyone else—and I'm a person,
too."*

*Elvis was on the verge of tears. "Do you realize I'll
never know if a woman loves me"—he pointed at his chest
with his finger—"or Elvis Presley?*

*"Me, not the image. I'm real. I have feelings. How can
I ever know which one they're loving? I'll never know."
Elvis glanced toward Ginger's room. "I'll never know."*

The Valentine's Day show in St. Petersburg was marred
by more death threats. Elvis had just gone onstage, and I
was walking to the wings, where I usually sat, when a fan
waved me over and told me someone was planning to kill
Elvis. I passed the word on to Dick Grob, the head of
security, who informed me that there was already a bomb
squad in the auditorium, and that we were all to intercept
any gifts handed to Elvis and pass them backstage. Elvis
didn't know what was happening, and as David Stanley,
Dean Nichopoulos, Ed and I grabbed the teddy bears,
cards, flowers and other gifts the eager fans passed to the
stage, Elvis looked at us but didn't pay too much attention.
Meanwhile we gave the packages to members of a special
police squad. There was a weirdness about the whole evening. A woman fell from a second-story balcony and broke
her leg. And when Elvis ran for his limousine, despite our
usually foolproof precautions a small mob broke through
and nearly caught him.

Inside the limousine, breathing heavily and drenched in sweat, Elvis exclaimed, "Good Lord, what the hell was goin' on tonight? I know something was up."

Joe told him of the death threats. Elvis listened, then said, "Wow!" Obviously relieved, he broke out laughing, and we all joined in. We were so tired, scared and relieved simultaneously, we couldn't even think straight.

FEBRUARY 17, 1977

DeSoto Hotel, Savannah, Georgia

Ed Parker, David Stanley and I were just being served our dinner appetizers when the host came over and asked for Mr. Geller. I identified myself, and he told me that "Mr. Presley" would like to see me right away. When I entered Elvis' suite he was standing in the middle of the room, wearing his bathrobe with the hood on. In one hand he was holding the Bible, and in the other he held an object that appeared to be a black wallet.

With all the drama of Barrymore, Elvis exclaimed, "Lawrence, get on one knee, raise your right hand and place your left one on the Good Book."

Dumbfounded, I went along, falling onto one knee as he requested. Al Strada, one of Elvis' aides, looked on silently, as if he wasn't sure what to make of us. Elvis eyed me sternly and said, "Hey, I have a certain power, too, you know," then solemnly added, "According to the powers vested in me by the State of California, I hereby swear you in as a police commissioner." His serious demeanor was quickly replaced by his old beaming smile. He handed me his personal police commission badge that had been presented to him by the Mayor of Los Angeles: a beautiful gold-plated badge with a brilliant electric-blue border and letters, and the seal of the City of Los Angeles in the center. At the bottom was just ELVIS.

FEBRUARY 20, 1977

Hilton Hotel, Charlotte, North Carolina

I was walking toward the coffee shop when my new friend Darlene approached me with a large manila envelope under her arm. She said, "Larry, I've got to talk to you; it's serious."

"Sure," I said, "what's up?"

Darlene looked around to make sure we weren't being overheard.

"Larry, you know the book that is supposed to come out by the bodyguards Elvis fired? Well, it's going to." She pointed to the envelope. "One of the fans got her little hands on this at Ballantine Books in New York and made a copy for me. And I made one for you."

She handed me the yellow envelope. "They're trying to crucify him. Wait until you read what I just gave you. My friend said the book will be out in paperback only in late July or August. Larry, I'm giving this to you because I know you'll handle it in the way you figure best."

I thanked Darlene, gave her a hug and told her to keep this to herself. She concluded by saying, "Are you kidding? This is top secret, and I'm glad to help Elvis."

I immediately went to my room and read the material. The Xeroxed pages look like galley proofs and speak of Elvis being wiped out on drugs and wanting Mike Stone killed for stealing Priscilla away from him. Judging from these two pages, the former bodyguards are twisting the facts so that it seems that Elvis would, in fact, do such an outrageous, ludicrous act as committing murder, or contracting it out.

A writer for The Star *and former bodyguards—my head reels to think how they can blow everything out of proportion. Elvis has mentioned going on a vacation to Hawaii in a couple of weeks. This information would kill that idea, and he desperately needs to get away from this maddening pace, relax, rejuvenate and hopefully, rethink everything.*

I told Joe and Ed about the galleys. Joe said, "Don't tell Elvis, whatever you do. This would really knock him out."

A few hours later I was sitting with Elvis in his room. He was propped up in bed reading a book. He peered over his glasses, put the book back on his lap and said with a self-conscious laugh, "It almost happened last night. I don't even believe I'm sayin' this, but it's true. I mean, we started kissing and all that—Larry, this was the first time since Ginger and I have been together that we both were so aroused. I mean, it was that close, but I stopped. I'm telling you, this is different, and I'll do my damnedest not to spoil anything. For the first time in my life I feel I'm doing the complete moral thing. No one would believe it, but it's true, and Ginger understands.

"I haven't heard one single cuss word out of Ginger's mouth yet, and I respect her for it," he continued, obviously pleased. "I want this relationship to be right. I know, others might laugh, but to hell with them. Sex energy is the strongest energy in the body, and if you don't learn to control it, master it, it will master and control you. Sex is one of the greatest gifts of God, but it'll remain a gift only if we don't abuse it."

Elvis picked up the book from his lap, *The Rosicrucian Cosmo-Conception,* and waved it in the air as he said, "All the teachings say it. You know, most people reject the spiritual side of life and escape through their five senses. They unconsciously allow themselves to be ruled by the strongest urge we have. I'm no prude, that's for sure, only I know that being ruled solely by our animal nature will never bring us true enjoyment."

Laughing, he said, "Remember when I told you about when I was drafted back in 1958? For about a week before I was to report I went hog-wild. I would screw anything in sight, and I did! But we're not machines, we need more than the physical act, and I needed to go through that and see it for myself. Ever since then I need much more: I need to feel something for the woman. Otherwise, to me, it's a waste and a bore. There's more to life."

Elvis was preaching to the converted, but I listened patiently. His devotion to the teachings was sincere, but his reason for talking about it ran much deeper. Elvis rarely mentioned it, understandably, but he had been physically impotent for some time, the result of the drugs and his generally poor condition. Rather than let his impotence eat away at him, as most men would, he tried to redefine his lack of sexual capability in spiritual terms. What other choice did he have? Just then Ginger walked into the room.

"Honey, where have you been?" Elvis asked sweetly.

"Oh, I was in my bedroom talking to my mom," Ginger replied. Then noting the look of frustration on Elvis' face, she added, "She needed to talk with me."

Turning to me and deliberately speaking loudly enough that Ginger would hear, Elvis quoted from *The Prophet*, " 'When love beckons to you, follow him, though his ways are hard and steep.' "

Charlotte Coliseum, Charlotte, North Carolina

Elvis just went onstage as they played his opening theme. I packed my hairstyling tools, then proceeded to the stage. As I did, I heard cries in the back of the building and saw two ladies being held back by several police officers. They were standing at the exit of the building among a crowd of people who didn't have tickets. The two ladies were wearing lace capelets and long dresses down to their ankles. They were waving their arms and pleading for me to come over.

When I approached them, they were both talking frantically at the same time. "Slow down," I said. "What can I do for you?"

The larger, more buxom one said, "You work for Elvis, don't you?"

"Yes."

She continued, her eyes bulging, "Please give him this if you want him to live," and she handed me a note.

"We've been praying for him; we were told he is going to die."

I asked, "Who told you that?"

The other woman, tiny and slender, replied with great fervor, *"The Lord told us."* Her friend cried out, *"Praise God! Praise God!"* as her eyes rolled heavenward.

The tiny lady continued her barrage: *"We were directed here tonight to deliver this message. Just give it to him, and he'll see us. We have to speak to him and tell him everything. We were told to see him and explain God's plan. If we don't see him, he will die!"*

I thanked them and said I would see what I could do. As I walked back into the building, I turned and saw them both with raised hands and heard them speaking in tongues. I read the note:

Dear Elvis:
We have been personally directed by our Lord to speak with you. Your life is in grave danger. We have a special message for you that can save you. Your own mother is very upset and concerned, and we have a message from her, too. Please take heed. We are not some nuts. This is for your good. Praise the Lord.

After holding on to the note for a day or so, I threw it away and never mentioned it to anyone. I didn't see the point. It had definitely been one of the stranger tours, and, as always, we were glad to get off the road. The first day after the tour ended we were back at Graceland, watching *The Return of the Pink Panther* on the videocassette player. Elvis had seen this dozens of times and was imitating Peter Sellers' Inspector Clouseau character, reciting the lines and laughing. Midway through the film Ginger called, and Elvis took the call in another room while Billy and I continued watching the movie. When he returned, he was angry, disappointed and disgusted.

"O ye of little faith," he said. Ginger had called to tell him she wouldn't be staying over at Graceland but would stay with her mother. "Damn, that girl's tearin' my head up. One minute she's here, the next minute she runs to her mother. I've told her to let go of her attachment. I've read to her all the teaching on growth and how negative attachments to the past will only hold you down."

Within a couple of hours, Elvis' anger gave way to total depression. "If for some reason anything should happen to me," he said sadly, "I've made sure that certain people will never have anything to worry about. Outside of Daddy, Lisa, Grandma and a few aunts, uncles and cousins, I'm talking about Billy, Charlie, David and Ricky, Joe, Jerry and you. You know how I feel about you. I don't know how to repay you. You gave me something money can't buy. You're responsible for my spiritual life, and if it weren't for you I would've been dead years ago.

"The rest of them, hell, they never talk to me. I mean, really come to me and talk. I'm not judging them, I know each and every one is here for a reason. Someday, what we're into, even the books they bitch about because they have to carry them, will rub off. They'll remember, in their own way, in their own time. Outside of you, at least I can talk to Billy, Ed and Charlie. David and Ricky are young, but they listen. They absorb a lot of information when they sit around us.

"The main thing I wanted to say, though, Larry, is that your ship will never sink. I've made sure of that. That's the least I could do. And if Ginger gets herself together, I'll have her butt covered for life, too."

I was deeply touched, though not surprised. After all, Elvis was so generous to all of us in his life. It only made sense that he would want to give something after he died. But as bad as things were going, I didn't make the connections. In my deepest thoughts, I worried about Elvis. I had even begun having dreams of saving him or Vernon from danger. The dreams bothered me, but I pushed them aside. Though all the signs were flashing, I simply couldn't believe that Elvis would die. All my hopes were tied to the upcoming vacation. Elvis loved Hawaii, and perhaps there he would find the impetus to get healthy, quit drugs, find out whatever was wrong with him and have it tended to.

MARCH 4, 1977

Rainbow Towers Hawaiian Village Hotel, Honolulu

*We're here at last on a vacation that was long overdue.
Everyone is drained from the grueling effects of being on
the road and the enormous pressures of working for Elvis
under unforeseen, horrendous conditions. The one-
nighters; the debilitating winter cold; taking care of Elvis,
an exhausting job unto itself—all have taken their toll.
Everyone looks older than they are.*

*Elvis is a driven man, and he needs this rest more than
anyone else. He desperately requires more than a short
vacation in Hawaii. Hopefully this will signal some kind
of change, because his condition is getting worse, and this
short surcease from agony is just the tonic—for the time
being. "The journey of a thousand miles begins with the
first step."*

*I can see on everyone's face the relief of just being in
this tropical paradise. The Rainbow Towers has a spec-
tacular view from the thirty-first floor. Elvis spent most of
the daylight hours on his balcony today with its panoramic
view of Waikiki Beach and Diamond Head. His suite was
open to any of the entourage, and their wives and girlfriends, who cared to come in and visit with him. He is so
happy being here, pointing out the various points of interest to all from his balcony. Ginger has two sisters, Terry
and Rosemary, with her, and Elvis is taking great pride
and joy in providing this trip for them.*

*Actually, there are thirty-eight of us: what a family Elvis
has adopted.*

*Everyone is hopeful that Elvis will take full advantage
of this golden opportunity to get outdoors, exercise and
eat better, instead of his typical fried-food diet and stuffing
himself with cheeseburgers and fried potatoes right before
he goes to sleep. Health and nurturing are everywhere.
The air is clean and aromatic, and the Hawaiian fragrance of pineapples and tropical flowers in this atmosphere has already enveloped all of us. It's so seductive.*

MARCH 5, 1977

Feeling fantastic in Hawaiian bliss, dressed loose and comfortably in my new Hawaiian floral shirt. As I entered Elvis' suite, he had just come out of his bedroom to have some breakfast. A few of the guys were hanging around on the balcony. As I approached Elvis, he smiled and greeted me with "Aloha, L.G."

"Aloha, E."

Some weeks ago, when I gave Elvis a complete kit of vitamins and minerals for his birthday, he took them for only two days. Now I felt this was an ideal opportunity to direct him toward a healthier regimen. I placed in front of him on the coffee table a packet of vitamins and minerals I had prepared.

"Take this power pack, Elvis. It will pick you up and give you some natural energy. I put in some extra E and a potent combination of the B complex, vitamin C and some minerals. If you take these every day, they will help strengthen you."

Elvis opened the vitamin pack and gulped them down with fresh orange juice. Then he looked over to me with a grin and said, "I want to get these down before Dr. Nick comes in. Remember last year when we were on tour and you came in with a load of vitamin pills like these for me? And Dr. Nick said, 'That crap doesn't work; he doesn't need those'? Well, you know, he's a doctor, and most of them are locked into the old traditional-medicine ways of doing things, that's how they've been trained. I don't want to hear him bitch and complain again. Doctors think they know everything."

For the remainder of the day Elvis stayed in his suite relaxing, spending a lot of time sitting on the balcony, enjoying the view and this incredible tropical air wafting through the open balcony windows. The majority of the group spent the day on the beach in front of the Rainbow Towers, went shopping and then went out for dinner at the various restaurants that are part of the Hilton Hawaiian Village Hotel.

MARCH 6, 1977

Oahu

Elvis decided to rent a beach house in Kailua on Kaapuni Drive, on the other side of the island. This will provide the privacy he requires, so that he can lie in the sun by the pool or go down to the beach. This afternoon we all played football together for the first time in well over a year. Elvis played so hard that Joe told him to go slowly, because he wasn't used to moving his body like that and it was dangerous for his heart. But there's no stopping Elvis once he has his mind set on something.

MARCH 7, 1977

Oahu

Elvis was sore today due to yesterday's vigorous football clash. In fact, most of us feel the effects of roughhousing it yesterday. We all sat by the ocean most of the afternoon relaxing and joking with one another, and by the expressions on everyone's face it looks as though we died and went to heaven. I can't remember the last time Elvis was outdoors in the sunshine, playing and enjoying himself so much. It's like the old days. God willing, this will shake him out of his stupor.

Strangely, he won't expose his body. No matter how hot it is, he wears his athletic pants, a short-sleeve sweatshirt, a terrycloth hat with the brim turned down and his sunglasses. Is there some other reason than the beach being open to the public?

MARCH 9, 1977

Kailua Bay

Author/inventor Bernard Benson invited Charlie, Celest and me to his beach house a few miles from Elvis'. Bernard has arranged a special meeting for us with the leading Tibetan Buddhist master of the Hawaiian Island, Rimposhe, who escaped Chinese invasion of Tibet. We first

*met Bernard in Las Vegas last December, and he's been
an avid Elvis fan ever since.*

*Rimposhe does not speak English, which, in the long
run, doesn't matter. He is a small, radiant man. I could
not take my eyes off him. He was clothed like a lama,
wearing the traditional saffron robe. His face was a very
fine Mongolian type, and beautifully formed: a high brow
with piercing yet happy eyes, and his face lit up as if the
energy of the sun was shining from it. He smiled a smile
of one who knows.*

*We all sat together in Bernard's large living room over-
looking the magnificent Kailua Bay. Everyone was silent
for an hour or so. The meeting had a tremendous healing
effect on me, and I realized that the silence and the electricity in the air were releasing layers of tension and frus-
trations that had gradually accumulated. I felt it slowly
melting and dissolving as I sat with this mysterious, still,
silent man. I saw him turn to his attendant devotee, a
young Tibetan clad in an orange robe and with a shaved
head. I saw his lips move but could not hear his softly
whispered words.*

*The young monk said, "Master said, 'One can never
"know" truth that is beyond the mind; the mind can only
create an idea of truth, an image of truth. Truth is the
creativeness behind all creation, yet that which is created
is not truth. Only the uncreated is creative, and that is the
truth. Therefore, discover in the silence of the mind the
true unity in all things. Disregard personal separation.
Live in the conscious realization of your oneness with the
Creator of all mankind.' "*

*The young monk then said to me, "You should do a
meditation, 'Om mani padme om.' " (Translated, it means
"The jewel in the center of the lotus," a symbol of the
divinity within the flesh.)*

Elvis' Beach House, Kailua Bay

*This afternoon Charlie and I related our experience at
Bernard's to Elvis and asked if he wanted an audience
with the Master. Elvis was hesitant.*

"Not now, Charlie. I have a little trouble with that one. I don't need to meet any masters right now. I'm on the right path." He waved a spiritual book he was holding and clutched the chai he was wearing around his neck. *"I'm sure you had a good experience and they're good people, but not now—maybe some other time."*

MARCH 11, 1977

Ed Parker, a strict Mormon who was raised in Hawaii, set up an evening for Elvis and the entire group to visit the Polynesian Cultural Center at the Hawaii campus of Brigham Young University. We all piled into a caravan of vehicles at about 8 P.M. and drove for about thirty minutes to the Center.

Through Ed's organizing with the campus and local security and Elvis' personal security staff, we were secretly ushered into the open-air pavilion, so that Elvis went unnoticed among the hundreds of tourists—until he reached his seat. Within moments his presence became known. News spread like wildfire, and most eyes were glued to our special section in the grandstands where Elvis was enjoying himself, instead of on the exciting show.

MARCH 13, 1977

Elvis decided it was time to leave paradise. The next tour begins on the twenty-third, and he wants to spend some time back home at Graceland. One by one, he presented everyone with a special gift. Afterward he said, *"I gave everyone gifts so that they would have something to remember our trip to Hawaii and us all, happily, being together.*

"This trip cost a good one hundred thousand, but money is not what matters. Before we left they even had me sign that will. Y'know, just in case, flying over the ocean and all that. Only it's the times like this, sharing not the money, but the good times, that transcend money."

Back on the mainland, we all returned to our homes to prepare for the next tour, a nine-day swing through Middle

America. Though everyone enjoyed the vacation, and Elvis did get to relax, it wasn't nearly enough.

MARCH 23, 1977

Arizona State University Center, Tempe, Arizona

Back on the road again, with great expectations of Elvis being healthier after vacationing in Hawaii. However, it's apparent that nothing has structurally changed. His face is already pale and puffy again. Backstage, moments before showtime, with his general demeanor unusually sluggish, and after Dr. Nick left the dressing room, Elvis said, "Larry, I need some help. Just put your hands on my throat and body and send me some light and energy."

During tonight's concert a young girl, no older than fourteen, who maneuvered her way through the crowd and the security officers approached me by the side of the stage. She smiled, gave me a sensual wink and said, "Larry [reading my name off my ID and picture tag], if you give me one of Elvis' scarves, you can do whatever you like with me. Just one scarf. We can go backstage or outside the building; whatever you say."

I stared at her for a moment and nodded at one of the security police, who briskly escorted her back to her seat. It's unbelievable. People will do anything to get a close glimpse of Elvis, or a memento. The bizarre requests are now everyday happenings, but they never cease to amaze me.

Miraculously, Elvis' voice seems stronger—more resonant, more beautiful—than ever. He's drawing an energy from the depth of his soul, not his weakening physical body.

We flew into Amarillo right after the show in Phoenix. It was after three in the morning when I got up to Elvis' room. Dr. Nick had just handed Elvis his nightly packet of pills, and he excused himself when he saw me. Elvis was lying on his back with a wet towel over his eyes. He began speaking to me, but his voice was weak, his words were garbled, and I couldn't make out what he was saying. When I asked him what was wrong, he fumbled for words, then said, "Oh, my damn eyes are killing me. They're burning like hell again, I can endure physical pain, but—"

He stopped, pushed away the towel, and slowly pulled himself up to a sitting position. Then he took a deep breath and started talking about what was really bothering him.

"What I can't handle is the thought of my baby Lisa and my daddy reading that blamed, lyin' book. I'm not concerned anymore about the fans. They're wise enough to see through any lies." His voice rose in panic. "But what about Lisa? What is she gonna think of her daddy when she grows up?"

"Elvis, listen to what you're saying," I said. "What's Lisa going to think when she grows up? What do you mean? Think of the implications of what you're saying."

His steel-blue eyes clouded with despair; he didn't bother answering me, but continued, "And Daddy, my daddy, reading bullshit lies about me. It will kill him. If anybody hurts my daddy or Lisa, God help them, for I'll personally do God's work for Him and send them to where they belong. And, Larry, don't get me wrong. I don't hate those guys; I hate what they're doing."

I massaged his neck and back, then Elvis asked me to meditate with him. After fifteen minutes of meditation, he said a prayer, during which he blessed Red, Sonny and Dave, and suddenly his mood was much lighter.

"You know what, Larry," he said brightly, "I'll bet that book is not coming out anyway. Look, we haven't heard anything in the press. And what publisher would want to take the chance? I mean, when we first heard about it we knew it was a bunch of distortion and fabrications, an attempt to smear me. No publisher will lie and face a lawsuit like that. I really don't think they could even find a publisher who would take their story."

Elvis went on and on, building a tower of rationalizations, trying to convince himself that he was correct. Believing that he might be wrong was too frightening for

Elvis. I sat listening, unable to tell him about the galley pages I'd seen, praying that something like the scenario Elvis had concocted really was occurring. Joe had to have told Colonel Parker, and Colonel Parker had to be working on this. Didn't he? Joe was right: knowing for certain that the book was being published would kill Elvis; but as time passed and there was no evidence that it would disappear, it became increasingly difficult to keep the truth to myself.

Elvis finally went to sleep, so I returned to my room.

MARCH 26, 1977

The Skirvin Plaza Hotel, Oklahoma City
4:45 A.M.
Elvis' Bedroom

About thirty minutes ago Elvis had taken his nightly pack of pills and was eating his favorite bedtime snack: a cheeseburger. As he ate, he began nodding off as the pills were taking effect. David and I heard him choking and ran over to him. I quickly put my fingers into his mouth, pulling out a large chunk of hamburger meat that had caught in his throat. After the piece of meat was extracted, Elvis, not conscious of what had transpired, was tucked in for the night by us. I returned to my room and cried my heart out. Is there much more time left?

MARCH 29, 1977

Rapids Parish Coliseum, Alexandria, Louisiana

I was at the foot of the stage directly below Elvis. About seven or eight feet from me I saw a young boy, approximately sixteen or seventeen, sitting in a wheelchair. He was wearing braces under his trousers, both arms were contorted, his hands were bent, his fingers twisted, and his head continually bobbed and weaved as he struggled to keep it straight. His wheelchair was stationed in the aisle beside the front row, midway between center and stage left. The young boy was wearing a flashy black suit with a pale-blue ruffled shirt and a flamboyant electric-

blue tie. His hair was dyed pitch black and styled exactly like Elvis', with the pompadour and the large curl falling on his forehead, and he had long sideburns running down to his jawbones.

I looked at Elvis, who was singing "Bridge over Troubled Water." The audience was spellbound as Elvis' voice rang out.

What was this boy thinking and feeling as he watched his hero? Was this his moment of glory? What was going on in this boy's heart and mind? If he only knew what is behind the facade.

I couldn't contain myself. I fled, and when I finally reached Elvis' trailer dressing room outside the building, I stood there alone, wiped out, crying.

On the thirty-first we were in Baton Rouge, Louisiana, having flown in after a show in Alexandria early that morning. Over the past few weeks Elvis' moods had swung from euphoria to dismay, and though he summoned the energy to get out onstage each night, only an idiot would believe that this could go on forever.

I was sound asleep when my phone rang at a quarter past seven in the morning.

"Larry, will you please come to my room?" Elvis sounded tired and frail, like an old man. I quickly got dressed and crossed the hall to his room. Ginger was asleep next to Elvis, who sat propped up by two large pillows. As usual, he wore his blue robe and his reading glasses. An open book lay in his lap.

"I haven't slept yet," he said grimly. "I took my medication, and it didn't help. I hurt, man; my body's in pain. There's something wrong. What should I do?"

Elvis sounded so afraid, so helpless, it was heartbreaking.

"Elvis, you have only four more nights to go on this tour, and you need your rest. You must go to sleep. And you shouldn't be reading now. It's only stimulating you to stay up. I'll make sure you're not disturbed. After you wake up you'll feel better, and we'll talk then."

"But I can't sleep," he replied, almost whining. "Get

Dr. Nick in here. You're right—I gotta get some sleep. He'll give me something to knock me out.''

"I'll be right back," I said, thinking I'd go fetch Nick.

"No, just call him on the phone and wake him up.''

I called Dr. Nick and explained the situation. He arrived within minutes, dressed in his bathrobe and carrying his medicine case.

"Nick," Elvis said urgently, "I've got to sleep.''

Dr. Nick nodded, opened his bag and took out a vial of sleeping capsules. With his back to Elvis, he opened two and let half the contents of each spill and disappear into the lush pile carpeting. He winked at me, then turned and handed Elvis his pills. I stayed with Elvis after Dr. Nick left, and within fifteen minutes he was fast asleep.

Sometime after three the next afternoon I entered the living room of Elvis' suite. I gently rapped on Elvis' bedroom door, opened it slightly, and peeked in. He was sitting up in bed and told me to come in. Ginger was in her room, talking on the phone to her mother, Elvis explained, although I hadn't asked. Despite six or seven hours' rest Elvis looked old, haggard; he seemed very weak.

Just then Joe walked in and said, "How you feeling, Boss?''

Elvis started, then responded softly, "Joe, I'm sick. I have to cancel tonight. I can't make it. You guys go into the other room while I call Daddy and explain to him what's happening. Then come right back in.''

Once we had closed the door behind us, I turned to Joe and said, "Elvis has never canceled a tour before.''

"I know, I know," he replied. "But he's going to cancel tonight, and that's it.''

I looked at Joe. Like so many things happening around Elvis, the real problem was never discussed. Everyone acted as if his canceling a date was the big issue. The solution was always to Take Care of Business—to massage the symptoms until they disappeared.

"Joe, no one will tell him the truth that that damn book is coming out," I said. "But when we go back into his bedroom, I'm going to tell him.''

"That's up to you," Joe replied, "go right ahead.''

Then as a gesture of support, I suppose, he added, referring to the Wests, "I'll never talk to those two guys ever
again as long as I live." Dave Hebler had been so new to
the scene that he almost didn't count.

When we reentered Elvis' room he was standing in the
middle of the floor, waiting for us. Dr. Nick came in after
us. As we stood around Elvis, he said, "I told Daddy."
Then he turned to Dr. Nick and said, "I'm canceling the
show. I can't go on; I feel really shaky."

"Well, Elvis," Dr. Nick replied, "you'd better get back
in bed."

As I watched Elvis walk unsteadily toward his bed, I
could bear it no longer.

"Elvis, I have to tell you something."

He stopped and turned.

"You're not going to like what you're about to hear, but
I have to tell you the truth. No one else here will, but I
have to. You might want to send me home on a plane
tonight, you might fire my ass, but I don't care."

Elvis took a deep breath and glared at me as if bracing
for a punch. In a low growl he said, "Well, go ahead.
Let's have it."

"Elvis, you know the book by Red, Sonny, and Dave
you think isn't coming out? I know for sure that it is.
Ballantine is publishing it this summer. I've seen parts of
it."

Elvis blanched. His eyes turned cold, and his nostrils
flared. He didn't utter a sound, but his expression said,
How could you do this to me?

"They're out to crucify you," I continued. "If you cancel this show, it will be a major news item in the press,
and tomorrow morning the publisher will go nuts. They'll
say, 'See? Elvis is doing drugs. Elvis this and Elvis that.'
You'll be verifying their story. They're waiting for something like this."

Elvis inhaled; it sounded like a death rattle. Then he
shouted, "Get Tom Hulett in here! Now! Call the Colonel!" He got into bed, then sat silently, enraged.

Poor Charlie Hodge walked in and, unaware of what

was happening, casually said, "I just heard you're canceling, Elvis—"

"Just sit down and shut up!" Elvis snapped.

Charlie and Dr. Nick drew up chairs and sat at the foot of the bed, while I took a seat next to Elvis. We remained silent as Joe placed the calls. Elvis leaned back against the headboard, his arms folded across his chest and his eyes fixed on the ceiling. The hard, watery sound of his breathing filled the room. In a few minutes Tom Hulett appeared, accompanied by an assistant. Tom was the representative assigned to Elvis from Concerts West, the concert-promotion firm that booked Elvis' tours. Of all the promoters and managers Elvis worked with, he liked Tom the best. He was smart, honest and truly concerned about Elvis. Tom didn't know it, but Elvis was planning to ask him to replace Parker as his manager.

"What's the trouble?" Tom asked.

"Tom, I hate to do this," Elvis said, "but I'm sick. I'm canceling the show."

Without a moment's hesitation and, more important, without giving Elvis a list of reasons why he shouldn't, Tom replied, "Well, Elvis, if you're sick, you have got to go to the hospital, though not here in Louisiana. They'll call in other doctors, and we want your doctors in Memphis. We have to get you to Memphis immediately and cancel the rest of the tour. This will be a major news story that will hit the wires tonight. We have to think about the insurance costs, and all the other costs, and refunds. The next shows are sold out, and the local—"

Elvis got up, and Tom stopped abruptly. Looking at me, Elvis raised his right hand and gestured for me to follow him. Everyone stared as we walked into the large bathroom. Elvis closed the door behind me, and as we stood face to face, he extended both arms in front of him. With tears in his eyes, he cried, "Larry, Larry, I'm sick! My legs are weak. Look at my hands—they're shaking."

At that moment one of his knees buckled and he grabbed the brass rail that encircled the room. As I steadied his swaying body with my arms, I said, "Elvis, Tom's right.

You have to go into the hospital. The insurance and everything else is secondary. You need to be checked out, thoroughly, and you need help. Now. These drugs are killing you! You've got to get off these damn drugs! They're no good for you. Your life is at stake.''

The two of us stood crying. Elvis nodded. He understood, but I sensed his feeling that I had hurt him by telling him the truth and forcing him to face it. My voice breaking, I tried to explain. "I had to speak up and tell you the truth about the book. I know the lies in the book are cruel, but I had to tell you because I love you. I love you, Elvis, and you have to know. We're speaking of your life—''

I couldn't go on. My every word, no matter how carefully phrased, how gently spoken, how well intentioned, how true, hit Elvis like a blow. He knew the truth. All I could hope for now was that he'd use it. He stood there, his eyes glazed and reddened from crying, and his face swollen. Touching my arm, he whispered, "Larry, I know you do, I know. I love you, too.''

Once we had composed ourselves, we returned to the bedroom. Everyone wondered what had been said, but no one asked. Despite his condition only a few minutes earlier, by the time Elvis got back under the covers he had transformed himself from the frightened, sickly man in the bathroom into a tiger.

"We're goin' home,'' he announced firmly. "We're not going on to finish the tour. We'll make it up later down the road.''

Elvis was furious, and in his mind everything was twisted and convoluted. He directed his anger at me, not only because I'd delivered the bad news but because I'd done so in front of other people. He knew there wouldn't be any charming or bullshitting his way out of it this time. For the first time in years Elvis was not in control, and everybody knew it. Now the game—Elvis' game, and everybody else's—was up. Every few minutes he'd stare at me, and without him uttering a sound I knew what he was thinking: I had betrayed him.

After the details of canceling were ironed out, Elvis said, "Now, if you gentlemen will excuse me, I need to call my daddy."

APRIL 1, 1977

12:15 A.M., the Baton Rouge Hilton, Baton Rouge

Everyone is scrambling to leave. The guys who pack Elvis' wardrobe and personal belongings are awaiting word to enter his bedroom, where he's been holed up with Ginger. As expected, the local news flashed Elvis' picture as their lead story, giving unconfirmed reports of his illness and hospitalization.

Around 2:30 A.M. Elvis boarded the Lisa Marie. *He didn't say a word to me. His hair was a mess, but he refused to have me fix it. Elvis and Ginger remained in his bedroom for the whole flight.*

Once we landed in Memphis, Elvis quickly got into his limousine with Ginger and security and sped off to Graceland. When I got there half an hour later, he was upstairs in his bedroom, eating fruit pies. Everyone was waiting for him to go to Baptist Memorial Hospital. I was waiting for him to talk to me.

Around 6 A.M., just before dawn, Elvis left quickly with security to go to the hospital. I'm going to stay at Graceland, get a few hours' sleep and go over there later.

APRIL 2, 1977

1:30 P.M., Baptist Memorial Hospital, Memphis

As I drove over to the hospital, I saw a crowd downstairs, pointing up at Elvis' floor. The newspapers are all carrying the story, with conflicting reports. I spoke to California earlier; the media everywhere is covering Elvis' sudden hospitalization.

7:15 P.M.

I've been waiting all day to see Elvis, in the anteroom that adjoins his room. Vernon visited him for about an hour, as did Joe and Charlie. Elvis knows I'm here and hasn't

*called me in. He's pissed over what I told him—I'm sure
of that—and I'm not leaving Memphis until we speak.
N was on duty for Elvis and said smugly to me, "Ya finally
fucked up, Geller. See what happens when ya shoot yer
big mouth off?"*

*Apparently the word is out that I spoke up. I strongly
doubt whether anyone knows the accurate story. If I have
to spend the night, I'll stay at Graceland and come back
here tomorrow.*

It wasn't until April 3 that I finally got to speak with
Elvis. As I waited in the anteroom to Elvis' hospital room
Lamar Fike said, "I don't know what you said to him, but
it must have been heavy. He knows you're here. He'll
probably see you when he gets ready. You know how he
is."

"Lamar! You still here?" Elvis shouted from his bed.

Lamar jumped up and ran into Elvis' room. Emerging
fifteen minutes later, he said, "He wants to see you now."

Elvis motioned me to sit in the chair at his bedside. For
the first few moments we were both quiet. Then he grinned
and said, "Larry, you probably know why I haven't talked
with you since the other night. I admit it—it was my pride.
You kinda took me by surprise, but I respect you for what
you said. I was pissed, man, but after I thought about it I
realized that you did the right thing. That's why you're
here and that's what I expect of you: the truth."

The tension evaporated, and for the first time in years I
actually believed there was hope. This was the turning
point.

"But, listen," he continued, "Lamar knew something
was up. He asked me what happened, and I told him you
told me some very heavy things. But I didn't tell him what
we said in the bathroom back in Baton Rouge the other
night. That's between us, all right?"

Elvis seemed more desperate than ever to maintain some
illusion of strength, of control. "Definitely," I answered.
"I won't tell anyone." Trying to change the focus to what
really mattered, I asked brightly, "How are you feeling?"

"Oh, *much* better," he said, smiling. "That tour was too much. I just got run down."

"Are they running any tests on you?" I started to feel like his guardian.

"Oh hell, yes," Elvis answered a little too quickly. "They're gonna check me out thoroughly, and if anything's wrong, they'll find it."

I wanted to press for more details, maybe a commitment that he was serious about getting straightened out, when a very attractive nurse came in. In a sweet Southern accent she said, "How y'all feelin', Elvis? Do you want another massage?"

Elvis blushed and stuttered, "N-not just yet, honey. I'll call you in a few minutes when I'm ready."

As she left the room, he turned to me and, grinning like a rascal, said, "Now, Lawrence, you give me great massages, but there's nothing like the warm hands of a beautiful young female." He winked. "If you want me to, I'll fix you up with her." He was back to his old self, it seemed, then he looked me in the eye and said, "I want you to know that I appreciate what you're trying to do for me. More than you know."

I ran into Lamar on my way out. He put out his hand and said, "Let me shake your hand. I wanna tell you you're the only one around here who had the balls to finally speak up."

I returned to Los Angeles a few days later, satisfied that something important was happening and Elvis was on the brink of making major changes. As for the book, even from the few pages I'd seen, it was so full of lies, so libelous, it didn't seem possible that it could be published. Of course, once Colonel Parker and Elvis' attorneys got wind of it, they would make the proper fuss, and that book would never see the light of day. But that isn't what happened at all, and *why* remains one of the great unanswered questions in Elvis' life.

There's no question that if Elvis' attorneys had requested to see the manuscript and pointed out the errors, the publishers would have been forced to seek documentation of the bodyguards' charges. When they failed to provide it, as surely would have been the case, no responsible publisher would have proceeded. But no such request was issued.

For one thing, Elvis was very unsophisticated when it came to anything to do with business or law. He never read anything he signed, for example. Success for Elvis meant never worrying about money or anything else. That's what he'd hired the best professionals to do, and he fully believed that they'd do what was best for him without his having to ask. It was a naive attitude, but that was Elvis.

Another thing that kept Elvis from going out of his way to do something about the book was that he knew he had a very dirty secret, and he knew that regardless of why he took medications or where he got them, the world at large would perceive him as a drug addict, even though he didn't see himself that way. He expected that in this instance he would be what he always felt he was, misunderstood.

These were the days before the Betty Ford Clinic, before confessing to a drug problem and undergoing rehabilitation earned you a cover of *People* magazine and public applause for being a ''survivor.'' In 1977 exposure of drug abuse—regardless of the substance, its source, its reasons—would have sparked a major, devastating scandal, particularly for Elvis, who, up until the last months of his life, had an impeccable image. In his illness and confusion, Elvis often remarked that the fans would understand his situation, but deep down he feared that they might not.

By April Elvis' thoughts about the book had evolved through several stages. Initially, he reassured himself with the belief that Red and the other two wouldn't betray him. He was, in so many ways, very childlike, and innocent in the true meaning of the word. Why would anyone want to hurt him like that? Elvis could not conceive of anyone being that wicked, least of all those three. Sure, they were pissed off; he understood that. But this was something else. He didn't believe they had it in them.

The second phase was his deluding himself into thinking. Well, okay, the book is being written, but it will never be published. In that phase Elvis was accepting the betrayal, but desperately trying to convince himself that it wouldn't matter, because the book wouldn't exist. Not only did this allow Elvis to sustain his fantasy of avoiding the public's rejection, but it gave him the green light to forgive the guys, particularly Red. It wasn't that Elvis was so goodhearted; he forgave because he had to forgive. He needed to feel that he was above petty fights and jealousies, that he was big enough, sufficiently spiritually involved to overlook wrongs done him and to forgive when others could not. It was one of the characteristics that made him a very beautiful man, but it was also his undoing.

By April the book was real. It was just a matter of time before it hit the stores. Elvis spent the rest of his life listening to time tick by, waiting for the bomb to go off. He believed that if he made a big noise about the book, everyone would interpret it as a sign of guilt. Though he tried to put it out of his mind, he knew that people were already laughing at him for being fat, for being slow and messing up onstage, and it killed him.

The crime was that no one in a position to do anything ever offered Elvis information on precisely how it might be handled. Elvis went to the Colonel, who in Elvis' eyes, for better or worse, was omnipotent. He didn't know specifically what the Colonel could do but there had to be something—after all, hadn't he always masterminded the details of Elvis' career?

So where was the Colonel? If Parker had decided to do something, it would have been done. But he didn't. All the way up until the very end of July, Elvis would say, like a child talking about the death of a pet, "It won't happen. It's going to be stopped. I just know it." Meanwhile, behind his back another member of the entourage remarked, "I'll bet Parker has a piece of that book." Perhaps they thought Parker was a gambling man, too smart not to realize that the game with Elvis—at least, a living Elvis—was winding down. We still don't know what really happened.

Even if any of the dream scenarios had come true, none would have changed the basic fact that Elvis had convinced himself he was a beaten man. He was dying, and

CHAPTER

10

Los Angeles

I called Graceland and asked for Charlie. When he got on the phone, I asked to speak with Elvis, but Charlie said he hadn't awakened yet. I asked about his condition and if he had had a thorough examination. Charlie explained that Elvis was feeling much better, that he had checked himself out of the hospital two days after I left, and that he hadn't undergone any extensive testing. I asked Charlie to let Elvis know I called.

    This week Elvis was on the front page of the tabloid The Star *in a scathing article. (In it, the writer offers examples of Elvis' "erratic" behavior, such as doughnut-eating binges.) The cover depicted him looking horrid. Each night during a concert, the tabloids snap hundreds of pictures, then select one that conforms to their story—the worst possible one.*

    After eleven tonight Elvis called from Graceland. "Lawrence," he said, "that hospital rest was great. I'm feeling back to myself again. We leave on tour in ten days or so, you can come to Memphis first. I can't find that copy of Rudhyar's astrology chart and that little book he wrote about me. Make a copy of everything, and check out the Bodhi Tree and bring me anything that pops off the shelf, if you get my drift."

APRIL 12, 1977

Los Angeles

I've been deeply disturbed since my conversation the other day with Elvis. Our relationship is certainly intact, but what bothers me is his refusal to do the right thing for himself. He had an ideal opportunity and let it dissolve. He's rejecting the ways and means to pull himself out of the undertow. How much longer can he go on?

I know he knows what's at stake. At the same time, he truly believes that God is leading and directing his path— and he knows and has even said that God helps those who help themselves. But he's not helping himself.

It's strange how the old clichés are so true. You can lead a horse to water . . .

At the Bodhi Tree bookstore I picked out some titles that weren't exactly what Elvis would want to read, but it seemed like a good opportunity to drop some hints. I picked up Edmond Szekely's *The Book of Living Foods*, Adele Davis' *Lets Get Well* and Alice Bailey's *Esoteric Healing*.

APRIL 20, 1977

Graceland

Elvis and I embraced as I entered his room. His spirits are good. Nevertheless, his physical condition seems to be worsening. He seems heavier than ever, and his eyes— which still sparkle—now have a yellowish tinge and are discolored.

Billy was with him, and they had been laughing. They were almost hysterical, with tears in their eyes, and Elvis couldn't hold a straight face when he released our hold on each other. He barely got out "How are ya?" before falling back on the bed, looking at Billy. Then they both broke into waves of uncontrollable laughter. On the TV screen was Peter Sellers as Inspector Clouseau imitating Humphrey Bogart. Elvis went into his imitation of Sellers doing

Clouseau doing Bogart. Soon we were all doing our imitations of Sellers and Bogart.

A couple of hours later Billy went home. As the energy subsided, Elvis said, laughing weakly, "We better calm down a few notches or we'll have a damn stroke or something."

He suggested it would be a good time for me to dye his hair. After I had shampooed it, he said, "Okay, Lawrence, don't keep me in suspense. What do you have for me?" I handed him the three health books, which he examined with a look of disgust. "Damn," he said, as if disappointed. He put on his glasses and opened *Esoteric Healing*, the book with the least "health"-oriented title. "This one looks interesting. Hey, what about the astrology material? Did you bring it?"

I dried my hands and took the materials out of my case. While I made the preparations to dye his hair, Elvis read through the pages, which he had read many times before over the years since I'd first given them to him in 1965.

"Lawrence, listen to this," he said excitedly, then proceeded to read Rudhyar's words:

"It [your horoscope] *suggests that you are open to inspiration and inner guidance and a channel for the fulfillment of a social human need. It may, someday, extend beyond what you at present bring to people. This 'beyond,' however, may not be reached or understood before you pass through some kind of crisis or self-repolarization. Perhaps after you are thirty-seven. In 1972 you might find yourself in circumstances, or in an environment, which will bring to your consciousness greater depth and maturity—and this might change your life—or at least your conscious approach to it. It may mean some sort of 'test.' "*

Elvis let the bound pages drop to his lap, peered over his glasses and spoke to my reflection in the mirror as I stood behind him doing my work. "Do you believe he wrote that ten, twelve years ago, and he pinpointed 1972?

Lord God, 'a test'; he was putting it mildly. I mean, 1972 was the worst year of my life since my mom died in '58.''

After a second he continued, ''I'll tell you this, no way—*no way*—will I get married again until there's not a shadow of a doubt of who I'm gettin' involved with. I went hog-wild at first with Ginger, and I still love her, don't get me wrong. But there will be no marriage until I'm sure it's right on all levels. And, by the way, when he says here . . .''

Elvis adjusted his glasses, then glanced over each page, looking for something. When he found it, he read aloud, '' '. . . a channel for the fulfillment of a social human need. It may, someday, extend beyond what you at present bring to people. This "beyond," however, may not be reached or understood before you pass through some kind of crisis . . .' I'm not saying I don't still feel the effects, the aftershocks, you know. I'd be a liar if I didn't admit that. Only I'm ready to be that channel, and I find, like Rudhyar says, it goes way beyond what I'm presently doing. I'm not sure yet what it is, but something's coming, and I know it.''

He thumbed through more pages, then said, ''Look at this. It says the symbol for my rising sign is 'a typical boy, yet molded by his mother's aspirations,' 'efficacy of overtones in life, or ideals in giving reality or depth to outer material things, conformity to inner light.' That's my symbol, and it fits me perfectly. I can't believe it. Every time I read this, it takes on a deeper meaning.

"This seems to be quite fitting as, apparently, you have been deeply influenced by your mother, and the degree of this symbol often suggests the way in which an individual comes to achieve his characteristics and contributions to society, thereby giving his most significant spiritual stature.

''Larry, I love it. Everything fits. It's all falling into place; my life, I mean. I've been dreaming about my mom recently. I've been remembering things that happened when I was a little boy. I'm not trying to remember, only sometimes, when I least expect it, certain events I haven't thought of in years flash through my brain like it was yesterday. Even onstage, when I least expect it . . .

"Well," he said, snapping out of a fleeting daydream, "let me read on. It says here, 'The moon in Pisces can indicate quite a "psychic" temperament, or at least a great sensitivity to psychic currents.' That's putting it mildly," Elvis remarked with a sigh. " 'This Moon-Saturn conjunction may be connected with the death of your twin brother, and perhaps also to the socially restricted environment in which you grew up as a child.' "

Elvis stopped and set the pages on the marble ledge. He put away his glasses and sat in deep reflection. Finally he said softly, "It all goes back to my mommy. She instilled so much in me.

"Jesse Garon is sure on me. I do think about him. I have certain questions. Maybe they can't be answered logically, but I do have my own ideas. Maybe—"

When he stopped talking I looked up and saw him crying. "What is it, E?"

Trying to hold back his tears, he searched for the words. Finally he said in a hushed voice, "There's a lot of possibilities. Maybe we'll never know for sure, not in this life anyway. I guess I'm just crying for what might have been."

APRIL 22, 1977

2:25 A.M., Detroit

We just arrived from the first show of the tour in Greensboro, North Carolina. The various tones and subtle hues that make up the emotional spectrum between black and white are diminishing into grays.

Elvis' voice last night had the entire audience entranced as he sang "Unchained Melody" sitting at the piano and playing with no accompaniment. Even every member of our group became paralyzed as they watched him. There is something so special since he incorporated this song about four months ago at the end of the show, just before

"Can't Help Falling in Love." I've never seen such a re-action as that he receives when he does this number.

The words have a special meaning for Elvis, and he wants this to be in his next album. We discussed the album cover Elvis would like: just him sitting at the piano, under the spotlight. Yet his physical body is a mess. He has to put so much effort into every move. It almost seems he's doing a parody of his old self, though he can't see it. When I blow-dried his hair on the plane tonight, he was breath-ing heavily. He shook his head from side to side and said, *"The spirit is willing, but the flesh is weak."*

Detroit is cold and bleak. I helped the guys unload the baggage from the belly of the plane. Though there was neither moon nor stars in the sky, the Lisa Marie was illuminated with a diffused light as clouds rolled close to earth. The tarmac was flooded from the recent rain, and the hazy airport lights were reflected in the black pools across the airstrip as in a lake. An icy chill went through my bones as the wind streaked across the open landing strip.

On the way to the hotel I sat next to Dean Nichopoulos. He said to me naively, *"Hey, great show tonight, huh?"* I looked at him in astonishment. Maybe he's blinded be-cause his father is Dr. Nick; I don't know.

I said, *"You're only twenty-one years old, Dean, and you're so lucky to be here. We all are. Let me give you a word of advice: Take in every moment to its fullest. Try to absorb everything that's going on, because nothing lasts forever. You're young. Someday you'll be grown-up and you'll look back on this, and it will all seem like a dream. Look around you, see what's happening. This won't last forever."*

Dean stared at me for a moment with a concerned look in his eyes. I thought that perhaps I had struck a chord in him. Then he said, *"What the hell are you talking about? Are you using that psychological stuff on me?"*

On the twenty-third we were in Detroit, and that after-noon I met Elvis in his room. As I wrote in the diary:

They [the hotel rooms] *all seem alike now. There are seven or eight of Elvis' books strewn about. Also, two pearl-handled Patton .45 automatics on the table next to the bed, along with the usual array of sprays, drops, tablets and atomizers. A large dictionary is on the bed, with his magnifying glass next to it. Bottles of Mountain Valley spring water crowd the floor, and, to complete an Elvis Presley bedroom, of course, the windows are covered with aluminum foil to keep out the daylight. Outside the hotel, in the lobby, in the coffee shop, even in some of the rooms, are the fans. They're everywhere.*

When I got there it was after four, Elvis had just finished his breakfast, and we were looking for Billy. This was Billy's first tour in a long time. Elvis wanted him along. He always felt most comfortable around his cousin, who lived with his wife, JoJo, in a trailer behind Graceland. Billy had traveled with Elvis in the fifties and sixties, and less often in the seventies.

While Elvis was talking to me, he bent over an open suitcase and took out some pills. Before he put them into his mouth, he made a point of telling me they were for his stomach.

"You know," he said, "everyone thinks I'm just plain fat. They don't understand that it's fluid; my intestines don't function right. I've got that spastic colon. Between that, my glaucoma and all the rest, it's a miracle I'm still in one piece.

"Lawrence," he said as he walked to where I stood and placed a hand on my shoulder, "I need your help. We have a mission, and if I know you're behind me all the way we can accomplish it. But I need to know if you're with me."

"What is it? I'm sure I'm with you, although I'm not sure what you're getting at."

"The world's changing rapidly." He began surveying the room, then stared into my eyes. "And this is only the beginning. Drastic changes are what is in store for this world, and millions of people will be turning, in the future, for guidance. I know it's all been said in many different ways, but using my name and influence, let's write a book and explain the best way we know how about the spiritual world. *The path.* I'll even reveal my conversion and initiation in the desert when I had my vision. If we got into my secret spiritual life and all the experiences—and ours together—people all over the world can be led to God. Not by preaching and all the stuff that turned me off to 'churchianity,' thank God.'' Elvis laughed.

"But the world knows Elvis," he resumed seriously. "Elvis the image. They have to know me, the real person. And that's where you come in. It's our special mission together. Larry, something big is going to happen, soon. I know. I'm not sure when, but I feel it in my bones. I'm dreaming a lot of things—some we'll go into later—but something's going to happen."

"You have my word," I said, and we shook hands.

From that point on, my conversations with Elvis assumed a different tenor. Although he wouldn't say, "Let's put this down for the book," he spoke of things he wanted included. The idea of writing such a personal book seemed to grant him even greater freedom to delve into his past and the meaning of his life. Most of the things he spoke of then he had told me years before or on several separate occasions over the years. But because he knew I'd be writing things down, he told me the stories again.

APRIL 25, 1977

Detroit

Elvis was finishing breakfast when I arrived. He excused himself from the entourage and asked me to come into his room. Once inside he handed me a copy of The Sacred Science of Numbers, *by Corinne Heline. We both sat down, and Elvis said, "Larry, start reading on the page that I folded back and start where it's underlined."*

" 'The I Am is the eternal and ever-existent principle of truth. Only as a man awakens this I Am consciousness within himself is he able to contact truth in all things about him. . . . The number seven is introspective and intuitive,

it is attracted to the unseen and mystic side of life and being. This is because the number seven is founded upon and centered in the very mystery of life and being.'"

"*Do you know what today is?*" Elvis asked.

After thinking a moment, I replied, "*No. Is it significant?*"

Elvis smiled and said, "*Today is April twenty-fifth. Methinks it's quite significant. It's my mama's birthday. She would have been sixty-five years old today if she would have lived. Her number is seven, and so is Priscilla's. Now, what I'm getting at is that my mom fits that passage to the letter. I mean, the very first time I ever heard about the Almighty I Am was from her when I was a little kid. She believed in the supernatural and the Holy Spirit. She was mystical, man. She just naturally knew things. She raised me on it.*"

Typically, after Elvis said something like this about his mother, he'd pause and reflect for a moment.

"*Wow!*" he exclaimed. "*Priscilla, when we were together in 1972, used to be against anything mystical. She rejected the spiritual. She tried to get me to stop reading and studying. I really think if it were up to her, she would have had me stop my search for God. But no way. That's my very life, my God-given right. That's what everyone is born for, to find out who they are, to get closer to God. You remember when we first got started, that was the number-one question burning inside me, and still is. Why am I Elvis? Why am I picked to be Elvis Presley, to be put in the position I'm in, and to have the kind of ministry I have?*"

"*What ministry do you mean?*"

"*You know, my fans! That's it. I'm not an evangelist, I'm an entertainer. That's how God has used me to get the message across, not by preachin' but by using the universal language of music. I couldn't go out there and preach; that's not my calling. It would confuse the hell out of my fans. You know, all these years that you and I have spent together, praying, healing, meditating and studying the greatest books the world has known were—ah, what's the word? It sounds like electric?*"

"Eclectic?"

"Yeah, that's it. Eclectic. Hey, I never preached to Priscilla, saying this book is the way, or my way is the way. I used the eclectic approach, on myself as well as on her, or anyone else through the years. All I attempted to do was help her awaken her own search.

"When I had that vision in the desert, when Jesus proved Himself to me, Priscilla couldn't relate to it. And that was the most holy experience of my life. What we're talking about has given my life meaning—Lisa, my career, my music, everything. I thank God for it. I'm the first to admit I'm imperfect. I've done things I'm not proud of. I've got a long way to go—we all do, we're all on Jacob's Ladder somewhere. And like it says in the Bible, 'And though I have the gift of prophecy, and understand all mysteries, and all knowledge, and though I have all faith, so that I could remove mountains, and have not love, I am nothing.' God is love, that's what it's all about. And that's my mama's middle name, Love. Gladys Love Presley.

"I've been kinda talking in circles in a way. But there's something I have to tell you. It's something I did with Priscilla years ago, and since you've been back the past few years, the guilt has been growing. And I've got to get it out. You know all the arguments Priscilla and I had about my books, and you remember when I slipped and hit my head. I was too ill, too weak, to fight back and protect you. Or myself. They pressured you to the point where you had to quit, and I was just too ill and confused to do anything about it."

He took a deep breath, and his eyes misted. *"You know, Larry, she made me burn those books we loved and learned so much from—sacred books. She said it would make her so happy. This was right after we got married, and I wanted very much to please her, so I did. She hated them and you, and she was plain, outright jealous of you and what you represented. And the books. Imagine seeing those great books burned because they bored her."*

APRIL 27, 1977

Milwaukee

As Elvis was taking his final bows and walking from one side of the stage to the other, receiving flowers, kissing girls, babies, elderly women, shaking hands, we were on-stage to protect him: holding back the crowd and grabbing anyone who broke through. As Elvis turned to exit through the back of the stage where the steps are, he put out his arm for F, who customarily waits there each night to assist him.

The people were nuts tonight, and it seemed like more than the usual confusion and hysteria. Elvis appeared lost; it was obvious he was blinded. For whatever reasons, F missed his cue, and Elvis slipped, twisting his ankle, as he attempted to climb down the few steps backstage to where his limo awaited. Security ran over and helped him up as the rest of us, along with the local and hired police, held back a stampede. Elvis limped into the limo, which sped off with a mob of excited people after it. I could hear on the loudspeaker Ed Hills' voice ring out: "Elvis has left the building."

Back in Elvis' bedroom, he was livid. When F got there, Elvis screamed, "Where the hell were you? You're sup-posed to be right there for me! I depend on you! You know I'm totally blind after a show, between all those damn flashbulbs and my eyes and the sweat. I can't see any-thing! I think I sprained my damned ankle, and I hope to God that's all that's wrong, and you better hope to God, too. Shit, you should know better!"

"Boss, I'm sorry. But when you started to come back I saw a mob of people who broke the security line. They were chargin' you. I had to help the other guys hold them back. If they got through, they would have been all over you—"

"Listen," Elvis interjected, "I don't give a fuck! You just keep your fool ass where you're supposed to, you hear?"

"I'm sorry, Boss. It won't happen again."

"You can bet your ass it won't!" With that, the case was closed.

Dr. Nick and I stayed with Elvis to tend to his ankle. Elvis could barely get to his feet to test it; it was swollen and sore. Dr. Nick suggested tape. I put Elvis' foot on my lap and shaved the hair off his ankle and upper foot. He started grinning and said, "It was a good time to lay into him. These guys get slack every once in a while, so I had to play boss."

After Dr. Nick wrapped the ankle, he gave Elvis his nightly pack of medication and left. Elvis was sitting up in bed and said, "Lawrence, we better go to work. Dr. Nick did all he could, so give me a healing, and let's meditate."

MAY 2, 1977

The Arlington Hilton, Chicago

What a relief! Elvis' performance tonight inspired a tumultuous response from the audience despite all the mental and physical problems that are eating away at him. Back at the hotel I went to one of Elvis' inner circle, a trusted friend and longtime associate with whom I could speak privately. He was lounging in his room, sipping a drink.

After a few minutes of small talk, I said, "There's something that's really troubling me, and I'm sure you're aware of what I'm about to say."

"Sure, what's bothering you?"

"I'm so worried about Elvis. He's more than sick. I'm afraid that something is going to happen. It's obvious in his performances that something is wrong. I want to know if you're aware of it."

He stared at me quizzically, then with an expression of self-satisfaction replied, "Larry, I think the problem is that you just don't understand. Let me explain it to you. It's very simple. See, if you were an entertainer, you'd see it, 'cause performers, especially singers, stay younger than other people. They get rejuvenated from their audiences. You'll see. In twenty years Elvis will be sixty-two, and

he'll look better then than he does today. He won't age.
You and everyone else will, but Elvis will be on that stage
singing, looking great.

"I know he's a little overweight, and he's been ill, but
don't worry yourself. It'll only make you older." He gig-
gled. "Nothing can happen to Elvis."

Stunned, I excused myself and went directly to my room.

I am writing down the conversation I just had. I'm flab-
bergasted, angry, frustrated, and distressed. Am I losing
my mind? No one is going to age? No one can become
desperately ill?

I am writing down this outrageous discussion not only
to capture in words how Elvis' closest associates are blind
and do not perceive or relate to his worsening condition,
but I must also hold on to myself and maintain my own
center. A few members of the group admit he's ill. I can
speak to Ed, who realizes the seriousness of the situation,
only his hands are tied, and he is unable to be effective.

Those around Elvis who have any authority seem not to
understand what appears to have become a moment-to-
moment life-and-death crisis.

MAY 4, 1977

Graceland

We flew back to Graceland early this morning from Sagi-
naw, Michigan. After this long tour, everybody is wiped
out and ready for a rest. Elvis was still sleeping when I
left word with Charlie that I had to catch a six-thirty flight
back to Los Angeles.

I was at the Memphis airport about to check my luggage
and get my boarding pass, when I heard my name paged.
I picked up one of the courtesy phones, wondering who
could be calling me here.

"Lawrence?"

"Elvis! Good heavens, man, I didn't expect to hear your
voice."

"Lawrence, where the hell do you think you're goin'?"

"I left a message with Charlie. My plane leaves at six-thirty."

Elvis just laughed. *"You're not going anywhere."*

"Elvis, I need to get back to L.A., to see my family and do some writing before the next tour."

"No way, son. I'll have them stop the plane if I have to. You're comin' back to Graceland. You can leave in a day or two. I need you to do something." Then he added quickly, *"My hair. And we can have some time to talk."*

Thirty-five minutes later I was in Elvis' bedroom. He gave me a sheepish grin and said, *"There's no escaping, Larry, so you might as well accept it."* We spent the evening relaxing, talking and watching videos. Elvis decided to have his hair done tomorrow; what a ploy to keep me in Memphis. I really want to go back to L.A., but I'm also glad he had me stay over. I'm so exhausted, yet time spent with Elvis is always special.

It was late the next night when I entered Elvis' room; he was sitting in front of the bathroom mirror with his feet propped up on the marble ledge. A few books lay on the counter next to a large bottle of spring water, of which he's been putting away at least two quarts a day. His eyes were red and puffy, and he looked at me anxiously as he said, "My eyes are killing me. I think what you better do is cut the sides of my hair so that when I'm moving on-stage it doesn't get caught in the sweat and catch the corner of my eyes. That's probably one of the reasons they're so screwed up."

While I cut his hair he asked, "Am I losing any on top? Is it getting any thinner?" He seemed extremely concerned.

As I examined the crown area, I couldn't stop thinking about how any physical deterioration is inevitably reflected by hair loss. Judging Elvis' agitated state, though, I decided this wasn't the thing to say.

"Elvis, just the *very* top," I replied carefully. "It's not as strong as it used to be. It's a little weaker, but don't be alarmed. When this starts, it's usually gradual and takes years to become noticeable."

I jerked back the scissors when Elvis quickly bent his head forward, trying to examine the spot in the mirror.

"What the hell am I gonna do?" he moaned.

"Don't worry. It's only very slight," I said, trying to assuage his fears. "That's why I always massage your scalp, and it's helped. You've got a beautiful, full head of hair. I add those special ingredients to your shampoos, but you also know that the most important single element for healthy hair is good nutrition—"

"All right, all right," Elvis interrupted wearily. "I get it, Lawrence. Just do your thing and make it look as good as possible. And trim my sideburns; they're too bushy."

I set to work. Elvis was obviously not in the mood to chat. When I glanced up I caught him scrutinizing his reflection with the cold eye of an appraiser. He slowly turned his head to a three-quarter profile, then examined his full face. I flashed back to the midsixties, to the first time I had witnessed this private ritual. He was then just thirty, and I remembered thinking how distant he looked as he examined every angle, every line, every tiny imperfection, of which there were then so few. He knew he was beautiful, and yet his attitude reflected none of the narcissism I'd seen in so many other stars.

Now the same motions in the same mirror—only the image in the glass had undergone a horrible metamorphosis. Deterioration awaits all of us eventually, of course— but over decades. For Elvis, it took only a few short years for something so magnificent to evolve into a bloated, blotched caricature of itself.

A few seconds later our eyes met, and he read my mind. Trying to deflect attention from the obvious, I said gently, "You know, Elvis, if we didn't keep dyeing your hair it would definitely get healthier. You're almost all white, like your daddy. You would look so dynamic. Can you picture yourself in one of your show suits, with long, flowing white hair? It would be classic."

Elvis said nothing for a minute, then chuckled softly and smiled. Shaking his head, he said, "L.G., you're something else. Naw, right now I think a change like that would be too drastic. But I'll give it some thought."

MAY 20, 1977

Stokley Athletic Center, Knoxville, Tennessee

We just flew into Knoxville for the first show of a long, fourteen-day concert tour. This was only the first night, and Elvis already looks as if it were the last. He was visibly shaky, and his face, especially his eyes, reflected the fear that his efforts might fail.

Standing next to him in the wings, I said quietly what I later realized was a foolish thing. "Elvis, tell me something. How do you do it? How do you get onstage and perform feeling the way you do?"

Elvis stood motionless, then said, "Larry, a man has to meet the occasion, no matter what it is. A real man rises to the occasion." He smiled, then bowed his head, bringing his folded hands in prayer fashion to his forehead, and said his nightly salutation.

He then walked away, onto the stage, where a sea of lights flashed all across the huge, sold-out auditorium. Women and men of all ages ran to the stage, handing up bouquets of roses, cards, personal letters, teddy bears and other gifts for Elvis and Lisa Marie. Shrieks were heard as usual from the packed house, while Elvis, dressed in his suit of lights, strutted grandly across the stage several times, letting the fans see him as he basked in their loud cheers. Clad all in white, sparkling with jewels, he stood there in the spotlight.

"Elvis We Love You" banners hung from the balcony. Someone yelled out, "Elvis, you're the King!" And he rose again and met the occasion. After a few songs, I looked up at Elvis from where I was kneeling at stage left and was astonished to see his face so radiant, the puffiness and pain gone. He had come back to life, for now.

He came toward me and gave me a look that said, "Don't ask me; all I know is what I have to do. The rest is Grace from Above."

The next show was in Louisville, and that afternoon I was alone, waiting in Elvis' suite to see him. Dr. Nick was in Elvis' bedroom. Suddenly the Colonel opened the front door and walked in briskly. As I stood to greet him, the Colonel stopped. With both hands firmly grasping his cane, he leaned his stocky frame over it and, scanning the room, demanded, "Where is he?"

I started toward the bedroom door, saying, "Colonel, I'll let him know you're here."

Parker brushed past me. "No!" he said forcefully. "I'm goin' in."

He threw open the bedroom door, and in the instant before it closed behind him I caught a glimpse of the horrifying scene inside. There was Dr. Nick kneeling next to the bed, holding up Elvis' unconscious body and working frantically to revive him. He kept dunking Elvis' head into a bucket of ice water. Eyes closed, jaw slack, Elvis looked helpless, as if he were in a coma. I could hear him moaning faintly. The door slammed shut.

Less than two minutes later the Colonel emerged, slamming the door. He stalked over to me, pointed his cane heavenward, looked coldly into my eyes and declared, "The only thing that's important is that he's on that stage tonight. Nothing else matters!" With that, he was gone.

I couldn't believe this. Naively, perhaps, I expected the Colonel to take some action, to react in some human way to the sight of "his boy" in that condition. Was his only fear for Elvis that he might not be able to perform? What about Elvis?

After Dr. Nick left Elvis' bedroom, about half an hour later, I rapped on the door. Elvis asked me in. He was sitting up in bed, looking watery and bloated. When I asked him how he was feeling, he sighed heavily and said, "I feel whipped, like a fondue." It was obvious he still wasn't out of his grogginess, but he said with irritation, "Larry, why did you let the Colonel barge in on me? Why didn't you come in and tell me he was here?"

"Elvis, I told him I would let you know he was here, but he just walked right by me and came in."

Elvis was furious. "Hey, I don't care who he thinks he is! This is my fucking ballgame, not his! He can't walk his big fat ass into my room like that, manager or not. This is my room. I'll take care of him."

By this point going to the hospital was out of the question. Elvis refused. Back in April he had come too close to facing some truths about his health, and he couldn't bear it and so he had checked himself out and run back to Graceland. He had come to the decision, consciously or subconsciously, that he was on this ride to the end, and all there was to do was close his eyes and hang on tight. Now and again he'd rage against someone, usually the Colonel, but more often he lost himself in his studies or in elaborate plans for the future.

For those of us who lived with him—at least the few of us who faced up to the severity of the situation—there were two options: stay or leave. I stayed because Elvis was my friend. The fact that he chose not to do the right things for himself didn't relieve me of a moral obligation, as his friend, to point those things out to him. He wasn't what so many believe, a man bent on self-destruction who became what he was to punish anyone. He needed to know that when and if he took charge of his life, someone would be there. But he also needed to know that even if he never did that, someone would be there, too.

During these times it was as if Elvis had retreated into a dark place inside himself where no one else was welcome, but he wanted us to see him there nonetheless.

The morning after Elvis' threats against Parker, I entered his room at the Baltimore Hilton and found a few guys scurrying around, Ginger painting her nails, and Elvis having breakfast: a giant banana split. When he was about halfway through it he said, grinning with boyish delight, "You'd better order me another one." A few minutes later the second dessert arrived: three large scoops of ice cream flanked by banana halves and topped with crushed pineapple, chopped nuts, hot chocolate syrup, whipped cream and a cherry. Elvis immediately buried his face in the second and a few minutes later exclaimed, "You'd better order me one more!"

The third, then the fourth were consumed. Elvis sat back, placed his hands on his bloated gut and, squinting his eyes as if considering the fate of the world, declared, "One more will finish me off!"

After spooning up the last bite of the fifth dish, he sat back again, shrugged, then let out a great belch. He spoke to no one, and I quickly excused myself and went to my room. What was he doing?

The next evening Elvis implored me to speak with Ginger, to explain to her what he was all about, what mattered to him, and why it was important for her to share these things with him. "She doesn't understand me yet," he said, looking troubled and hurt. "Maybe if she did, she wouldn't be so damned concerned about her family, which is really only an excuse. I want her on my team—all the way."

My initial reaction was, This is pathetic: Elvis infatuated and desperate to impress a twenty-year-old. The prognosis wasn't good, but Elvis pleaded. I agreed to speak with Ginger, and we had a pleasant conversation that consisted mostly of me talking and her nodding her head. I told her of his spiritual quest, how important the studies were to him, how he planned to communicate what all this meant to him through movies and books, and why he needed her to be with him in these endeavors. Elvis was listening through the bathroom door the whole time, and when he emerged he winked approvingly. I excused myself and went to enter the whole lengthy conversation in my diary.

Ginger was a very sweet girl, but she wasn't going to follow Elvis in this any more than Priscilla had. At least Priscilla spoke up and let you know what she thought; Ginger didn't do even that much. What was Elvis falling in love with? An image, an ideal, a chance to relive some part of his life?

The next day he seemed in a happy mood. When I got up to his room in Portland, Maine, he waved me over to where he was standing at the window. He had folded back a tiny corner of foil and was peeking out.

"Man! There are sure a lot of people down there!" he exclaimed as if he'd never seen his fans before.

He stepped back so that I could look. Down in the Hilton's parking lot stood hundreds of fans, all looking up at his bedroom window, which was easy enough to find because of the foil. One of the fans spotted us, and suddenly we heard shouts and saw people pointing.

"If it weren't for them, I wouldn't be where I am now, God love 'em."

Watching him, dressed in his hooded bathrobe, ensconced in a penthouse, all the windows covered with aluminum foil to keep out the sun, I often flashed back to 1966, when after the desert experience he had proclaimed his intention of becoming a monk. Here he was, eleven years later, living in his own monastery. He didn't know what was going on out there, except for what he saw on the TV news; he knew intellectually, but by 1977 he had spent more than half of his life, and nearly all of his adult life, several steps removed from the daily business of living. Elvis loved the world, but he feared it, too.

He pressed the foil back in place and started talking about his acting career, and his regrets. We had discussed these things a dozen times before, but he wanted it down for the book. Charlie Hodge came in and sat with us. Then we discussed how he might get back into the movies, a prospect that excited him.

"You could have a script tailored to your specifications," I suggested. "All you have to do is put a tape recorder on the table and throw out your ideas."

"Exactly! Now I want to do it my way, and here's where you come in. Not the next tour, but the one after. You bring your tape recorder, and we'll have our own think-tank sessions, then we can hire a professional script-writer."

Elvis was pleased with the plan, as farfetched as it may have been. Thinking about movies brought to mind what had stood in the way of his last thwarted attempts in that direction, and he became very serious.

"What I'm about to tell you is top secret," he said slowly. "And I don't want you to tell anyone. But—"

He paused and, stammering slightly, said, "I'm going to get rid of the ol' Colonel. I need a change, new blood. I've always been loyal to the Colonel, and I appreciate what he's done. But nothing can last forever. The times are changin' and I don't think the Colonel is up-to-date with what's going on like Tom Hulett is. I've had it with him.

"And I also want a different lifestyle. I don't want the Memphis Mafia anymore," he said disdainfully. "I don't need that scene anymore. I've had it with all the little jealousies, the infighting. I know who my real friends are. I want to live a different kind of life; this one has gone on long enough. After the next tour, or the one after that— I'm not sure yet, but by the end of summer—it will happen. A drastic cut. Daddy's been on me a long time about it. This will make him very happy. He feels too many people have taken advantage of me for too long." Elvis then listed the guys who'd be fired, and asked Charlie and me to promise not to say a word. When he finished he opened his eyes wide in mock astonishment as if to say, "Isn't this a surprise."

MAY 26, 1977

Binghamton, New York

Most of the guys were sitting around in the living room when Dr. Nick and Elvis came out of the bedroom. Elvis was in a pensive mood at first, declaring, "Well . . . Ginger and I need a rest from each other. That's why I sent her home . . . for a few days." He added angrily, "Actually, she'd better think things over very carefully and choose between me and her whole damn family. She's still young, but she'd better grow up a little faster, or there'll be no wedding."

Several hours later, around 2 A.M., I was in Elvis' room when Dr. Nick delivered the nightly packet. Elvis was in pain and depressed.

"I'm glad Ginger is back in Memphis," he sighed. "It has to be that way right now. But, damn, I can't sleep alone. I need someone next to me. I just need some companionship. I can't be alone tonight. Call Joe in here. He's good at that. Maybe he can figure something out."

I dialed Joe's room, and a few minutes later he was there, drowsy, dressed in his bathrobe.

"What's up, Boss?"

"Joe, I need someone. I can't sleep alone. I need someone in bed with me. Can you find someone?"

Joe shrugged. "Elvis, it's late. How the hell am I going to find someone now?"

"Joe," Elvis said evenly, "you're in touch with a lot of girls. What about calling the West Coast? I'll have them flown in if I have to charter a damn plane out there."

"Elvis! It's almost three in the morning. What you're asking me to do is a project." Joe chuckled, trying to impress upon Elvis how impractical his request was. "I'll get on it tomorrow, Elvis, but there's no way I can get you someone now."

"All right, all right," Elvis replied, conceding defeat. "Only I do need someone."

Joe was on he way out as he said, "Elvis, tomorrow you'll have someone. I'll check into it when I get up."

"Lawrence," Elvis said forlornly, "what am I going to do?"

"I've got it—Kathy Westmoreland."

"You're right, you're right," Elvis replied, brightening. "Kathy."

His lids grew heavy as the medication kicked in. "Call Kathy for me and explain the situation and get her up here."

I rang Kathy's room and she answered the phone, obviously still half asleep. "It's Larry, and I'm sitting here with Elvis, and he asked me to call you because he wants to see you now."

She replied that it would take her about twenty minutes to get dressed, and I cut her off.

"Kathy, listen, don't bother with that. Just put on your bathrobe and come up to our floor right now. I'll meet you at the elevator and explain everything."

Five minutes later I met Kathy. I told the security police that she was allowed on the floor, that she was part of Elvis' show. As we walked away down the long corridor, both officers grinned at me slyly; one winked. On the way to Elvis' room I explained the situation to Kathy and told her this wasn't about sex. I promised her that nobody else would find out about this or get the wrong impression. Elvis was groggy but happy to see her. I said good night.

The next afternoon I wrote:

Elvis decided that for the time being Kathy would stay with him and travel with us. I was in the living room, and Kathy entered carrying her luggage. When she saw we were alone, she sat down next to me with a concerned look on her face.

"Larry," she said, "Elvis made some remarks last night after you left, and I'm really worried about him." She lowered her voice so that we wouldn't be overheard. "He was talking about himself, about the changes he's been through, and suddenly he said, 'Kathy, I know I look fat now, and I'll look terrible for my TV special coming up. But I'll tell you this: I'll look good in my casket.' "

Over the next few days Kathy and Elvis passed their time reading from the books. Of all the women Elvis ever knew, spiritually speaking, Kathy was the most attuned to him. The three of us had several long conversations about God, which, at Elvis' request, I recorded in my diary.

MAY 29, 1977

Baltimore Civic Center, Baltimore

Before Elvis began his show tonight, it was obvious that something was wrong. He barely spoke to anyone, and when he did his speech was slurred. He was drained and had to put extra effort into every move getting ready for the show.

As I styled his hair at the hotel, Elvis sat quietly with his eyes closed. When I finished, he said weakly, "Larry, my body hurts. My leg is killing me, my throat feels raw. Man, I'm a wreck. Before I get up, please, just put your hands on me. I need some extra energy."

When he went on stage at the Civic Center, thirteen

*thousand people cheered wildly. Elvis was desperately ill—
his eyes were swollen, his body movements lethargic—and
the more effort he put forth to get in gear for that old magic
to transform him and bring him to life, the worse it got.
As he sang, he slurred his words. He struggled to stay on
his feet, his body swaying.*

*From where I was kneeling on stage left, I saw a man
shake his head and heard him exclaim, "Man! That boy's
plain drunk!"*

*Elvis simply couldn't continue; he was about to col-
lapse. The orchestra was getting ready to begin the next
song, when all of a sudden Elvis announced to the audience, "There's a lot of talent on this stage tonight, and
I'd like Sherril Nielson to sing to you—one of my favorite
songs, 'Danny Boy.' "*

*During "Danny Boy" Elvis motioned to security, left
the stage and went back to his dressing room. The audience didn't know what was happening. Charlie took charge
onstage, buying time for Elvis. I was so proud of Charlie.
He assumed command like a seasoned pro. He didn't know
what was going on in the dressing room, neither did he
know if Elvis would be able to return. In spite of the pressure, Charlie emceed the show, calling on Kathy to sing a
solo, and on J.D. and the Stamps to sing a couple of
gospel numbers.*

*Backstage in the dressing room Dr. Nick did his best to
revive Elvis. Thirty minutes later Elvis emerged from the
dressing room looking refreshed and pumped up to finish
the show. As we walked by his side, he whispered to me,
"Just send me some energy so I can finish this show and
get the hell outa here. Man, I hurt bad."*

*When Elvis appeared onstage, the audience went wild.
They wouldn't stop clapping and stomping. Elvis apologized to everybody and said kiddingly, "Hey, when ya
gotta go, ya gotta go." The audience cheered. They sensed
he was ill, and they responded with enthusiasm, letting
him know how much they cared for him.*

*Elvis said under his breath when he turned around to
sip some water, "Man, sometimes it hurts so fuckin' bad."
He completed the show sitting on a stool, playing his gui-*

*tar and singing. The audience was thrilled. In spite of his
illness he did his best to entertain them, and they loved
him all the more for it.*

It was a quarter after four in the morning, just a few
hours after we'd flown into Jacksonville, when Elvis called.

*I got to Elvis' room and was surprised to see him dressed
in his black jumpsuit. He had a long black flashlight in his
hand. He walked up to me and said, "Don't tell anyone;
most of the guys are sleeping anyway. Let's take a fast
flight to Memphis. We'll be back before anyone wakes up.
I wanna get Ginger and bring her back on tour. I already
told Kathy's what's happenin'. We'll just bring Dick and
Billy. Let's hit it."*

*Without anyone knowing, we left the hotel and drove to
where the Lisa Marie was waiting and set to go. Elvis and
I sat in his bedroom. He had with him his case containing
medications he'd collected from various doctors.*

*"Man, if anyone goes into your room and finds you're
not there, they'll go out of their minds!" I said.*

*Elvis laughed. "Yeah, it'll tear their heads up," he said,
grinning.*

*I knew we were in for a long night—what was left of
it—and that I'd probably get no sleep until tomorrow night,
late. We've been on the road for eleven days, and I was
feeling the effects. "E, man, I'm tired. This tour has been
a long one."*

*Just then Elvis happened to be taking some tablets from
his case. He selected a small pink one and handed it to
me. "Take this. It will keep you up."*

*"No, I don't think so, E; you know I don't like to take
that stuff."*

*"You won't feel it. It's very mild. It'll just keep you
up."*

*Feeling like a hypocrite—an exhausted hypocrite—I
swallowed the pill with some coffee. Elvis was right; it was
so mild that I took a short nap.*

*When I awoke the sunrise was illuminating the inside of
the plane and I was made aware again of how far outside*

the boundaries of the conventional our lifestyle was. We landed in Memphis and got into the waiting limo. Elvis instructed the driver to go to a medical building before we went to pick up Ginger. We arrived at the medical building around 7:45 A.M. The office was empty except for an assistant, who turned white when she saw Elvis. She explained that the doctor [one I'd never heard of before] should be in soon. Elvis asked her if we could wait in his office. She said yes and escorted us into the inner office, where she left us alone.

Elvis sat down and started nervously drumming his fingers on the desk. Then he quickly got up, went behind the desk, opened a drawer and said, "This is where he keeps my medication."

He selected a vial of pills, looked at the label and emptied half its contents into his pocket. When he saw me staring, he grinned and said, "He won't miss 'em. I know what they are; they're what I need anyway."

About five minutes later the doctor arrived. I left them alone for about fifteen minutes. As we were leaving the building Elvis said, "That worked out good."

Next we drove over to Ginger's house, where she was waiting anxiously, her bags packed. Her mother was overjoyed when she saw Elvis—flying in specially to pick up her baby, Ginger, making up with her after he had sent her home.

CHAPTER

11

A couple of psychics were in the news, predicting Elvis' death, and the press had picked up a few leaks from the bodyguards' book. Elvis' appearance and bizarre behavior only intensified speculation. Sadly, there was little to rebut the rumors. Though Elvis' voice rarely wavered, there were nights when everything else betrayed the truth. He was a very sick man.

Colonel Parker had made a deal with CBS to tape several shows from Elvis' next tour, a ten-day swing through the Midwest. Everyone knew the taping would be done in late June, but Elvis didn't really focus on it until early in the month, and once he did he became as nervous as I'd ever seen him. Elvis was back in Memphis from the third until the seventeenth, when we would be leaving for what would be the last concert tour of his life.

It was early in the evening on June fourth, and Elvis and I were sitting on Graceland's front steps, just relaxing and talking. He was dressed in his black jumpsuit and wearing gold-rimmed sunglasses. Out beyond the gates were dozens of fans, waving and yelling at Elvis, who smilingly returned their greetings. Elvis was carrying his big police flashlight, and he pointed it down the driveway to where Kathy Westmoreland and Ginger were looking over a brand-new white-and-blue Lincoln Continental Mark V, a present for Kathy.

"I'm so lucky to be in the position to give. It's really a gift to give." He grinned, then said, "Lawrence, now it's your turn. I was going to get you a Mark V like Kathy's. Only problem is, there's not one new one left in Memphis. I mean, I looked and I looked. I wanted you to have a car." With that, Elvis pointed the flashlight down the other side of the drive, and I saw Billy drive up to the porch in an old beat-up heap, its paint peeling off in sheets and the hood so warped it barely closed on one side. Elvis, embarrassed and unable to look me in the eye, apologized. "I'm sorry, Larry. This is all I could get. But at least it has wheels and runs."

This has to be a joke, I thought. But when I saw Elvis and Billy playing it so straight, I was afraid that maybe it wasn't.

"Elvis, that's all right," I answered uncertainly. "I appreciate the thought—and the car."

Elvis put his hand on my shoulder and gave me one of those deep, sincere looks, but once he caught Billy's eye they both exploded with laughter. Ricky drove up in a beautiful new Lincoln Continental Mark V. Speechless, I stood there amazed, and Elvis said, "Larry, you gotta admit, it was a perfect setup. I couldn't resist. So this is yours. Check it out. Let's get in."

I sat behind the wheel, and Elvis, sitting in the front passenger seat, said, "Larry, you know I wanted you and Kathy to have these new cars. You deserve it. It's my way of thanking you. It's the least I could do. You know what I've always wanted to do? Tell someone I was gonna buy them a new car, and when the car was delivered the person would get in, and when the motor was turned on, the car would slowly break away. First the doors would fall off, then the tires, and slowly the whole car would collapse, piece by piece." He laughed.

Elvis hadn't been in a better mood for weeks. He was showing Kathy and me all the cars' features when another of the guys came out on the porch. Apparently jealous, one of the other guys snidely remarked that we were receiving what he deserved. Elvis stopped, turned away as if he were going to ignore it, then swung around and caught him on the bridge of his nose with a backhand. Then, realizing what he'd done, Elvis ran up the steps and into Graceland, leaving the guy standing there, stunned, blood pouring down his face. This was the first time I'd ever seen Elvis hit anyone.

Ricky had left his car at the dealership, so I drove him there to pick it up. When I returned, someone had washed the blood from the steps, and Elvis was upstairs in his room. He'd been crying.

"Damn, damn. I'm sorry that stupid shit ruined our moment. I mean, he said the wrong thing at the wrong time. I lost it for a second. I thought I was beyond that, but that asshole gets on my nerves, and he should have known better. I was looking forward to today. I had it all set up, bringing up that old car and all that. Damn, he ruined it for us. Now I'm worried about him. I never hit any of the guys before. Do me a favor. Go downstairs and check on him. Make sure he's all right and call me back."

The aide Elvis hit, X, was back from the emergency room, and I found him in his room, lying on the floor, obviously drunk. Crying and moaning pathetically, he said, "He never hit me before, he never hit me before. Why? Why did he hit me? I love him. I know he loves me."

"Of course he loves you," I said patiently. "I just left him, and he feels as bad as you do. He can't believe he actually struck you. But you need to understand why. The truth is you offended him. You had no right to spoil his pleasure like that."

The phone rang; it was Elvis. I told him what had happened, and he asked me to stay downstairs for the night and keep an eye on X. This seemed like something two adults should have worked out between themselves, but Elvis simply wasn't capable. His violent outburst terrified him, and he was ashamed. "I'll talk to him tomorrow," Elvis said. "Tell him that, and tell him that I love him."

JUNE 5, 1977

I spent the night with X. This afternoon he walked around in a solemn mood, recovering from the shock of yesterday. I called Elvis' bedroom to say goodbye.

"Larry, how's X?"

"He's doing better, E, he's just waiting for you to talk with him and patch everything up. Listen, E, I'm getting ready to drive my new car back to L.A. It's a long drive, and I want to get started."

"Larry, look: You've gotta drive carefully; we don't want anything to happen to you. Now, I know how you feel about taking pills, but I'm sending you something just in case you get tired. So promise me that if you get too sleepy you'll take them—they'll keep ya up—or that you'll pull over into a motel and sleep.

"I'm feeling really bad. I'm not coming down or seeing anyone for a few days. Man, that scene wiped me out. I'm tired and need to recharge. Billy's up here fixing my video; just wait a few minutes, and I'll send him down."

We said goodbye, and I told Elvis I'd call when I arrived in L.A. Fifteen minutes later Billy came downstairs and handed me two Dexedrines. I drove out of Graceland around 7 P.M., headed west on an eighteen-hundred-mile journey.

Two days later I called Graceland to leave word for Elvis that I'd arrived home safely. It had been several years since I'd had the time to drive cross-country, and going through the desert had brought to mind all the wonderful times we had had during the sixties, traveling by night, laughing and singing. When Elvis picked up the phone he sounded very disturbed. The taping for the TV special was drawing near, and he was distraught.

"Man, I don't know how the hell I got into this one," he said. "It's another one of the Colonel's greedy deals. I guess there's no limit to how he'll use me. I wonder if he's still losing bundles of money in Vegas.

"I don't know; I don't get it," he said in a resigned tone. "I guess it comes with the territory. Damn, I've only got a little over a week to drop some weight. I can imagine how I'll look on camera. They'll all think it's fat. Of all the times he picks for me to face that camera. But I'll tell you this, no matter what, I'll give 'em their money's worth."

"Elvis, why don't you go on that liquid diet we talked

about before, with protein, vitamins and minerals? If you do that until we start the tour, you're bound to lose a little weight and you'll feel a little better, at least psychologically.''

"Yeah," he replied, "that's a good idea. Listen, when you come to Memphis, bring me some books about all that. I've gotta do something. In the meantime I'll have them make me those protein shakes.''

"I'll bring some books," I promised. "You must take care of yourself and relax. I know you—you'll sit up there and worry yourself to death.''

Elvis had heard enough, and he quickly changed the subject. "You know, that Mark V I gave you is the best-made American car. You really like it, huh?''

"Elvis, I can't tell you how much I love that car. I don't know how to thank you.''

"Hey, you don't have to. Don't you get it? The car is my way of thanking *you.*''

I asked how X was feeling, and Elvis replied, "Oh, he'll be all right. It was just one of those things. That's behind me now; there's more important things on my mind. It seems that everything hits the fan at once, Larry. To say I'm having second feelings about marrying Ginger is putting it mildly. She's always letting me down. I don't know whose team she's on. She's not after money, but I do suspect—you know me—I suspect someone's behind it, filling her head with all sorts of things. One minute she's here, and as soon as everything is together she runs home to Mama and her sisters. That's why it says in *The Prophet*, 'For even as love crowns you, so shall he crucify you.' ''

Elvis sighed loudly. "Lawrence, I just wonder if she's seeing her old boyfriend. Damn it to hell! This girl has me on fire. I don't wanna lose her. I just hope to God she sees the light before it's too late. All I know is I've gotta get some peace and harmony into this situation. At least Daddy has that with Sandy. I'm gettin' too old for this. Well, anyway, I'm gonna talk to Ginger now, so Larry—''

"Just promise me you won't be so hard on yourself, Elvis. It will only create more problems.''

"I promise. You know me. Didn't I come up with T.C.B.?"

JUNE 16, 1977

Graceland

When I arrived, Elvis was sitting in front of his bathroom mirror, looking heavier than ever. Aurelia and Shelley [his makeup artists] were with him to help a new problem that has surfaced recently: his eyebrows. Due to his failing health and years of using hair dye, his eyebrows are shedding, becoming uncommonly sparse. On the surface Elvis seemed to be in a good mood, but I could see his pain and anguish.

When the ladies left, Elvis' spirits sank, and for good reason. His face was bloated, his eyes were sickly, and his general countenance was worse than ever. His inner, private world was expressed as he got up, shot me a deep, penetrating look and said, "Fuck it; somehow I'll make it through this damn ordeal."

"I know how I look—fuck that. And Red and Sonny's book coming out to get me—fuck that. Ginger's been a blessing and a curse—fuck that! My throat hurts, my body's in pain, the TV cameras, the fans, Daddy's sick, I'm worried about Lisa . . .

"I've been having crazy, mind-boggling dreams. When I can finally sleep."

Elvis sat on the edge of the bed, exhausted. "Just be there for me? We've got to meditate every day. I need all God's help I can get. Just stay close at hand. The Almighty is the only solution there is.

"It just proves that things aren't as they appear," *he went on.* "The fans, the fans—they don't know my pain. And there are some people here around me who see me every day, yet they don't know what I'm all about. Life's a paradox." *For a moment, Elvis' humor prevailed.* "That's two doxes." *He laughed to himself.*

"Well"—*his mood turned grave again*—"it's all part of

the master plan. There are some things that can't be explained; not yet, anyway.''

The next day Graceland was chaotic; everyone running around gathering things together for the tour. Large trunks stood in the den, where several of the guys were packing Elvis' costumes. Suddenly Vernon came down the staircase. Though greatly weakened physically, in some way Vernon appeared stronger than ever, as if all the things he'd wanted to speak up about over the years suddenly exploded inside him. He was visibly angry. He stopped in front of a photograph of his son, taken during the 1973 "Aloha" concert. Everyone turned to look at Vernon, who was obviously furious.

"I just had a long talk with Evis," he said, staring at each person in turn. "He's plenty hurt, and I don't blame him. Don't think my boy doesn't know who his real friends are—y'all are not foolin' anyone 'round here!

"You've all had a good thing goin' here, and Evis is real hurt. He told me that y'all run away every night and never go in and talk with him, or just plain sit 'round and listen to what's goin' on. Y'all supposed to be his friends, and he can't understand why you leave him. He said the only people he feels care are Larry, Billy and Charlie. They're the only ones that stay with him or wanna be with him and keep him company. Now, sometimes Ed does, too, but the rest of ya do your job and get the hell out as fast as you can.

"He's not askin' too much. And I'm just givin' you some good advice. I know Evis. He's fed up, and so am I."

No one said a word, but once it was evident that Vernon was finished they all busied themselves in the embarrassed silence. Vernon walked over to me and said, "Larry, I appreciate you being there for Evis. So does he, I just wanted you to know."

JUNE 17, 1977

Hammons Center, Springfield, Missouri

Elvis' fifth tour of 1977. Everyone around him is on edge. Events cascaded upon one another. Days washed one another out. So the following has been entered in my diary whenever I had a moment away from one emergency or another.

The first nights of the tour were spent preparing Elvis for the forthcoming filming of his CBS television special in Omaha, Nebraska, his first since the great "Aloha from Hawaii" special in 1973. Elvis has been putting extra effort into his performances, getting ready to face the cameras again, but he is plagued by his weight. The contrast between his sylphlike figure in the "Aloha" special and his present appearance is shocking. Elvis is acutely aware of the transformation. His movements onstage are slower, more methodical. His costumes can no longer camouflage the approximately fifty pounds excess baggage covering his frame. His puffy face and swollen eyes mirror his inner torment.

Yet in spite of all this, the adulation never dims and the electricity that flows between the fans and Elvis onstage is as charged as ever. The buildings quiver from the pounding of thousands of feet rhythmically accompanying Elvis—"their" Elvis.

But the fans' love and hysteria can only be contrasted with the grim reality that worsens day by day. It seems that Elvis is constantly talking in cryptic terms that have an ominous ring to them. Last night, just before he was about to walk onstage, he turned to me and with quivering lips said, "I'll give 'em what they want if it's the last thing I do." After the show, while he was lying on his bed with a wet towel covering his face, totally exhausted and full of medication, he said hoarsely, "Now they have something to remember me by. Larry, was it me at my worst?"

Elvis has been reminiscing a lot recently. The other day, before he was scheduled to get ready for the show, a few

*of us were sitting with him in his living-room suite along
with Vernon.*

*Elvis' eyes shone as he was transported back in time.
He spoke of when his asthma was so bad that he had to
take off his shirt and rub his back up and down against
trees to ease the unbearable itching. Vernon would say,
"That's right, son, that's right. I haven't thought of that
in years."*

*"Daddy, remember back in Memphis when you took me
to see my first movie, and we couldn't let the church know
anything about it?"*

*Vernon looked puzzled. "Evis, that was when we were
livin' in Tupelo." Though he never said anything, Vernon
realized that his son's memories reflected a disturbing in-
coherence.*

The *Lisa Marie* taxied to a space reserved for Elvis.
Although his landing was supposed to be a secret, many
fans were on hand to greet him. There was a tremendous
commotion from the hundreds of them roped off by police
security. At the bottom of the ramp stood media people,
the CBS film crews, airport staff, and police, all awaiting
Elvis' appearance. I stood at the front door of the plane
watching as the police held back the fans and attempted
to impose some degree of order. Suddenly the crowd
parted, and Colonel Parker stalked through, pushing people out of his way. With cane in hand and his ever-present
cigar sticking out of his mouth, he stormed up the ramp
and with characteristic brusqueness barked, "Hello,
Larry. Where is he?"

"Hello, Colonel. Elvis is in his bedroom, having his
makeup applied."

As Parker imperiously marched down the plane's aisle,
everyone snapped to attention. He entered Elvis' room,
and when he emerged a couple of minutes later he proceeded purposefully toward me.

Putting his arm around my shoulder as if I were his best
friend, he said, "Larry, you gotta do an important job
tonight. I'm countin' on ya!"

Standing so close that I could feel his breath on my ear,

he said, "Tonight CBS is filming a very important television special. And I need you to help us. You gotta get Elvis up for this show. Now, remember, Larry. Make sure his attitude is right. Talk to him! Talk to him! He listens to you. You know how to do it. I know you do. Just make sure he's in good shape psychologically."

As Parker waddled back down the ramp, I wished that I had the power he attributed to me. If I had, Elvis would not have been sitting before his mirror, anxiously tapping his fingers, watching someone paint on his eyebrows, and dying inside. He would have been someplace else, very far away from Tom Parker.

The two concerts CBS filmed, in Omaha on the nineteenth and Rapid City, South Dakota, on the twenty-first, captured Elvis at his best and his worst. His nervousness was painfully obvious. From where I sat, just a few feet away from him, I could see him rolling his eyes, and pausing at unusual spots. And when he spoke, he sounded very subdued and anxious. The fans, of course, loved him as much as ever, and he returned their love, particularly during a moving, powerful version of "How Great Thou Art." Each time he sang that song or "Unchained Melody," especially the line "I'll be coming home, wait for me," I'd find myself thinking, He's singing to God, and to death.

Elvis never left a stage to less than a standing ovation and thunderous applause. I might hear a random person commenting about how fat Elvis looked or how screwed up he seemed, but most audiences were won over by his presence, his good humor and, of course, his voice. Elvis lived to perform, and although I place much of the blame for his later unhappiness on Parker's insistence that he tour, I'd be less than honest if I didn't admit that even without a Colonel, Elvis probably would have found a way to get back on the road. He needed the fans; he lived for their love. Many stars pay lip service to the so-called little people, but Elvis truly loved them. Except for a couple of ill-advised appearances early in his career, Elvis Presley was never booed, a record most other performers would envy.

Elvis was a consummate showman; he knew what to do

and how to turn even the worst moment into something his audience would perceive as magical. Not only did everyone love the image of Elvis, on the rare occasion the real Elvis appeared before them, they were blind to him. Something that happened before the CBS cameras demonstrated this with painful clarity.

During the show Elvis said, "I'm gonna actually play the guitar. I know three chords, believe it or not. I faked 'em all for a long time." He sounded almost wistful. "They may catch me tonight. And if you think I'm nervous," he continued softly, "you're right."

The audience applauded loudly. I looked up at Elvis and saw his pain. "Gonna do a song called 'Are You Lonesome Tonight,' " he continued sadly. "And I am, and I was."

He sang the first two verses, then began reciting the now-famous monologue. "I wonder if you're lonesome tonight. You know, someone said the world's a stage, and each of us play a part. Fate . . ." Then he stammered for several seconds, unable to speak clearly, but recovered by ending the line with "plus tax." Laughing, he continued, "You read your lines so cleverly," then, having almost stammered over the last word, laughed again, "you never missed a cue. Then came act two, I forgot the words, you seemed to change, you fool, and why I'll never know—why I ever did it."

My heart stopped, and I looked at him. He caught my gaze and flashed me a panicked look that said, *I'm out of control.*

"Honey," he went on, "who am I talkin' to? You lied when you said you loved me, you . . ." Then he chuckled again. "And I had no cause to doubt you. But . . ." Then, stumbling and laughing, he continued, "But I'd rather go on hearing your lies than living without you. Now the stage is bare, and I'm standing there, without any hair—uh, no. And if you don't come back to me, well, to heck with ya!"

He resumed singing, and the audience cheered more loudly than ever. They thought it was part of the act, and Elvis, pro that he was, pulled it off. I had sat there dread-

ing every second, certain the crowd would turn on him. It
was so obvious that Elvis was out of it, and yet by laughing in the right places and inserting his little asides, he
had turned this brief descent into his dark, troubled world
into a comedy bit. Elvis never mentioned this incident,
and, despite the fact that every person in the entourage—
including the musicians and the singers—had been morti-
fied by it, neither did anyone else. Looking back on that
night, I can't help but wonder what might have happened
if he had been booed.

JUNE 26, 1977

The Netherland Hilton, Cincinnati

*Elvis was sitting on his bed cross-legged, wearing his blue
silk pajamas. He was physically exhausted, and because
tomorrow is the last concert of the tour he's feeling relieved that the filming went as well as it did, particularly
after all the built-up anticipation.*

*He had just finished taking a handful of pills from his
nightly medicine packet when Billy walked in. In the past
several months Elvis has been taking his pills in front of
me, as if he doesn't care or the effort of maintaining any
pretense is wasted. The three of us sat on the bed, with
Elvis in the middle. In front of him was a stack of books
including a small black book issued each year from the
U.S. Justice Department, listing the names of all narcotics
agents by city.*

"Look, here it is," Elvis said, opening to the page containing his name. "Every year this special black book
comes out, and only the agents who are listed are allowed
to have a copy." He flipped the pages and read names at
random to Billy and me.

"Here! Here's the agent that we have at the Vatican.
Can you imagine? The Vatican! Man, the illegal flow of
drugs connects every government in the world; even the
Vatican. Man, I love this country. I believe in what we
stand for, and there's a conspiracy to flood America and
ruin the lives of our youth. It's the dark forces using drugs

*to weaken their minds. There's a war going on. I mean,
behind the scenes it's a spiritual war of the light versus
the darkness, and I'm proud to be part of it. I'm ready to
do whatever they call on me for.''*

For the next hour Elvis went on talking about the government's role—and his—while he slowly turned from page
to page. He was getting groggier by the moment, stuttering
and slurring his words as he read name after name. He
was half asleep when he turned a page and a small yellow
tablet fell out onto the bedspread. Elvis picked it up, examined it, grinned and—as he put it into his mouth and
swallowed it with a gulp of Gatorade—said, ''Well, it's
from the government antinarcotics book, so I guess it must
be okay. Anyway, it came from Dr. Nick.''

Within fifteen minutes he was nodding off, mumbling
Lisa's name: ''. . . Lisa . . . don't let 'em . . . stay away
from those cameras.''

''Elvis, what are you talking about?''

His eyes were closed as he murmured, ''They're going
to trap her . . . I see it coming.''

''Elvis,'' I said louder, squeezing his shoulder, ''what
the hell are you talking about?''

Suddenly his body jerked, his eyes opened, and he said,
''Larry—wow!''

''Elvis, you were talking about Lisa. Do you know what
you were saying?''

Elvis' face had a puzzled look. ''Yeah . . . yeah . . .
It's . . . just . . . ah . . .'' He couldn't express himself.
''Let's forget it for right now. Only I want Lisa at Graceland while we have some time off.'' He quickly changed
the subject. ''Who's on duty tonight? I'm hungry. I want
some hamburgers and french fries.''

The medications were starting to wear off. Thank God.

Elvis sought meaning in everything, particularly his
dreams. A couple of years before he had told me of a
dream that made an especially distinct impression. In it he
and Lisa Marie are somewhere in the Holy Land following
Armageddon. There's destruction everywhere, and they're
traveling around in a large armored vehicle, like a tank.

Typically, Elvis' armored vehicle is being driven by a chauffeur. Lisa begins crying.

"Larry," Elvis said, "I look at her and I say, 'Don't worry, honey. Don't worry, honey. Nothing's going to happen to your daddy. There's always going to be an Elvis.' "

Unlike many of his dreams, this wasn't one Elvis had to ponder too long to understand. In his own mind, outside of his very self, there was *another* Elvis.

Elvis was visibly relieved when the tour finally ended. The last day, in Indianapolis, I asked, "You know what today's date is?"

"No, what is it?"

"The Colonel's birthday."

"Of all days," Elvis said, smirking. "Another 'coincidence.' "

The next afternoon we were back at Graceland. I was in the kitchen, having a cup of coffee with Elvis' Aunt Delta, when Vernon came in.

"Larry, what are you up to?" he asked.

"I'm waiting for Elvis to wake up so I can say goodbye before I fly back to Los Angeles."

"Well, I'm goin' up there to wake him. Come on with me if you like."

As we neared Elvis' bedroom door, we heard his voice. Assuming he was talking to Billy or Ginger, we knocked on the door, but when he didn't answer we went in. Elvis was lying alone in bed, delirious, speaking in fragments, some clear, others garbled. Vernon looked at me helplessly. It was the drugs.

"No! No, no! She did it—oh, I know, I know. They told me, yeah, they told me. They all know! They know! Sh-sh-she—she had an abortion. She did it! She did it!"

"Evis! Evis!" Vernon shouted, trying to rouse his son. Tears were running down Vernon's face, and he kept crying out, "Evis! Son! Evis!"

"I can't tell 'em," Elvis kept saying, "I won't—I won't. Red'll tell—in the book—the book. Whoring—in the book. My baby Lisa—oh, Lisa!"

Vernon vigorously rubbed Elvis' shoulder and arm, trying to wake him. "Evis! Evis!"

Suddenly Elvis was jolted into consciousness. "What's goin' on here?" he asked groggily.

"Oh, nothin', son," Vernon replied, trying to wipe his eyes. "You were just havin' a nightmare. Larry, why don't you go back downstairs. I need to talk to Evis privately."

Twenty minutes later Vernon came downstairs. His voice trembling in fear, he said, "Listen, Larry, you got to keep this to yourself, what went on up there." I promised I would.

I postponed my flight until after I saw Elvis. Following dinner I buzzed his room, and at around nine we got together there. He was unusually passive and withdrawn.

"Lawrence, I thought you were going back to L.A. today," he said weakly.

"I wanted to say goodbye in person," I replied.

My book was almost completed, and over the past several weeks I had been approached by investors willing to help me launch my line of hair products. I had kept Elvis posted on my progress, never imagining that he'd want to be involved, but one day he suggested that I use his name to promote my products. All that was left to do was draw up some legal papers for his signature. I knew that Elvis' handshake was good; his word was always his bond. But my backers were understandably cautious, and when I approached Elvis with their concerns, he understood and offered to get things rolling with his attorney, Ed Hookstratten, in Los Angeles. In the past year Elvis had lent his name and some capital to Joe Esposito and Dr. Nick, who were planning to launch a chain of racquetball courts; things hadn't come together, Elvis lost some money, and Vernon was now tighter than ever.

"I thought you had to get back to see Mr. Hookstratten," Elvis said. "You know, in all the years I've been in showbiz, I've never done a single commercial for anyone's products; I've never lent my name for an endorsement. But I want you to use my name for your book and your products. Just don't tell the Colonel about this. He'll only try to screw it up. Just call Hookstratten, tell him what you need on paper, and I'll sign it."

His mood changed, and he sat back, chuckling softly, and remarked, "Oh, your book will come out, all right, but not the way you think." It was as if he knew something I didn't know, as if there was some surprise awaiting me. It so unsettled me, I didn't press him to elaborate, for fear he would really say what I knew he meant.

For the rest of the evening we watched videos—*Dr. Strangelove* (for at least the fiftieth time), some Monty Python programs—and then talked for a while. The sicker Elvis became, the more he relied on Billy, who really understood him. During those last months, Billy was Elvis' anchor, a link with the past, someone who understood what Elvis used to be, what Elvis longed to believe he still was.

Throughout July I felt myself being pulled in several directions simultaneously. Exhausted from the tour, frightened by what I'd seen, I was relieved to be home in Los Angeles with Celest and eager to work out the final plans for the book. I called Ed Hookstratten, and we made an appointment, following which I called Elvis in Graceland. Unfortunately, though I took notes in longhand of our conversations, they aren't dated. They're presented here in the order in which they occurred.

This evening I called Graceland, and when Elvis came on the line he said, "L.G., good timing. I knew you were gonna call tonight. I got the vibes. Earlier I even told Ginger, 'I bet Larry calls tonight.' So what's happenin'?"

After I told him that I'd be meeting with Hookstratten, he said, "Well, I'm sure I'll be gettin' a call from him after you see him. He'll probably call the Colonel too, you know, to check out what this is all about. But don't worry; he's my lawyer, he works for me, and he's only doing his job if he calls the Colonel. If the Colonel calls me, I'll tell him the way it is. This will tear his ol' head up.

"Listen, Larry, I want you to get me a good book on the Holy Shroud of Jesus. I know there's a lot of them, so *pick one out that you feel really covers the subject. I don't know what it is, but I know there's something there for me. So after you finish your business with Hookstratten, you should be able to come back here by the end of the month. Then we got to get ready for the next tour.''*

I was sitting at my desk when the phone rang. It was Charlie. "Larry, Elvis wants to talk with you." Elvis' mood was apparent from his first words. I heard him ask Charlie to leave him alone for a while, and when I asked what was going on there he said, "Good God, don't I deserve some happiness from a woman? Like other people have? Is that asking too much? Man, I'm a human being, you know. There's a real person behind Elvis, who has feelings like everyone else.

"Oh, I know, I realize it's a one-sided love affair. Only I know we're supposed to be together. Son of a bitch, man! You know what she's pushin'? To set a date to get married! And I can't be pushed, you know that. My natural instinct is to rebel. I've always been that way. I can't believe she doesn't know me better than that by now. No matter how I feel about her, I'm not getting pushed into marriage unless she comes around on her own and stops those damn tactics like she laid on me last night. Threatenin' me! She'd better wake up. I don't know what's goin' on in her fool head, but threatenin' me into gettin' married is a big mistake. She doesn't realize who she's dealing with.

"She said that going on tour bores her, and she doesn't know if she's going on the next tour with us. Hey, I strongly detect someone's filling her head and telling her what to say. Larry, I can see right through it. That's not Ginger. I know it. For some reason, I know it's not her words. It's just not her." He sounded hurt, but his voice was level. "Man, I don't want to make another mistake. Hey, I asked you to marry us, so I guess what I'm trying to tell you is that we're in a holding pattern."

"Okay," I said. "Are you still hung up on Priscilla? Is there any way you would ever get back together?"

Elvis laughed. "No way!

"The only thing I care about is Lisa. Priscilla's been a

good mother, but I'll tell you this: I don't appreciate the fact that Lisa knows that other men sleep in the same bed with her unwed mother. It's not right. It can only confuse her head. Lisa's only a nine-year-old kid. I just hope Priscilla isn't foolish enough to get pregnant and have an illegitimate brother or sister for Lisa.

"I've been thinking, though," he said, suddenly optimistic, "if everything works out with Ginger, and we get married, how do you think the court would view it? I mean, if I wanted custody of Lisa, and she wanted to live with us, maybe they'd allow it. You know, me being married, and Priscilla being single, maybe it can make one helluva difference. You know, Larry, I never said anything in court about her fuckin' around. You never know: maybe they'd do me a favor.

"My love for Lisa comes first; she's number one. I want a family now more than ever. It would be perfect, you know? Lisa and Ginger, and I've always wanted a son. If I knew then what I know now, things would be different.

"But the point is . . ." He laughed. "I lost the damn point of all this. Oh, the real point I'm gettin' at is that I've come to realize some hard, cold facts. Certain things I buried within myself go back to when I was a kid. Man, I used to fantasize about everything—about being a star and having money. We were so poor, at least I had my imagination to live off of. I used to fantasize about the things I would do for my folks if I were rich. I made certain promises to myself then, and one of them was to give my mom all the material things in life she never had. Man, I dreamed of showerin' her with furs, jewelry, homes, you name it.

"I used to see my mom slave her life away, suffering and struggling—I could tell you stories that would tear your head up. And growing up the way we were—I mean, no one was poorer than us, my mom made less than half a dollar an hour. But in spite of all that, she kept our family together, put food on the table, instilled in me the real basics in life. She literally lived for me.

"I've told you about this many times, but the point I'm trying to make is: About a year or so later, I was in Ger-

many, in the Army, when it happened. I saw in Priscilla, and I don't know why, certain things that my mama was like. You know, my mom was never educated, but she had a natural way of knowin'. She had natural musical abilities, but she could never afford to have lessons. So I put Priscilla in school to educate her. Drama school, etiquette, dance; the whole bit. I was fantasizing. I was trying, in my own way, to give her what I wanted to give my mom. I wanted Priscilla to take advantage of all the opportunities that my mom was denied.

"I'd never tell this to Ginger—it would only hurt her— but I'll say this for Priscilla: Of all the women in my life, she definitely has the most beautiful face. Her features are classic. I remember back in 1964, I was falling in love with Ann-Margret. You remember. It was serious, and I had to make a choice between Ann and Priscilla. What's really strange is that they look so much alike, like they're sisters. But I chose Priscilla. I'll tell you why. I didn't think it would work with Ann and myself. Priscilla wanted to be a mother and raise children."

Elvis paused, then said, "Larry, I think I hear the pitter-patter of Ginger's feet. We got more things to go into, as you can see. So when you finish up with Hookstratten, you can fly back with Lisa, or I'll have to have security fly out and bring her back. I want her here. That fuckin' book will be out any day now, I want to protect her. So do what you gotta do, and get here with her. I really need to talk with you."

Sometime around the middle of the month I called Graceland to tell Elvis that I hadn't completed my writing and wouldn't be coming to Memphis for another couple of weeks. Elvis was so preoccupied, he hardly heard a word I said. He immediately began talking about the bodyguards' book.

"My so-called friends turned Judas on me. As far as I'm concerned, in the long run it won't matter. I've already let that fuckin' no-good book take its toll on me. You know how the mind has so many preconceived ideas. I've been through the whole gamut. Larry, I tell you, I pity those guys. I wouldn't want to be in their shoes; they have to live for the rest of their lives with what they're doing. So my attitude is, 'Father, forgive them, for they know not what they do.'

"Only what's eatin' away at me is, what is Lisa Marie going to think of her daddy when she grows up?"

Although I'd said it before, I replied, "Elvis, you said it again. What do you mean, what will Lisa think when she grows up? What does she have to think? You'll tell her, you'll explain to her if they exaggerate or blow things out of proportion. Or if they out and out lie, you'll explain that to her also. She'll understand. She'll believe you."

Though he said nothing, I could hear Elvis becoming overwrought and fighting back tears.

"And what if I'm not here to tell her, Larry?"

The *click* reverberated in my ears. The line went dead. I sat at my desk, shaken. Some fifteen minutes later the telephone rang. I barely got out "Hello" when I heard "Hey, Larry, did I hang up on you, or what?" Elvis sounded foggy, uncertain of himself. "Man, my damn brain went dead on me or something."

"Elvis, I heard a click, then a dial tone. I wasn't sure if you hung up or we were disconnected."

"Larry, it's my fault, man. This thing has got me way off center." Elvis stammered, "Man, I—ah—feel like I'm going to explode. Yeah, it's the book, and other things. Good God, why does everything happen at once? Well, like it says in the Desiderata, 'Do not distress yourself with dark imaginings; many fears are born of fatigue and loneliness.' "

Then Elvis laughed to himself and said, "You know, it's weird when you really think about it. Supposedly, all the women in the world want to be with Elvis, and my own so-called lady doesn't.

"I found out she's been in touch with her old boyfriend. I want to believe she's moral and she wouldn't do anything, but what really hurts is she's not standing by me. And of all times—with that fuckin' book comin' out—you would think she'd really understand and be with me all the way. I don't want to lose her.

"Listen, Larry, there's something else. I told you a few times that we've never gone all the way. Well, it's true. Hey, we fool around," he added quickly. "It almost got to that point a few times; I mean, I got hot and heavy. Oh, man . . ."

After a few seconds' silence, he continued. "You know all the stories that have circulated about me over the years. I mean, I'm supposed to be *Elvis* the World's Womanizer, having anyone I want, as many as I can handle in one night. No one, I don't care who it is, can live up to that image and survive. Man, I'm barely running on one cylinder."

"Okay, Elvis, okay. I hear you."

"Larry, just listen. You know this isn't easy for me, so let me get this out. Man, what I'm talking about is so heavy. I don't have the strength within me to make it with her. Shocking, isn't it? There's just too many pressures right now. Can you imagine how that makes me feel? It's tearing my damn head up. Ginger hasn't said anything about it, but that's what's probably confusing the hell out of her and probably that's why the temptation of her old boyfriend . . .

"Larry, this time I'm going to just hang up. I need to. We'll talk about this later. Thank God, at least we'll be able to write about this. In the meantime, I'll just hang in there. You know, I'm not the only one. Everyone has their own cross to bear, but when you start bleedin', it's a mess."

"Elvis, I just want you to know I love you."

"Larry, I love you, too. I'll just talk with you later."

On August 4 Elvis dialed my house direct, which was unusual for him; usually Charlie or one of the guys placed his calls. "Larry, you're still in L.A. What's goin' on? I know Hookstratten already checked the situation out."

"I just got the papers," I explained. "I was going to call you as soon as I wrap everything up here, then I'll fly back. It'll probably be in a week or so."

"You know, we have to leave on the sixteenth," he answered, "and I really need you here."

"Don't worry, E. I'll be there. By the way, when I went to Hookstratten's office to pick up the papers, you should have seen the look on his face as he handed them to me. He looked startled. He said, 'I'm sure you realize what Elvis is doing for you. No one has used his name like this. He certainly thinks a lot of you.' He told me he'd be sending a copy to your father for you. Elvis, thank you so much."

"You gotta be kidding," Elvis replied. "What you've done for me over the years goes beyond the call of duty. Giving you permission to use my name is the least I could do. If you didn't me get on the spiritual path, I would've been dead years ago. So I'm happy to help you with your book. But I did something else that will be everlasting, that really represents how I feel. I've already told you, you're in my last will and testament. I've told Daddy—"

I had to stop him.

"Elvis, you know well enough how potent our thoughts are, how we create by thinking, that our thoughts are living things that determine our lives. What I'm really getting at is—"

"Look, Larry, I'm on fire, man," Elvis interjected forcefully. "Why me, Lord, why me?" he murmured to himself. After a few seconds' silence, he said, he said, "You just have to keep the faith. I know what I'm talkin' about. You know the book Rudhyar wrote? I wanna read you something.

"All right, listen to this: He says on page ten, 'A very important time for you, and also for the whole world, and you may play quite a significant role in what will happen then all over the globe.'"

Though from earlier conversations I knew that Elvis was proud about this passage, as he read it his voice betrayed his doubts. I don't think he realized how transparent his attempts to throw me off the track were. He was a master at diverting attention from things he didn't want to deal with and creating whatever impression he desired.

"Here," he said, flipping to another section, "I'm skipping over this Rudhyar astrology jargon that I don't know anything about. Ah . . . here! My charts show a potential conflict between social forces and friends working upon me, and a deep quest for superpersonal values. 'Friends working upon me'—that's putting it mildly. He says, 'The tensions indicated could conceivably affect your health, or your most characteristic work, at some periods, especially between 1972 and 1977.'

"Well, Priscilla and I broke up in 1972. My so-called friends are tryin' to crucify me with their book in 'seventy-seven. And tensions have definitely taken their toll. Then it says here, 'You seem eager, and also able, to leave permanent records of your personality and its ideals in a really enduring form.'' And you can see from what he says about the conflict between social forces and even friends that this is exactly what Cheiro says in *The Book of Numbers*. Listen to this . . .''

Elvis obviously had the book nearby. ''This is for number eights, like us: 'These people are invariably much misunderstood in their lives, and perhaps for this reason they feel intensely lonely at heart—and they generally play some important role on life's stage, but usually one which is fatalistic or as the instrument of fate for others. And such persons often are called on to face the very greatest sorrows, losses, and humiliations.'

''Larry, I'm not saying we're bound by all this, but it sure explains my life. So I guess what I'm sayin' is, it's been written and so shall it be done. And that reminds me, don't forget to get me the best book on the Holy Shroud of Jesus. I really need to look into it. It seems to me that it's definite proof that Jesus, or Yeshua or whatever His real name is, definitely did walk the earth and for some reason left behind His own cloth that they wrapped His body in that made His imprint. His spirit. The Christ is eternal and now we have physical proof, because whoever it was that had a body so highly charged with that degree of energy left it as a permanent record of His existence.

''Man!'' Elvis exclaimed after talking nonstop for almost half an hour. ''Good God, I've been yackin' away. Only I had to.''

"Hey, E, don't worry about that. We've talked this long many a time."

"Yeah, it's like those times, Larry. Only I hope you remember all of this. You know what I mean?"

"Are you kidding? I've got it all down here."

AUGUST 8, 1977

Los Angeles

Today is my thirty-eighth birthday. Usually it's a happy, joyous occasion. However, this day I find myself overwhelmed as my mind keeps turning to Elvis. What is destroying him? And what about Ginger? Does she honestly love this man who is more than twice her age? I wonder if that's the reason Elvis has been telling me more and more about what happened when he was a child and as he was growing up. And more and more about Gladys and what she meant to him. And more and more he seems to be in tears as he remembers those things.

Around 10 P.M., I couldn't sit still; I had to get out. As I drove my Mark V I had no destination in mind. I was driving around for about forty-five minutes, oblivious to where I was, when suddenly, from the pit of my stomach, a nauseous wave swept over me. There I was, driving and crying, and I found myself in front of the Musicians Union on Vine Street. My mind conjured a picture of Elvis. Dead.

I drove home as fast as I could and dialed Graceland. God, I thought, it's three-thirty in the morning there; what am I doing? As I was about to hang up, the maid answered sleepily. I asked what was going on there. She said simply that she'd brought up some food to Elvis and that Graceland was quiet. I told her I'd see her next Sunday.

AUGUST 12, 1977

Charlie called for Elvis, asking me when I'm coming back to Graceland and to not forget the book on the Jesus shroud. I asked Charlie to convey to Elvis that I will be leaving here the day after tomorrow. All my business ac-

*tivities are now under control. And, of course, the book
he wants will be with me.*

AUGUST 14, 1977

*I stopped by the Bodhi Tree to select the books for Elvis.
There was a large selection on the subject of the Holy
Shroud of Turin. I knew that there was a growing interest
in it and that many scientific studies have been done; however, I was still surprised by the wide range of books within
this category. Of all the books on the shelf,* The Scientific
Search for the Face of Jesus, *by Frank O. Adams, beckoned to me, and I knew this was the one. I also selected
two others,* The Second Birth, *by O. Mikhail Aivanhov,
and* Music: The Keynote of Human Evolution, *by Corinne
Heline.*

Later that day my father drove me to the airport. He
noticed that I was unusually quiet.

"Larry, is there something wrong?" he asked.

I thought for a moment. Usually I told my father and
mother almost everything, but they weren't aware of how
serious Elvis' situation was. They both loved Elvis. During the sixties, when my father used to visit the movie
sets, he and Elvis would talk between shots about all kinds
of things.

"Dad, I just hope he's alive by the time I get there."

"Is it that bad, son?"

"Dad, it's worse than you know. And I'm really
scared."

*I arrived in Memphis late Sunday night. I took a taxi
directly to the Howard Johnson's motel, a short distance
from Graceland, down the road on Elvis Presley Boulevard. I realized the significance of this date: It was nineteen years ago today that Elvis' mother died. I wondered
about that a few times today and had some ominous feelings as well. Why, of all days, did I fly in on August 14?*

*I dismissed my feelings as negative doom and gloom.
Everything's all right. I'm in Memphis. Elvis is here. And*

*we're leaving on tour Tuesday. Perhaps this tour will be
the last one before Elvis makes the new changes in his life
he spoke about in Portland, Maine.*

*Elvis' room was buzzed for me, and when he answered
he sounded weary. "Hello, who's this?"*

"It's me, E. I just checked into my room."

*"Finally, huh? Well, I guess everything is timing. I'm
in bed, trying to get rested and ready for the tour. Would
you mind if I called it a night?"*

*"Of course not. I'm sure you know best. So get plenty
of rest."*

*"Lawrence," Elvis said before hanging up, "I'm glad
you're finally here, but I need to recharge the ol' batteries.
So I'm going to knock myself out and sleep as much as I
can. All right?"*

"No problem, E, I'll talk with you tomorrow."

It was after nine o'clock the evening of the fifteenth,
and I was having dinner in the kitchen when Joe walked
in. Elvis phoned the kitchen from his room and told Joe
that he wanted to see *MacArthur*. "He's going over to Dr.
Hoffman's to have a tooth filled, and he wants us to make
the arrangements and set up the film," Joe explained.
Around ten, Elvis, Ginger, Billy and Charlie left for Dr.
Hoffman's in Elvis' black Stutz, while Joe and I stayed
behind, calling all over town, trying to set up the screening in a local theater. Everything was arranged, but it was
impossible to find a projectionist, and when Charlie checked
in with us around eleven-thirty we gave him the news. I
remember thinking it was probably all for the best, since we
were scheduled to leave for Maine tomorrow anyway.

Around twelve-thirty we heard the Stutz pull up the
drive. I hadn't seen Elvis in six weeks, and when I saw
him I was horrified. He walked through the front door and
stopped in the foyer, about fifteen feet from where I was
standing in the dining-room doorway. He removed his
glasses and shook his head from side to side. He never
said a word, but the look that he gave me spoke volumes.
I saw fear and pain. He put his sunglasses back on, then

with Ginger at his side slowly ascended the staircase to his room.

I'd seen him in bad shape before but nothing like this. Charlie and Billy said hello; I didn't hear them or anyone else. I sat down on a sofa and for the next forty-five minutes tried to absorb what was happening. I snapped out of it only after I heard my name and had a telephone receiver pushed into my hands.

"Hello?"

"Lawrence," Elvis said very softly, "did you bring that book on the Holy Shroud of Jesus?"

"Do angels have wings?"

"Yeah, and don't forget: Angels fly because they take themselves so lightly."

We both laughed longer than we should have; it must have been nerves. When we finally settled down, I said, "Wait until you feast your eyes on the other books I brought you also. You'll love 'em."

In his Inspector Clouseau voice, Elvis replied, "I know that already," sending us back on another giggling jag. "Well, what do you think we should do, Larry? Do you wanna come up here and talk, or do you think we should wait until tomorrow?"

I was struck by the tone and texture of his voice. It sounded so light and pure, the way I imagined he spoke when he was a very small child. I had never heard him sound so peaceful.

"Well, E," I said slowly, still trying to figure out what he wanted, "it's really good hearing you like this. Maybe we should wait until tomorrow. It's already past one-thirty in the morning. This way you can get some rest for the tour, and I'll come up when you wake up tomorrow, do your hair, give you the books. And we have the rest of the tour. I'm sure we have a lot to talk about. How does that sound?"

"Well, whatever's right."

I hesitated for a moment. Elvis was many things, but never so passive. It was unusual for him not to ask to see me or at least get his new books right away. "All right,"

I answered, "I'll see you later, E. I'm going back to my room at Howard Johnson's. I'll be there if you need me."

"I knew that," Elvis quipped à la Clouseau. Laughing, we both hung up, never bothering to say goodbye.

As I walked to my car to leave Graceland, I felt my heart pounding, and yet I wasn't troubled. About an hour later I was reading in bed when my phone rang. It was Al Strada.

"Elvis decided he wants the books now. He says he can't fall asleep without them."

"Well," I answered, "I'm already in bed. I guess I could get dressed and bring them over."

"No, I'll come over and pick them up. I'll be there in ten minutes. This way you can go back to bed."

Sure enough, ten minutes later I handed Al the books. I was careful to put *The Scientific Search for the Face of Jesus* on the top of the stack, and I had marked with paper clips the pages Elvis would find most interesting.

I fell asleep, and woke after eleven the next morning, feeling tired and sluggish. I went back to sleep and experienced a terrible nightmare, in which a hideous monster pursued me. Just as I came within inches of its grasp, I levitated and, flying above the beast, looked up to see Elvis. He was reaching out his hand to lift me up and kept talking to me, telling me something important, but it was drowned out by the beast's screeches and howls. When I finally escaped into consciousness, I was soaking wet with sweat, and all my muscles ached.

I took a long shower, then walked to the coffee shop. As I sipped my coffee, I looked out the window and saw helicopters hovering down the road, over Graceland. It struck me as odd but not alarming. Maybe someone was filming him, I thought. Perhaps they needed some footage for the CBS special. I went back to my room and got ready to go to Graceland. I was riding in a shuttle-bus-type taxi when I saw the crowds milling around the Music Gates. There were always fans around there anyway, and the crowds seemed to swell whenever Elvis was leaving for or returning from a tour. We were driving up to the gates when Uncle Vester spotted me from the guardhouse. As he approached, I said, "Vester, don't worry. They're just going to drive me up to the house and leave."

He looked at me blankly for a second, then said, "Didn't you hear what happened?"

"No. What happened?"

"Elvis died."

It didn't register. I looked up at Elvis' bedroom window, then back to his uncle. *"Elvis what?"*

"He just died, Larry. Elvis died."

CHAPTER

12

Stepping across Graceland's threshold, I was assaulted by the mournful sounds emanating from the house. I hadn't been inside more than a few minutes when I spotted Vernon, ashen and looking very small, sitting in a chair crying loudly. When he saw me he extended one arm and gestured for me to come to him.

"He's gone! He's gone, Larry," Vernon wailed. "What am I gonna do?"

I put my arms around him and held him tightly as he heaved with sobs. He felt so weak and frail, like a tiny bird. "Vernon, I love you," I said.

"Larry, he's gone! He's gone!"

As her grandfather continued crying, Lisa Marie walked around in circles, sobbing and repeating, "My daddy is dead. My daddy is dead."

At one point Vernon tried to rise from his chair, and collapsed. Several of us ran to his side, helping him up. His face was wet with tears.

Before long, the story of what had happened after I left Graceland the night before was pieced together. After Al Strada had come back to Graceland with the books, Elvis, Ginger, Billy and Billy's wife, JoJo, went out to the racquetball court to play a game or two. Around 4 A.M. Elvis and Ginger returned to his room, where she fell asleep and he stayed up to read. He was still up when Ginger awoke at around nine. Elvis told her he was going to read

322

in the bathroom. Ginger advised him not to fall asleep in there, then went back to sleep.

Sometime between then and when Ginger discovered Elvis' body after one that afternoon, Elvis died. Ginger found him lying on the floor and not breathing. Several medical people would later say that it was obvious that Elvis had been dead for some time, but everyone at Graceland, the ambulance attendants, Dr. Nick and a special resuscitation team at Baptist Memorial Hospital valiantly tried to bring him back to life. It was too late. At 3:30 P.M. on August 16, 1977, Elvis was pronounced dead. By eight that evening the official cause of death was announced: cardiac arrhythmia, or erratic heartbeat, possibly precipitated by mild hypertension and coronary-artery disease. During the course of the day Charlie, Billy, Al and David each approached me to tell me that Elvis died clutching the book I had just given him, *The Scientific Search for the Face of Jesus.*

The phone wouldn't stop ringing, and for a while I answered a number of calls, saying the same thing countless times, "Yes, it's true. Elvis died today of a heart attack." Before too long, I just broke down. I got up and paced the floor from room to room, crying incessantly. When Aunt Delta saw me she said, "You know, Larry, stranger things have happened." What a peculiar remark, I thought. Looking back, though, I realize she was right. Stranger things had happened.

Lisa asked Sam Thompson, who had come to Memphis so that he could accompany her back to Los Angeles that day, where she could reach his sister. In the years Elvis and Linda were together, Lisa and Linda had developed a close relationship. Though Lisa was just a little girl, she seemed to realize that Linda had taken good care of her daddy. With Sam's help she dialed Linda in California.

"My daddy's dead!" Lisa cried the instant Linda answered.

"Honey, your daddy isn't dead," Linda replied, trying to calm her.

Sam took the receiver from Lisa and said, "Linda, you'd better come home. Elvis is dead."

By five o'clock Graceland was filled with mourners: ex-employees, old friends, relatives, special fans. Of course everyone is upset by death, but the thing about Elvis' death was that no one could believe it. Elvis Presley dead? It didn't seem possible. As more people crowded in and the reality began to fully sink in, I felt I was suffocating. I stepped out on the porch, and the sight beyond the gates was bewildering: tens of thousands of people gathered there. People were stationed throughout the grounds to maintain some control. Weeping and moaning, these countless strangers would keep their vigil until Elvis was laid to rest, and after. Some reporters, as taken with the scene as we were, wondered why. After all, they knew who Elvis was, but an outpouring on this scale? It didn't make sense. To those of us inside, there was no mystery about it: they loved Elvis, as they always had, as they always would love him.

Back inside, Vernon and Joe Esposito were meeting with a funeral director and making arrangements. Later Joe and the director approached me and asked that I help prepare Elvis' hair the next morning. I agreed.

By early evening Lisa Marie began to calm down. Some of us were sitting in the den when she walked in, sat down and remarked dispassionately, "You know, I just can't believe it: Elvis Presley is dead." We all looked at one another in disbelief. It seemed so bizarre, and yet it was just one of many strange, unsettling incidents.

Around 2:30 A.M. Priscilla arrived with her family and Jerry Schilling, having flown in from the West Coast on the *Lisa Marie*. Ed Parker, Linda Thompson and a few other friends of Elvis' based in California had assumed they'd also be flying back to Memphis on Elvis' plane, but Priscilla had refused to permit them aboard. The bad feelings her action engendered caused needless pain.

It was nearly four when those of us lucky enough to find accommodations in Memphis (there was a Shriners' convention that week) left to get some rest. Though rooms were scarce, several hotels kindly made special arrangements for those attending the funeral. By then, even more distraught fans had joined the crowd outside. It took the police twenty minutes just to escort me through the gates. During that time I was surprised to hear strangers calling out my name.

The morning of the seventeenth I picked up my wife, Celest, who had flown in with Linda Thompson, at the Memphis airport. I was so relieved to see them, and happy that they'd been able to make this painful journey together. Next I went to the Memphis Funeral Home, where I met Charlie Hodge, and we attended to Elvis. Driving back to Graceland, I found everything about the day—the sight of people crying everywhere I looked, my thoughts, the heat, the wails, the dark tension that blanketed the city— impossible to absorb. The only thing that seemed real to me was the fact that Elvis was gone.

Graceland was relatively quiet inside and, except for the maids, Aunt Delta, Grandma Minnie Mae (who was confined to her room) and a few of the guys, strangely empty.

At noon sharp the long white hearse came down Elvis Presley Boulevard, flanked on either side by six motorcycle policemen, their lights flashing and sirens blaring. The procession swept through the Music Gates, up the long drive, and came to a stop at the front steps. Several of us helped the attendants carry in the nine-hundred-pound copper coffin, which was placed in the living room and opened so that the family, friends and staff could pay their respects. The lid was raised, and there was Elvis, dressed in a white suit, a white tie and a pale-blue shirt. His face looked so serene.

Grandma was led in first, supported by Vernon and Aunt Delta. The moment she saw Elvis she collapsed. As we carried her back to her bedroom, she sobbed and cried out, "Oh, God! Oh, God! He was the prettiest thing I ever did see," repeating it over and over. Leaving her room, I recalled Elvis saying ten years before, "She'll probably outlive me."

Lisa Marie lovingly stroked her daddy's forehead and ran her fingers through his hair. I stood close by, and every time she stepped away I remodeled his hair. One by one, people approached the coffin to be with Elvis, to touch him for the last time, to gaze upon his face.

That afternoon Vernon decided the fans should be allowed to view his son for the last time. We moved the coffin into the foyer and placed it just several steps inside the front door. A massive security force, consisting of 150 uniformed officers plus a unit of Air National Guard and military sentries, maintained order as a single line of fans entered the house. I sat up on the staircase and watched as people from all over the country and all over the world filed past Elvis. Their grief was palpable; so was their love.

Out on the lawn lay people who had collapsed from heat, exhaustion, hunger, thirst or grief. One woman suffered a heart attack. Inside and out, Graceland was blanketed by flowers, sent from all over the globe and arranged in all kinds of shapes—guitars, hearts, Bibles, teddy bears, TCB insignias, crowns. In the oppressive heat, their sweet, heavy scent wafted through the air. Millions of insects added to the eerie atmosphere with their loud, incessant screeching.

Despite our petty jealousies and disagreements, all of us who had worked for Elvis were united, as he had always wanted us to be. During the next few hours, we shared stories and fond memories of him. Interestingly, some of the group remarked about witnessing strange phenomena around the time of Elvis' death, which they attributed to some kind of spiritual doing on Elvis' part. Suddenly they were seeking answers of their own. Elvis must have been pleased, wherever he was. I was sitting with Vernon, watching as the procession of twenty thousand people professed their love for his son. Vernon turned to me and said softly, sadly, "Larry, now Evis is in heaven."

After six, when the police shouted through their bullhorns that the gates would be closing, the crowd nearly rioted. "No! No! We want to see Elvis!" Once order was restored, the gates were closed, and we moved the coffin back to the music room, where it would remain. As touched as we all were by the crowd's outpouring of sympathy, there was a potential for the situation outside to turn ugly. Later that night a drunk driver plowed through the crowd, killing two people and seriously injuring a third.

James Brown called when he heard about Elvis' death, and arranged to come and pay his respects. That day he sat near Elvis for what seemed like hours, lost in his own private thoughts. He said very little, and was obviously very upset. Because Elvis had respected him so much, this private tribute held special meaning.

The funeral service was scheduled to begin at two on the eighteenth. I arrived just minutes before noon. As I drove through the gates, I noticed souvenir hawkers out selling T-shirts and buttons commemorating the event. One hundred vans had come that morning to carry the flowers to the cemetery where he would be entombed in a mausoleum several hundred yards from his mother's grave.

The first thing I did was walk into the music room. Elvis looked blissful, his face radiating a state of grace. Other times in the last two days I had glanced at him and seen what I was sure was a smirk. As the hour of the funeral approached, people began arriving. Ann-Margret, who had flown in from California with her husband, Roger Smith, appeared badly shaken. Ginger, who understandably hadn't yet recovered from having found Elvis' body, was devastated. She stayed near her family the whole time. Linda Thompson drew some disapproving glances when she arrived wearing a lavender dress.

"I don't care what anyone thinks," Linda remarked to me in her typical forthright manner. "Elvis told me a few years ago, 'Black is worn at funerals for mourning. At my funeral I want people to dress in colors and be happy for me.' Elvis always told me that purple and violet are the highest spiritual colors. I know this is the way Elvis wants it. He always said, 'I want to know about God, about life, and life after death.' And now he does."

Many of the women Elvis knew came carrying spiritual books he'd given them.

About forty-five minutes before the service, I went into the maid's bedroom, where Vernon was dressing.

"Come in, Larry. I'm glad you're here. I want to talk to ya. I just want you to know that Tuesday I was waitin' for Evis to wake up so I could go upstairs and have him sign the letter form Hookstratten. I know he wanted to sign it for you. I had it in my coat jacket all ready for him."

Vernon pointed to his inside pocket, then his voice cracked, and the tears began to well up in his eyes.

"And, Larry, ya know how Evis felt about ya. You were one of his favorites, and there was only a couple. You know what I mean.

"Ya know, Larry, I've got to admit somethin' to ya. It took me a long time to realize that both you and Evis were kindred souls—spiritual. I didn't know it at first, and I'll tell ya somethin' else I want ya to know. When ya first came here years ago and ya gave Evis all those books, I couldn't figure ya out. I wasn't sure. I was suspicious of ya. I even told Evis of my feelings, and ya know what he said? 'Daddy, he's a great guy.'

"And when he told me that, that was good enough for me."

"Mr. Presley," I said. "As far as the letter from Hookstratten goes, it doesn't matter. That's not important now. And as for what you told me about Elvis and me, I'm so glad you recognize that. I always felt that you did, and it's important to me that you told me. And there's something that I want you to know: I love you. You mean so much to me."

Placing his hand on my knee, Vernon said, "I know, Larry, I know." Fighting back his tears, he said, "Well, I guess Evis found what he was always searchin' for. Now he's at peace, and he's with God, where his heart was all along.

"There's one more thing." Vernon took a picture out of his coat pocket. "I received this in the office on Monday. I don't know who sent it."

The picture showed a saintly figure, wearing a long white robe. The face was blank, as if it had been erased. The image was the same one that appears on the cover of the book Elvis was reading when he died.

"When I saw the picture, I knew it meant something," Vernon said, shaking his head. "Now I know. It was like a sign of what was to happen."

I left Vernon pondering the strange picture.

I had barely absorbed that when Colonel Parker made his entrance, attired in a loud short-sleeved Hawaiian shirt and a baseball cap. There were rumors circulating among the guys that he was already pressuring Vernon to sign a deal to continue his management of Elvis. As always, I observed Parker closely, noticing that he never once approached Elvis' coffin and never even set foot in the room where Elvis lay. Parker loyalists have attributed his questionable behavior to his deep and profound grief. My favorite was Priscilla's excuse for Parker: "He disguised his emotions as best he could," a statement that can be read two ways. Another Parker sympathizer explained the old man's actions thusly: "He just wants to remember his boy the way he was." "The way he was" when? Lying in a hotel room with his head being dunked in ice water? Stammering through lyrics with his eyes half closed? Working Vegas to cover his manager's gambling debts? Elvis' death changed nothing for Parker. He showed the same "respect" for Elvis in death as he had in life. I turned away in disgust.

By two o'clock, over two hundred people had taken their places in the music room, the foyer and the dining room, and the service began. Statements were made by the evangelist Rex Humbard (whom Elvis briefly had met with on one of the last tours) and comedian Jackie Kahane. Vernon's pastor, C. W. Bradley of Whitehaven Church of Christ, gave a beautiful and honest eulogy, during which he said, "Elvis was a frail human being. And he would be the first to admit his weaknesses. Elvis would not want anyone to think that he had no flaws or faults. But now that he's gone, I find it more helpful to remember his good qualities, and I hope you do, too.

"Thus, today I hold up Jesus Christ to all of us."

During Kathy Westmoreland's rendition of "My Heavenly Father Watches Over Me," the pianist lost his place. Later, on the way to the cemetery, Kathy said, "I closed my eyes when he lost his place, and I swear I could hear Elvis say, 'Would you believe it? That poor old guy is messing up my funeral.' " She also sang "How Great Thou Art," with J. D. Sumner and the Stamps Quartet,

Jake Hess, Elvis' favorite gospel singer, then sang "Known Only to Him" with the Statesmen Gospel Quartet, followed by J.D. and the Stamps singing "His Hand in Mine" and "Sweet, Sweet Spirit." Though Elvis was not there singing, many of us heard his voice.

As the service drew to a close, Vernon rose from his seat at the very front and screamed, "Son, I'll be with ya, soon! Son, I'll be with ya soon!" Grandma became almost hysterical with grief, and poor little Lisa sat crying, frightened and confused by the outbursts. Many people walked outside to wait for the cortege to assemble. Inside, several of us said our last farewells. Vernon and I embraced, sobbing.

"Larry, this is the final curtain," Vernon said, weeping. "This is the final curtain."

Joe Esposito removed the diamond TCB ring from Elvis' left hand. I stepped to the head of the coffin and gently pulled down a lock of Elvis' hair, arranging it so that it rested on his forehead in the familiar curl. Despite the occasion, I suspected that Elvis would have wanted to leave us like that. The coffin lid closed for the last time.

In seventeen white Cadillac limousines, we followed the white hearse out through the Music Gates, down the middle of Elvis Presley Boulevard, past thousands of people lining the streets, to the cemetery. Our motorcade, flanked on each side by police motorcycles in a moving barricade, never slowed or stopped, despite countless hysterical people running toward the hearse. Along the way law-enforcement officials and average people saluted Elvis. Flags flew at half staff in Tennessee and Mississippi.

Once inside the cemetery, the procession stopped at a large white marble mausoleum. It appeared to float on the sea of flowers that washed over the lawn. Elvis' coffin was carried inside, where, after another short service, it was slid into its presumed final resting place in the crypt.

We returned to Graceland and spent the next few hours consoling one another. Priscilla approached me and kindly offered to take me back to Los Angeles on the *Lisa Marie*. I declined, and stayed in Memphis a few more days.

* * *

I recall Elvis saying many times over the years, "I'm not afraid of death. Only the ignorant, the unenlightened person is afraid of death. And that's because they're afraid of living. People, man, they go to funerals and everyone wears black, and everyone's crying. They should be rejoicing. The soul's free. The soul is going back to God, going home again."

Elvis always referred to death in terms of going home again. And I suppose it's a comfort to those of us who loved him to know that he felt that way. Certainly Elvis found his place with God, and he was home. Only years later, when I'd look back over the last year or so before his death, did I see how strongly death beckoned Elvis. With his lifestyle, he could have died a thousand times— on his plane, in his sleep, on the road. But he didn't. Death came to Elvis in one of his few private moments, and he surrendered.

Several times I drove to the cemetery and stopped outside the mausoleum. Yet I could never bring myself to go inside; I knew Elvis wasn't really there. Now and again, I glanced through the loose papers that made up my "journal," but it was too soon. Without explaining to my father what the papers were, I gave them to him and asked him to keep them in a safe place for me.

Not long after Elvis' death, Charlie called me. He was living at Graceland then.

"Larry, I just found out something that would shock the world."

"I know, Charlie."

"No, Larry, you don't know. I know you know everything, but you don't know this."

"Charlie, Elvis had cancer."

'How do you know?'' he asked, amazed.

"I don't know how I knew, but I did. I can't answer you, but I knew."

"Yeah, well, we just found out today. I was there when the doctor told Vernon. He said, 'Mr. Presley, it's a good thing Elvis died the way he did, because the end would have been horrible. He had cancer of the bone marrow, leukemia.' ''

Recalling Elvis' complaints of pain, fatigue, the bruises,

it made sense to me. Because Elvis' death was determined by the medical examiner to have resulted from natural causes, the family was allowed to keep the autopsy results private, which they did. The secrecy has only added credence to reports of Elvis being an addled junky whose sole interest in his prescriptions was pleasure. When lab results indicating quantities of prescription drugs present in his system were leaked to the press, charges of a cover-up seemed all the more plausible.

On August 22, 1977, Elvis' last will and testament was filed with the Shelby County Probate Court. Vernon said to Charlie, "I want you to come down to court to verify Evis' signature on the will, because you signed a page, too, as a witness that day. So did Ginger. But we just need one person.

"And, listen, Charlie," Vernon added, "I can't take care of everything. I can't take care of everything in Evis' will. It's just too much. It's too much."

Charlie went down, was sworn in, and testified that the signature on the last page of the thirteen-page document was Elvis'. Shortly thereafter, Charlie was fired and was asked to leave Graceland immediately. No further explanation was offered.

Elvis' beneficiaries under the will are Lisa Marie, Vernon, Minnie Mae, and any other relatives who, in the opinion of the executor—Vernon—were in need. Nothing was left to Priscilla, Parker, any of Elvis' girlfriends or any of his other friends or employees.

Vernon and I spoke almost every week for a while after Elvis died. One day he called me and said, "Well, Larry, we've got all that life insurance behind us now."

Vernon started crying. "He had cancer, Larry. He had cancer. I can't do everything Evis wanted to do, Larry. I can't do it. It's too much."

In early 1985, Billy Smith, Elvis' cousin, claimed that the probated will was a fake. In an interview published in England, Billy told of Elvis explaining to him who would be included in his will. Billy's account corresponds with Elvis' conversations with me.

"On page seventeen," Billy is quoted as saying, "as I recall, [the will] talked about bequests to a number of people. Among them was my name, and it said he was leaving me fifty thousand dollars. Elvis told me to find a hiding place for the will, and I hid it in his bookcase under a pile of books."

No one except Billy knew where this handwritten, original version of the will was hidden. After Elvis died, someone from Graceland called Billy and asked him where the handwritten version was. Billy described the location, and, according to someone referred to as "another member of the household," Vernon then went upstairs alone, locking the door behind him. The probated will, the one Charlie verified Elvis' signature on, is just thirteen pages long.

Billy said of his uncle, "I believe Vernon decided that Elvis had given us enough." When I read that, Vernon's cryptic remarks "I can't do it, it's too much" made sense to me. He was lost without Elvis, frightened and confused. Vernon did what he thought best for Lisa Marie.

Several weeks after Elvis died, I had a dream: My younger son, Kiara, and I are together. Suddenly Elvis appears, looking radiant and peaceful, and takes me by the hand. I'm holding Kiara's hand, and together we walk toward something.

"I have to take you somewhere," Elvis says. "I'm going to tell you all the mysteries, Larry. Only you're not going to remember this when you wake up."

We walk into a cathedral even greater than St. Peter's Church in the Vatican. The ceilings are so high they can't be seen, and the stained-glass windows are larger than skyscrapers. It's magnificent, more beautiful than anything I ever imagined. Far off in the distance, I see other people in the cathedral, standing in shafts of light.

"All right," Elvis says. "Now I'm going to tell you things that you want to know and you need to know."

The next thing I knew I was awake—my phone was ringing. It was my sister, Elaine.

Vernon and I continued to speak every so often. He was

growing weaker each day, and he never got over Elvis' death. He asked me for a copy of *The Impersonal Life* because, he said, he wanted to understand his son.

In June 1979 I had another dream about Elvis. Vernon, Charlie, Billy and I are all sitting together in a room, when the door opens and there stands Elvis. It isn't Elvis from the seventies, but Elvis as he was in the sixties: slim and handsome, wearing a gorgeous black suit. We recognize him, but nothing is said. He looks at no one but his father, whom he walks toward. When they're standing toe to toe, Elvis reaches out to Vernon and, holding his face with both hands, softly kisses him on the lips. A second later Vernon clasps his chest and falls down, dead.

Three weeks later Vernon died of a heart attack. His girlfriend, Sandy Miller, was at his bedside. In Vernon's characteristic style he said, "Well, Sandy, I'm goin'." And he left. It was June 26, "coincidentally" Colonel Parker's birthday and the second anniversary of Elvis' last live performance. As Elvis predicted, Grandma Minnie Mae outlived them all. She died nearly a year after her son, at the age of eighty-six. She and Vernon now lie with Elvis and Gladys in the Meditation Garden.

EPILOGUE

For all of us who knew Elvis, his death marked a change in our lives. After a period of grieving and reassessment, I collaborated with Jess Stearn on a book that presented an overview of Elvis' spiritual quest, then turned my attention to finally finishing the book I had been working on during the period of my diary, *The Hair Care System.* It was published in the United Kingdom and marketed along with the special line of hair-care products I had developed. I became the spokesman for a British hair-care clinic and in that capacity traveled widely, being interviewed for radio, television and print. People wanted to hear about the products, but inevitably the interview always came around to Elvis.

In the early eighties I was working with a charitable organization in Los Angeles when I met Joel Spector, just returned from London, where he had produced a number of hit plays and musicals. It was he who encouraged me to make the diary material public and, for the first time, to share with others all of my Elvis experiences, something I had been reluctant to do for reasons that will be obvious to the reader. Until then, even my own father did not know that the papers I had asked him to keep safely for me were my diary.

This particular book might never have come about if it weren't for three separate forces at work. The first is the seemingly endless stream of misinformation about Elvis that has made its way out lately. Ridiculous stories, such as the claim of one best-seller that I pasted fake sideburns on Elvis for his funeral, seem to take on lives of their own, growing from erroneous details to full-blown "facts" to gospel. As I write this, that particular piece of "information" is being repeated on national television by someone else. Mentioning me by name, she presents it as part of her doubtful "proof" that Elvis is still alive.

Generally speaking, what has been written about Elvis' spiritual involvement suffers from the same lack of understanding and tolerance that Elvis endured in his life. I certainly didn't expect the critics of that involvement to undergo a sudden change of heart toward the subject simply because Elvis died, but I was disappointed that rather than admit that they didn't understand it, they attacked the subject by showing Elvis as a fool for pursuing it.

The impact of this began to hit home for me very early on, but I believed it would eventually run its course. It's very painful to have your own children ask if you are really "the Swami" (as one best-seller put it) their friends have read about. It's embarrassing to sit across from someone with whom you're negotiating a major business deal and have him ask, "What is it about you that aroused so much suspicion among Elvis' people? I read that . . ." I finally realized that, rather than quietly fading, the misinformation was being etched in stone when a book appeared that inspired my aunt to ask my mother, "Are these horrible things about Larry really true?" It was 1985. It was time.

The second force is the fans, who deserve to know the whole story. The third is, of course, Elvis, who deserves, in a word, better. I promised him I would help him tell his story. With this book, the promise is kept.

Elvis once said, "Once I go, the world is going to really start changing. That's when it will all start." Of course he didn't mean that his death would set off global pandemonium or mark the beginning of the apocalypse. He was simply expressing his opinion that sometime after he died—and at the time he said this he had pretty much accepted that he hadn't long to live—there would be changes in the world, specifically changes in people's attitudes toward the things that Elvis felt so deeply about.

Elvis wasn't a prophet, but he was smart. And in this instance he was absolutely correct. We are living during a period of spiritual reawakening that's been attributed to everything from the economy to the planets. Whatever its source, it is real. People are looking for answers from a wider range of beliefs, philosophies and religions than ever before. The seeds of these new attitudes were sown during the sixties, have taken root over the last two decades, and blossom today.

Although it would have been a great change for Elvis, I believe that had he lived he would have been part of this new spiritual resurgence. Through the movies he wanted to make, the charity he dreamed of building and the book he hoped to write, he would have revealed and shared his own personal quest. He was too humble to have assumed the role of a leader, but, considering the impact of the Beatles' interest in Transcendental Meditation in the late sixties, it's not farfetched to imagine Elvis as an influential figure, if only because the world so loved him.

And it still does. If, with the help of one of Charles Dickens' ghosts or Frank Capra's angels, Elvis had glimpsed the events that unfolded after his death, he certainly would have been deeply touched and comforted, and probably quite surprised and more than a bit amused. While it's now popular to blame Elvis' fate on his success and the imprisonment his celebrity imposed, he would have been as shocked by that assertion as by claims he'd been abducted by Martians or was seen frequenting the Burger King in Kalamazoo eleven years after his death.

The almost religious atmosphere that has grown up around Elvis since his death amazes me, not only in its size but in its range of expression. On one hand, members of his fan clubs quietly demonstrate their love for Elvis by raising millions of dollars annually for charity. On the other, there are people whose love for him finds expression in public claims that their child is Elvis reincarnated or that Elvis has spoken to them from the beyond.

It is as if Elvis never really left us, and in a sense that is true, for his image, his music and the force of his personality remain. Through his greatness, his fans' love and a once-in-a-lifetime confluence of circumstances, he evolved into a reflection not only of our hopes and dreams, but of our struggles and weaknesses. Elvis didn't radiate purity, yet something about his innocence has always shown through. And I believe that is because he was an honest man who sincerely cared about those he loved and about those who loved him. And in view of all this, I don't think it a contradiction to say that Elvis was an ordinary man who did the most heroic things any of us ever do: he tried, and he believed.

APPENDIX:
ELVIS' BOOKS

Throughout his life, Elvis read over a thousand different works, encompassing a wide range of subjects related to philosophy, spiritual teachings and esoteric arts. His private collection, largely lost or destroyed since his death, consisted of nearly a thousand books, three hundred of which he took with him wherever he went. For those readers who wish to judge this material for themselves I have prepared the following list of Elvis' favorite books. Included here are the titles Elvis read and reread, thought about often, and gave copies of to his friends.

Some of these titles were originally published decades ago, and a good number of them were out of print for many years. The recent interest in so-called New Age topics has brought many long-forgotten works back to print, usually with different publishers. Because of these recent developments, they are listed here by author and title only.

Many large bookstore chains now carry a wide selection of metaphysical, spiritual and religious titles, and you may find some of these books there. Nearly all of the titles are readily available from either of these two leading bookstores:

The Bodhi Tree
8585 Melrose Avenue
Los Angeles, California 90069
213/659-1733

Weiser's Bookstore
132 East 24th Street
New York, New York 10010
212/777-6363

Both have mail-order catalogues available on request.

Adams, Frank. *The Scientific Search for the Face of Jesus.*

Alder, Vera Stanley. *The Initiation of the World.*

———*The Finding of the Third Eye.*

———*The Fifth Dimension.*

———*The Secret of the Atomic Age.*

Augustine, Saint. *The City of God.*

Bailey, Alice A. *The Light of the Soul.*

———*Initiation of Human and Solar.*

———*Glamour: A World Problem.*

———*The Reappearance of Christ.*

———*Esoteric Healing.*

———*From Intellect to Intuition.*

———*The Externalization of the Hierarchy.*

Bayne, Murdo Medowald. *Beyond the Himalayas.*

Benner, Joseph. *The Impersonal Life.*

———*Brotherhood.*

———*The Way to the Kingdom.*

Blavatsky, Helena Petrovna (Madame). *Isis Unveiled.*

———*The Secret Doctrine.*

Brunton, Paul. *Wisdom of the Overself.*

———*Hidden Teachings Beyond Yoga.*

———*In Search of Secret India.*

———*The Secret Path.*

———*Discover Yourself.*

———*A Hermit in the Himalayas.*

———*The Quest of the Overself.*

Brydlova, Bozema. *Ten Unveiled: The Brydlovan Theory of the Origin of Numbers.*

Bucke, Richard Maurice, M.D. *Cosmic Consciousness.*

———*The Lost Books of the Bible and the Forgotten Books of Eden.*

Cheiro (Count Louis Harmon). *Cheiro's Book of Numbers.*

———*When Were You Born?*

———*Cheiro's World Predictions.*

———*Fate in the Making.*

Eddy, Mary Baker. *Science and Health with the Key to the Scriptures.*

Fisher, Martin (trans.) *Gracian's Manual.*

Geller, Larry. *The New Age Voice* (magazine).

Gibran, Kahlil. *The Prophet.*
——*The Spiritual Sayings of Kahlil Gibran.*
——*Thoughts and Meditations.*
Goldsmith, Joel. *The Infinite Way.*
The Gospel According to Thomas, from the Nag Hamadi Library.
Gurdjieff, G. I. *Meetings with Remarkable Men.*
Hall, Manly Palmer. *Man, Grand Symbol of the Mysteries.*
——*The Mystical Christ.*
——*The Phoenix.*
——*Twelve World Teachers.*
——*The Secret Teachings of All Ages.*
——*The Lost Keys of Freemasonry.*
——*Old Testament Wisdom.*
Heindal, Max. *The Rosicrucian Cosmo-Conception.*
Heline, Corinne. *America's Invisible Guidance.*
——*Color and Music in the New Age.*
——*Music: The Keynote of Human Evolution.*
——*The Sacred Science of Numbers.*
——*New Age Bible Interpretation,* Volume I.
Hodson, Geoffrey. *The Hidden Wisdom of the Holy Bible,* Volume I.
——*The Hidden Wisdom of the Holy Bible,* Volume II.
Holy Bible. Old and New Testaments, King James version.
Krishnamurti. *You Are the World.*
——*The First and Last Freedom.*
Leadbeater, C. W. *The Masters and the Path.*
——*The Inner Life.*
——*The Chakras.*
Levi. *The Aquarian Gospel of Jesus the Christ.*
Long, Max Freedom. *The Huna Code in Religions.*
Mata, Sri Daya. *Only Love.*
M.C. *Light on the Path.*
Metaphysical Bible Dictionary.
Morya. *Leaves of Morya's Garden,* Volumes I and II.
——*Agni Yoga.*
——*Aum.*
——*Brotherhood.*

——*Hierarchy.*

——*Heart.*

——*Fiery World*, Volumes I and II.

——*Infinity*, Volumes I and II.

Nicoll, Maurice. *The New Man.*

Ouspensky, P. D. *In Search of the Miraculous.*

——*The Fourth Way.*

Percival, Harold. *Thinking and Destiny.*

——*Masonry and Its Symbols.*

Pike, Albert. *Morals and Dogma.*

Ramacharaka. *Fourteen Lessons in Yogi Philosophy.*

Roerich, Helena. *Letters of Helena Roerich*, Volumes I and II.

Rudhyar, Dane. *New Mansions for New Men.*

——*Fire Out of the Stone.*

Russell, Walter. *The Secret of Light.*

Rutherford, Adam. *Pyramidology: The Science of the Divine Message of the Great Pyramid.*

——*Pyramidology: The Glory of Christ as Revealed by the Great Pyramid.*

Satprem. *The Adventure of Consciousness.*

Spaulding, Baird. *Life and Teachings of the Masters of the Far East*, Volumes I–V.

The Urantia Book.

Waite, A. E. *The Holy Kabalah.*

Yogananda, Paramahansa. *Autobiography of a Yogi.*

——*How You Can Talk with God.*

——*Science of Religion.*

——*Man's Eternal Quest.*

Yukteswar, Sri. *The Holy Science.*

ACKNOWLEDGMENTS

The person I would like to thank first and foremost is Larry Geller. In the two and a half years of our collaboration he allowed me to confront and coax him into discussing the raw, personal, intimate, painful and sometimes joyous events in the life he shared with Elvis. And now the fruit of that collaboration is finally in print for the world to share.

Working together bonded Larry and me into a relationship that I shall always cherish and helped me to understand why Elvis placed his trust and faith in Larry—his perception, his spiritual strength and his illuminating spirit. Elvis truly loved Larry, and in our short time together I have learned to as well.

I am so thankful to my family, loved ones and friends who gave so generously of their love and support during the road to the publication of our book. My deepest gratitude to my son Neal and his wife Alice and the gurgles of my new grandson Ian Jonas; to my son Marc and his wife Arlene; to Hilda; to my brother Ed; and to my sister Renee and my brother-in-law Harry.

My loving thanks to my doctor and dear friend Daniel Wohlgelernter, who, with his staff at the Daniel Freeman Hospital in Marina Del Rey and in Inglewood, California, pulled me through a life-threatening crisis, and to Dr. James M. Kanda, Dr. W. Grant Stevens, and their staffs for their comforting ways.

My eternal gratitude to my love Jean Westland and to my special friends Lynne and Chuck Lockwood. My thanks to Kim and Ian Sillars and the staff at Flexi Media Systems, Inc., and thanks to Paula Cahill and Rose Young for their caring support. Also a thank you to Cori and Kandice Gibson, and to Mr. and Mrs. Peter Hayaschi for cheering me on.

343

A special thanks to Robert Zentis for creating a lovely atmosphere for all of us to work in, and to Dr. Trisha Sandberg for helping me to realize my spiritual quest.

As always, with deep love, my work is dedicated to my parents, Fannie and Jacob, and to the memory of my beloved brother Ben, my sister-in-law Florence, and my dearest Aunt Ida.

Joel Spector

It was through the friendship and guidance of my collaborator Joel Spector that this book came into being. He was the first person I came to trust enough to reveal that I had kept a "secret diary" of Elvis' last days and it was he who insisted that it be published. His shaping, structuring and extraordinary insight have made working on this book a rich experience. He is one of those rare human beings who are able to inspire and ignite. My deepest appreciation and a toast to Joel.

I am eternally grateful to my parents, Bernard and Annabelle Geller, for, through their undying love, faith and strength, they have been my example—my Beacon Light.

To my children, Jova, Kabrel and Kiara—they are truly God's gift to me—wonders to behold.

To my sister and brother-in-law, Elaine and Bernie Rothman, I am especially grateful for their years of intimate friendship and fascinating in-depth conversations providing insights beyond price.

To my sister Judy, who has always been my close confidante and friend. Her loving advice will always be deeply appreciated.

To my sister Kitty, who is one of a kind—a kindred soul on the path.

The special bond between Christian Dome, Chuck Lederman and myself was joined in the early 1950s. We continually grow closer—a blessing beyond words.

And, of course, Stuart Schoen, Monty Landis and Mary Lou Kimp, who have nurtured me and who have been there over the years—special mirrors.

To Stevie—my eternal friend—her words of wisdom are truly pearls.

Kathy Westmoreland and Ed Parker hold a special place in my mind; they have my deepest respect.

Celest has always been a bright light. Her beauty and genuineness I'll never forget.

Johnny Rivers has always been a true friend; his input has been remarkable, as always, at the right time.

I am deeply honored to call myself a friend of Sri Daya Mata, who touches my life so deeply, providing the most extraordinary guidance and inspiration.

In memory of my two mentors—Dane Rudhyar, Brother Adolph—words disappear.

Some of the following list of people are in my life now, the others will always remain in my fondest memories—close friends of Elvis in a never-to-be-forgotten time and place: Joe Esposito, Charlie Hodge, Jerry Schilling, Billy Smith, JoJo, Sandy Silverberg, Aurelia, Patsy Presley, Aunt Delta, Uncle Vester, Alan Fortas, Richard Davis, Mike Keaton, Marty Lacker, George Klein, Dick Grob, Linda Thompson, Sam Thompson, Dee Stanley, Lamar Fike, Dr. Nick, Dean Nichopoulos, Tom Hulett, Al Strada, Sal Orifice, Marilyn Brown, Pat Perry, Ginger Alden, Steve Smith, Dr. Elias Ghanem, Jackie Kahane, Joe Guercio, James Burton, Ronnie Tutt, Felton Jarvis, Sean, Donnie, Carol Bourtiere, Elwood Davis, Jim Manning, Sue Wiegart, Bernard Benson, Tobias, and Eddie Fadal.

To Shelley—who holds a special place in my heart.

Larry Geller

Our love to Patty Romanowski, a most sensitive and extraordinary collaborator, for helping us to bring about the totality of our book in spirit and substance, we pay our deepest and fondest appreciation. We are grateful to her beyond words.

Our gratitude to Sarah Lazin, our agent, whose belief in our work was the turning point toward our book's seeing the light of day.

Our deepest gratitude to Nancy Nicholas. Her love for our work was an inspiration to us from the moment we met. How fortunate for us to have an editor whose love, perception, knowledge and pinpoint guidance sharpened our work ever so beautifully. In the process we have gained a most wonderful friend in her and another in her brother, Daniel Wolff, who has also contributed to this book as a fan and *homme de lettres*.

Our sincere appreciation to everyone at Simon and Schuster, whose special talents endearingly brought our book to the world. In particular we are grateful to Patty O'Connell, Marcella Berger, Karen Weitzman, **Marie Florio**, Lisa Kitei and Kathy Kik-kert.

We are most grateful to our attorneys Jack Dwosh and Neal Spector and our accountant Sidney B. Palley for their distinctive support.

Our gratitude to Sean Shaver for his photographs, which enriched our book.

We are grateful to Salley Rayl and Roger Helms who guided us to our agent, Sarah Lazin.

A special thank you to David, Ricky and Billy Stanley for their years of friendship.

With gratitude and love to Clara Rudin, a constant and loving friend, and our deepest gratitude to Herman Rudin for his zeal and diligence in overseeing all during this long and hectic period of time. Our true friend and associate.

Larry Geller and Joel Spector

Sharing your life with a collaborator can be a difficult, emotional and, at times, painful experience. I'd like to thank Joel and Larry for their support, encouragement and, most of all, their profound trust in me. Especially Larry, who openly and honestly answered questions no one really had a right to ask and who proved to me that Elvis was a fine man as I'd always longed to believe that he was.

Larry, Joel, Nancy Nicholas and my wonderful agent, Sarah Lazin, made it all possible. For that, a million thanks.

My undying gratitude goes to my mother, the late Marjorie Streller Romanowski, who would have loved this. She liked telling people about me screaming from my high chair whenever I saw Elvis on TV. She collected his records from the jukebox in her Wichita bar and brought them home, where, along with wall plaques of the Hamms Beer forest animals and a Coors waterfall clock, they provided the best environment any fifties toddler could have had. I think.

Most of all, though, my love to my husband, Philip Bashe, for living with the results.

Patricia Romanowski